From Antagonism to Re-engagement:
Zimbabwe's Trade Negotiations with the European Union, 2000-2016

Richard Kamidza

Langaa Research & Publishing CIG
Mankon, Bamenda

Publisher:
Langaa RPCIG
Langaa Research & Publishing Common Initiative Group
P.O. Box 902 Mankon
Bamenda
North West Region
Cameroon
Langaagrp@gmail.com
www.langaa-rpcig.net

Distributed in and outside N. America by African Books Collective
orders@africanbookscollective.com
www.africanbookscollective.com

ISBN-10: 9956-762-34-2

ISBN-13: 978-9956-762-34-7

© Richard Kamidza 2017

Table of Contents

iv

Acknowledgements

I owe a debt of gratitude to many individuals and institutions that provided financial, intellectual, and moral support during the research that has resulted in this book. My special thanks go to KwaZulu-Natal University for providing a supportive environment, the freedom to explore critical ideas and fieldwork assistance in the form of a bursary and funding. Special thanks go to Prof Patrick Bond, who has long been my supervisor and role model for decades. Further, I will always be indebted to organisations and institutions, especially the Economic Justice Network of the Fellowship of Christian Councils in Southern Africa, the Hub and Spokes project and the Southern African Development Community (SADC) Secretariat for intellectual Economic Partnership Agreement (EPA) engagement that culminated in series of publications; facilitation of internal SADC EPA and joint European Union-SADC EPA negotiations; capacity building dialogue sessions with regional trade officials and activists; and exposure to contextualised EPA related politics, dynamics and complexities within the configurations, and between Europe and its former colonies, a mirror of the EU-Zimbabwe trade power relationship.

It would have been impossible to complete the book without the support of many close friends and loved ones: my wife (Agnes Kamidza), mother (Edna Gwenzi) and children (Kudakwashe, Rumbidzai, Chiedza, Tariro, Panashe and Ruvimbo) for their unwavering support throughout the research process and its financial challenges. I am specifically indebted to Anne Derges who meticulously edited the book for publication, benefitting significantly from her extensive experience and expertise. Finally, I would like to thank the publisher, Langaa Research and Publishing Common Initiative Group, for their unwavering support and commitment throughout the entire process of producing this book.

I dedicate this book to the Lord God Almighty!

List of Acronyms and Abbreviations

ACP	=	African-Caribbean-Pacific
AfDB	=	African Development Bank
ANSA	=	Alternative to Neo-liberalism in Southern Africa
ATN	=	Africa Trade Network
AU	=	African Union
BOP	=	Balance of Payment
CAP	=	Common Agriculture Policy
CARIFORUM	=	Caribbean Forum
CEMAC	=	Economic and Monetary Community of Central Africa
COMESA	=	Common Market for Eastern and Southern Africa
CRs	=	Committee Rooms
CSOs	=	Civil Society Organisations
CTA	=	Chief Technical Advisor
CTAs	=	Chief Technical Advisors
CZI	=	Confederation of Zimbabwe Industries
DFQF	=	Duty-Free and Quota-Free
DG	=	Director General
EBA	=	Everything-but-Arms
EC	=	European Commission
ECOWAS	=	Economic Community of West African States
EDF	=	European Development Fund
EEC	=	European Economic Commission
EIB	=	European Investment Bank
EPA	=	Economic Partnership Agreement
EPAs	=	Economic Partnership Agreements
ESA	=	Eastern and Southern Africa
EU	=	European Union
FA	=	Fisheries Agreements
FAO	=	Food and Agricultural Organisation

FDI	=	Foreign Direct Investment
FTA	=	Free Trade Area
FTAs	=	Free Trade Areas
GDP	=	Gross Domestic Product
GFIs	=	Global Financial Institutions
GNU	=	Government of National Unity
GPA	=	Global Political Agreement
Hivos	=	Humanistic Institute for Development Cooperation
IAS	=	Impact Assessment Study
IDP	=	Industrial Development Policy
iEPA	=	Interim EPA
IGAD	=	Inter-Governmental Authority for Development
IMF	=	International Monetary Fund
IOC	=	Indian Ocean Community
LDCs	=	Least Developing Countries
LEDRIZ	=	Labour and Economic Development Research Institute of Zimbabwe
MAR	=	Market Access Regulation
MCs	=	Multinational Corporations
MDC	=	Movement for Democratic Change
MERP	=	Millennium Economic Recovery Programme
MoFEDP	=	Finance, Economic Planning and Development
MPs	=	Members of Parliament
MSME	=	Micro, Small and Medium Enterprise
MWENGO	=	Mwelekeowa NGO
NANGO	=	National Association of Non-Governmental Organisations
NDTPF	=	National Development Trade Policy Forum
NGOs	=	Non-Governmental Organisations
NIP	=	National Indicative Programme
NSAs	=	Non-State Actors
NTP	=	National Trade Policy

OECD	=	Organisation for Economic Cooperation and Development
RECs	=	Regional Economic Communities
REIS	=	Regional Economic Integration Support
RIIP	=	Regional Integration Implementation Project
RISP	=	Regional Integration Support Programme
RNF	=	Regional Negotiation Forum
SACU	=	Southern African Customs Union
SADC	=	Southern African Development Community
SAP	=	Structural Adjustment Programme
SAPRIN	=	Structural Adjustment Programme Review Initiative Network
SEATINI	=	Southern and Eastern African Trade, Information and Negotiations Institute
SQAM	=	Standards, Quality Assurance and Metrology
TDC	=	Trade and Development Committee
TNCs	=	transnational corporations
TNF	=	Tripartite Negotiation Forum
TRADES	=	Trade and Development Studies
WDDR	=	WTO Doha Development Round
WTO	=	World Trade Organisation
ZANU-PF	=	Zimbabwe African National Union-Patriotic Front
Zim-Asset	=	Zimbabwe Agenda for Sustainable Socio-Economic Transformation
ZIMCODD	=	Zimbabwe Coalition on Debt and Development
ZIMPREST	=	Zimbabwe Programme for Economic and Social Transformation
ZNCC	=	Zimbabwe National Chambers of Commerce

List of Boxes, Diagram, Figures, Graph and Tables

Chapter One

Where Trade Negotiations Competition Begins

Zimbabwe began negotiating an Economic Partnership Agreement[1] (EPA) with the European Union (EU) in 2004, as part of the Eastern and Southern Africa (ESA) configuration[2]. However, the arrangements rapidly became mired in controversy. This was because the new ESA[3] was a significant departure from the January 2004 Mauritius EU-ESA joint EPA roadmap, which promised to conclude the new trade regime as a bloc. The trade talks culminated in the signing of an interim EPA (iEPA) on 4 September 2009 by the Government of National Unity[4] (GNU), as prescribed by the Southern African Development Community's (SADC) negotiated Global Political Agreement[5] (GPA).

The trade talks coincided with eight consecutive years of negative economic growth in Zimbabwe; from 1999 there had been a fall of nearly 50% of the Gross Domestic Product (GDP), coupled with significant capital flight and reductions in private sector investment.

---

[1] EPAs negotiations are meant to replace the thirty-year-old Lomé trade preferences with unprecedented reciprocal market access between the world's largest and most powerful single markets on the one hand, and many of the poorest and least developed countries on the other.

[2] The ESA group which comprises Burundi, Comoros, Djibouti, Eritrea, Ethiopia, Kenya, Madagascar, Malawi, Mauritius, Rwanda, Seychelles, Sudan, Tanzania, Uganda, Zambia and Zimbabwe. From the group, Burundi, Kenya, Rwanda, Uganda and Tanzania (which joined the EAC in 2008 having originally negotiated under the SADC-EPA configuration), signed as a bloc while Madagascar, Mauritius, Seychelles and Zimbabwe did so individually.

[3] This comprises Comoros, Djibouti, Eritrea, Ethiopia, Madagascar, Malawi, Mauritius, Seychelles, Sudan, Zambia and Zimbabwe.

[4] The new government includes both formations of the MDC led by Morgan Tsvangirai and Arthur Mutambara, and Robert Mugabe's Zimbabwe African National Union-Patriotic Front (ZANU-PF) party. Thus, the formation of GNU resulted in the former ruling party being faced with the reality of sharing power for the first time since it assumed power in April 1980

[5] This is the SADC negotiated political settlement that paved the way for feuding political parties (ZANU-PF and two formations of the MDC) to work together in the Government of National Unity formed on 11 February 2009.

Investment all but ceased after the Millennium, resulting in scarce inflows of foreign reserves and a corresponding tight exchange rate regime. As a result, the economy severely reduced its manufacturing capacity utilisation from an already desultory 35.8% in 2005 to as low as 4% at the trough by the end of 2008. Zimbabwe's industrial sector, which at Independence in 1980 was third largest in the world (Bond, 1998), measured as a share of GDP (after Korea and Germany), was reduced to a shadow of its past (Nyakazeya, 2009). Unemployment soared and largely as a result, the opposition, Morgan Tsvangirai's Movement for Democratic Change (MDC) defeated Mugabe's Zimbabwe African National Union-Patriotic Front (ZANU-PF) in the first round of the 2008 presidential election[6].

Meanwhile, the authorities in Harare were searching for new East Asian markets, especially in China. As Bond (2007) observes, the government's 'Look East' policy was both a trade diversification strategy and part of a broader foreign policy in response to deteriorating relations with Europe and other western powers.

Yet Zimbabwe-EU trade talks continued, notwithstanding the regime's vehement anti-colonial rhetoric and its repeated claims of 'EU meddling in the country's political affairs.' Mugabe was also annoyed by donor and western countries' continued support for civil society organisations (CSOs)[7] working on basic social, economic, and cultural rights, as well as democratic and constitutional principles. Meanwhile, the EU, as a donor, citing democratic and governance deficits, withdrew direct financial and technical assistance to the Zimbabwean government, channeling more funding to civil society. Individual EU member states also suspended all direct financial and technical assistance to the Zimbabwean state. Further, the EU

---

[6] Tsvangirai and Mugabe won 47.9 and 43.2% of the vote respectively, necessitating a 27 June 2008 run-off (wikipedia, 2008).

[7] Raftopoulos (2005) argues that donors have since 2000 been supporting liberal CSOs working on human rights, democracy, good governance and constitutionalism with unlimited resources but reject funding to those pursuing redistribution discourse and politics not only with respect to land, but also economic development including the EPA process. This translates to dilemmas of participation/resistance and rights/distribution in state-civil society relationships, as discussed below.

2

imposed 'targeted sanctions'[8] against 200[9] leading ZANU (PF) officials and their associated companies, a move which along with Bretton Woods Institution blacklisting (due to vast debt arrears), the state blamed for the lack of external trade financing. The EU also cut direct government-to-government contact except for purposes of negotiating the EPA in the context of the ESA group.

Still, trade negotiations continued, while civil society split into two distinct camps: one supportive of land reform and other state initiatives, comprising mainly small farmers, war veterans, and indigenous business advocates (Moyo and Yeros, 2007, and Mamdani, 2008), and the other comprising groups which emphasised democracy and governance. The latter group included those who championed broader struggles against neo-liberalism and criticised ZANU (PF)'s brand of 'crony capitalism' (Bond, 2006b and Raftopoulos, 2005).

Bond (2008; 2009) blames the government for wavering between market liberalisation, crony-capitalist corruption, and state interventions – which not only exposed state shortcomings, but also alienated most civil society groups. The tense political climate discouraged activists and scholars - who held various views on trade talks, the economy, and other developmental necessities - from formally engaging the state on these issues; many preferred

---

[8] The EU invoked the Cotonou Agreement Article 9 which deals with the maintenance of the rule of law, human rights, democracy and good governance when the bloc imposed targeted sanctions on Mugabe, ZANU (PF) officials and companies linked to the regime covering visa restrictions and the freezing of their assets in European banks. The EU also suspended economic cooperation and development aid towards the Zimbabwean government (Darracq, 2011). Further, the USA, Australia and other western governments imposed similar restrictive measures on the same persons and companies (Hove, 2012). But trade officials such as the former Minister of Trade and Industry, Samuel Mumbengegwi were allowed to attend EPA-related meetings in Brussels and Geneva. The removal of these sanctions is directly linked to the full implementation of the GPA. However, since the formation of the GNU, the AU and SADC leadership, as the guarantors of GPA, made numerous calls for the removal of 'smart sanctions' without any success.

[9] However, since February 2013, Brussels has suspended sanctions against more than 100 ZANU (PF) leaders and a dozen firms. By end of 2013, only 10 ZANU (PF) leaders and the army supplier, Zimbabwe Defence Industries remained on the sanctions list.

delegitimisation. Furthermore, the state-civil society relationship became increasingly contentious as the state became uncomfortable with the latter's advocacy of greater democratisation. This not only worsened EU-Zimbabwe bilateral relations, but also fueled countrywide state-civil society tensions, resulting in weak, narrow and often partisan strategic engagements during the trade talks. Meanwhile, the GNU between Robert Mugabe's ZANU (PF) and MDC formations led by Morgan Tsvangirai as Prime Minister and Arthur Mutambara as Deputy Prime Minister was confronted with internal neo-liberal versus protectionist struggles (with overlapping camps in both parties), resulting in disunity in the economic policy-making processes and undermining efforts to negotiate a better trade regime.

During the 1990s, the Zimbabwean government had invited representatives of some CSOs[10] with resources to join (as observers) various regional, bilateral, or multilateral trade talks, and consulted them on key strategic issues, positions, offers, and interests. For example, two representatives from the Southern and Eastern African Trade, Information and Negotiations Institute (SEATINI)[11] were sponsored by the EU through the Common Market for Eastern and Southern Africa (COMESA) to participate at the Regional Negotiating Forum (RNF) as well as joint ESA-EU meetings held in the region and in Brussels. However, this support was withdrawn in December 2004. Similarly, the Trade and Development Studies (TRADES) Centre, through COMESA, was commissioned to undertake the country's impact assessment study (IAS) whose findings were used to prepare the country's interests, offers and positions. Even though two national dialogues were organised (in Harare and Bulawayo) to engage the IAS findings, most CSOs could not strategically and collectively coordinate their activities, and failed to share plans, processes, and outcomes in support of the process

---

[10] These included SEATINI, Mwelekeowa NGO (MWENGO), the TRADES Centre, the Zimbabwe Coalition on Debt and Development (ZIMCODD), AFRODAD, the Community Technology Development Trust, the Trade Capacity Building Project, ANSA and LEDRIZ - a research arm of ZCTU.

[11] SEATINI monitored remarks by government officials, Ambassadors and EU officials and generated advice about "fault-lines" and "complementary lobbying entry points".

(Kamidza 2006). Limited resources also prevented government from deepening and widening its consultations with all the key stakeholders working in the diverse areas of trade and development.

Zimbabwe's few CSOs working on trade (including the EPA) had limited space and resources to improve their own strategic networking, synergy building, and citizen sensitisation, especially compared to the civil society struggles of the 1990s against the one-party regime, its neo-liberal policies, and the undemocratic constitutional order. Similarly, limited donor funding directly undermined all the CSOs advocating for a fair global trade system, including EPA processes, with SEATINI specifically defunded because of its hostility to multinational corporations. This not only compromised effective engagement and activism around the EU's institutions and structures, the EU member-states and the Zimbabwean government negotiators, but also limited efforts to galvanise the views of broader sections of civil society and social movements. Limited donor support undermined CSOs' efforts to build the necessary EPA-related technical and policy analytical capacities to lobby other constituencies. Furthermore, CSOs could not participate in the RNF and joint ESA-EU meetings held in the region and in Brussels, since the available EU resources only supported government officials and/or one representative from the private sector. As a result, there was limited interaction between CSOs' representatives and government officials during the national, regional, and Brussels meetings. Government and CSOs failed to share crucial information such as calendar events or published information of mutual interest. They failed to do coherent outreach regarding issues, positions, strategies, and interpretation of texts. There was a distinct absence of strategic networking, synergy building and systematic engagement, mobilisation of critical constituencies, collaboration, advocacy and policy research analysis.[12] This worked in favour of both the EU and those in the government who did not want civil society oversight.

Sam Moyo (2010) argued that the liberal rights agenda has marginalised redistributive concerns by instead promoting private

---

[12] This includes EPAs-related materials such as policy briefs, fact-sheets and analysis of positions and interests.

property rights, partnerships with donors, a bourgeois judiciary, and the privately-owned press. This expression reveals not only extreme ideological division within the non-state actors between redistributive and liberal rights, but also politically-induced polarisation that splits civil society into two distinct camps: 'collaborators,' who emphasise direct interaction with the state in their engagement and participation in the EPA and other economic process, or 'resisters' who repudiate any formal interaction and consultation, instead opting for confrontational tactical engagement. McCandless (2011) showed how redistribution of wealth, land and other natural resources in least developing countries (LDCs) and developing countries, was advanced by nationalism on the basis of contested civil society influence. In Zimbabwe's case, the critical question is whether CSOs are aligned with the state, or against it. Some very explicit leftwing institutions (most vocally, the International Socialist Organisation of Zimbabwe) are against ZANU (PF), while many indigenous business people are supportive of the ruling party. This makes advocacy on broader economic policy spaces, governance systems, and democratic participation processes confusing, and occasionally discomfiting for a Zimbabwean government long used to 'talking left, walking right.'

This is not new, for Dorman (2001) observed that state-society relations in Zimbabwe have long been a product of the ruling party's use of both coercive and consent-generating mechanisms[13] aimed at establishing its hegemony. The state turns regularly to silencing, discrediting, and undermining CSOs' activities. As a result of the deep divisions, activists' mobilisation strategies typically fail to woo those unwilling to challenge the regime's control over social and economic policy-making processes. Moyo (2010) accuses CSOs critical of the ruling party of becoming increasingly donor-driven, pursuing foreign 'neoliberal' agendas, albeit under the guise of traditional progressive goals such as democratic values and constitutionalism against authoritarianism. The government regularly accuses critical CSOs of simply reflecting outside interests and serving as dangerous distractions from the unfinished business of

---

[13] The regime provided financial incentives to civic bodies willing to cooperate while it excluded and vilified defiant ones.

building a national economy based on control over the country's resources, particularly land and minerals. It considers CSO critics to be urban elites with no constituencies beyond the internet café.

In any case, the CSOs have not been sufficiently capacitated to make much difference. Kalima-Phiri (2007) argues that Zimbabwe's CSOs working on the EPA processes could not access European Development Fund (EDF) resources meant to support the so-called "Non-State Actors" (NSAs) and their developmental goals. This is because the disbursement of EU resources to NSA activities is done through the national authorising officer located in the Ministry of Finance, who is assisted by the Project Management Committee comprising officials from other relevant ministries, representatives of CSOs, and the EU delegation in Harare. The EU's decision to withhold financial transfers to the regime therefore equally denied NSAs the resources necessary to build capacity to effectively advocate for transparent, fair, and inclusive participation in EPA negotiations.

Though some of the EPA-focused CSOs actively participated in the Africa Trade Network's (ATN) coordinated 'Stop Economic Partnership Agreements Campaign'[14] (aimed at building strategic alliances with African governments negotiators with the view to resist the initial iEPAs), the prevailing conflictual relationship with the Zimbabwean government on broader issues of democracy and governance translated into a weak alliance during the trade negotiations. The ATN's related global trade campaign, 'Our World is not for Sale' (a broad-based international network of left-leaning CSOs), also failed to make links with the Zimbabwean negotiators, in spite of the important role Zimbabwe's former trade and foreign minister, Nathan Shamuyarira, played opposing the World Trade Organisation (WTO), especially at the 1999 and 2003 summits (Bond and Manyanya 2003). All this reflects significant gaps in strategic networking and engagement between Zimbabwean trade negotiators on the one hand and national, regional, continental and global civic

---

[14] This was first launched by a vast coalition of CSOs from European and ACP countries in Brussels in April 2004, who believed that EPAs would disrupt the latter economies' production and fiscal revenues, thereby generating unemployment and poverty.

bodies on the other during the trade talks, a natural outcome of the division within Zimbabwe between pro- and anti-Mugabe CSOs. Also lacking was open and transparent interaction with specific government issues, positions, strategies, tactics and shared interpretations of offer texts. Unlike the WTO talks, Zimbabwean civic bodies working on trade justice and their networks in Africa and beyond failed to advocate for a collective and united voice capable of achieving a better deal when it came to EU-Africa EPAs. Within the ESA group, Zimbabwe lacked the political and moral authority to 'unite group negotiators' in a manner that could support the EU-ESA joint EPA roadmap, as had been the case in Seattle[15] during the WTO trade talks (Bond, 2006b). As a result, ESA countries were divided, leading to varied trade offers and signatories to the new trade regime, with South Africa playing an especially complex role, what with the pro-WTO stance taken by its trade minister prior to 2005, Alec Erwin, and the hostile stance to EPAs taken by trade minister, Rob Davies, after 2009. Ironically, despite the huge economic challenges that greatly undermined the country's industrial production and export competitiveness, Zimbabwe was one of four[16] countries to initial and subsequently sign the iEPAs. But, as noted by Keet (2007), the process and signing ceremonies did not reflect the consensus that had been evident during the Cancun and Doha WTO trade talks.

This configuration prompted Shivji (2004) to criticise donor-driven policy-making processes that compel states and peoples to surrender their right to self-determination to the WTO and Bretton Woods Institutions: the World Bank and the International Monetary Fund (IMF). In this respect, he argues, civil society's participation in the EU-EPA-driven trade negotiations legitimises imperial power and confirms governments' abdication of their primary responsibilities to define national and regional trade agendas. These claims relate to those CSOs which have a neoliberal orientation, who therefore have difficulty in claiming to represent the views of ordinary people, and to speak or act on their behalf. The most active such CSO in Southern Africa is based in Johannesburg: the South African Institute of International Affairs (long considered the think

---

[15] See section 2.2, second paragraph from bottom.

[16] Madagascar, Mauritius, Seychelles, Zambia and Zimbabwe.

tank of the Anglo-American Corporation and English-speaking white capital).

Given the tense state-society relations as well as cold bilateral relations with the EU because of democratic and governance deficits, there are many complicated factors to unpack: the ZANU (PF) government's anti-EU stance (based in part on claims of meddling in the country's political affairs); the contradiction-ridden macro-economic policy environment; the politically-induced polarisation that splits civil society into two distinct camps; the conflicts within the coalition government from February 2009 to July 2013; and the limited resources available to engage the EU institutions. In addressing the complexity, this enquiry into the EPA debate in Zimbabwe also shows how the EPA process provided a strong lobbying platform on which a new state-society trade relationship can potentially be built. CSOs' participation in these negotiations, however, are beset with challenges and frustrations.

European donors and investors lost confidence in the economy, especially by late 2008, due largely to *inter alia*, hyperinflation[17], tight liquidity conditions, and massive shortages of commercial basic daily goods and services, which resulted in the plummeting of industrial and export capacity to the lowest level in the country's modern history. This coincided with an economic meltdown that not only undermined the country's industrial capacity, export potential, and competitiveness in the market[18], but also generated massive social and humanitarian crises, at a time when Europe itself was suffering from a sustained economic crisis.

The period was characterised by conflictual state-civil society relationships given the Mugabe government's undemocratic practices; Tyrannical rule overshadowed collective strategic wisdom in trade negotiations as well as the state's pro-poor and pro-development initiatives, especially land reform, and indigenisation and economic empowerment programmes. Further, state-civil society antagonism undermined constructive, consultative and collective engagements, as well as strategic networking and synergy building. Poor relations between the former ZANU (PF)

---

[17] Estimated at 231,150,888.87% in July 2008.
[18] Local, regional and global.

government and other key regional and global constituencies working on trade negotiations undermined the prospect of achieving any potential pro-poor and pro-developmental EPA outcomes. In fact, the process exposed both state shortcomings and civil society advocacy inadequacies. The challenges facing the GNU's economic transitional trajectory were formidable.[19] And there was simultaneously a failure to exploit unfolding benefits from SADC's regional integration and trade agenda, as well as from Africa's growing trade relations with Brazil, China and India. Even the inclusive government – the GNU of 2009-13 – struggled to normalise its relationship with Europe in particular, and western governments and donors in general. This was largely due to 'pockets of resistance' (Kamidza, 2009a and 2009c) in the former ruling party bent on frustrating full implementation of the GPA. These instigated in-fighting within the GNU, resulting in the transmission of conflicting policy directives and messages not only to the international community, but also to national producers, exporters, merchants and investors. Foreign governments, investors, and donors are looking for value-enhancing opportunities that are sustainable and predictable and that guarantee protection for invested social and economic capital, all of which were hard to find in early-21st century Zimbabwe.

This book argues that in future, probably after Mugabe's reign ends, a hastily-concluded EPA negotiation, without sufficient consultation with civil society groups and members of the public, is likely to worsen the de-industrialisation and impoverishment of Zimbabwe's once well-balanced economy. EU commercial interests could particularly affect the agriculture and manufacturing sectors in the short to medium term, against a backdrop of severe rural turmoil. Since 2000, political upheavals affecting Zimbabwe have been witnessed in the near-cessation of 'white' commercial farmers' agricultural activities, the downsizing of production activities and

---

[19] Questionable trends in the rule of law with respect to private property and the newly enacted 'Indigenisation Law' that seeks to force foreign companies to surrender 51% shareholding to Zimbabweans. However, Charles Abugre argues that the new law violates the 1992 WTO principles which call for equal treatment of both foreign and local traders by governments.

closure of numerous industrial companies, the brain drain (migration of skilled personnel), and withdrawals of donor funding from the state (though around US$500 million per annum supported food aid) as well as foreign and domestic disinvestment. At a time of drought for most food crops, and as world tobacco overproduction and rapidly falling prices have lowered the yield on most farmers' output to unprofitable levels, the EU's potential penetration of what remains of local production is therefore a crucial economic threat. There is little hope for revival based solely on mining diamonds (which appear to have peaked in the Marange area in terms of surface-level alluvial output), platinum (whose price fell dramatically after 2011) and gold (whose price has been highly volatile since the 1990s) (Nyakazeya, 2009). The book, therefore, suggests that the withdrawal of European donors and investors from Zimbabwe since 2000 may have had a short-term logic – the loss of confidence in unfolding political developments, the fast-track land reform programme and the economic crash – but nevertheless, Brussels' 50-year scenario assessment of the potential for each African-Caribbean-Pacific (ACP) economy's subjection to European exports is far more important. This more dangerous longer-term engagement is, therefore, the lens through which we should view the iEPA.

The process of EU-Zimbabwe trade negotiations could continue to be contested, and not only by state actors. Zimbabwe's major national fault-lines will continue to include conflict in state-civil society and state-private sector relations. There have been inadequate consultative processes in virtually all economic policy making, not just the EPA debate. The Zimbabwe State came under sustained pressure from an enlarged ACP (most of whose members were in support of EPAs)[20] and business lobbies including transnational corporations (TNCs) and multinational corporations (MCs) as well as from the IMF and the World Bank. At the same time as the EPAs were under negotiation, the Bretton Woods Institutions denied the Mugabe regime balance of payment (BOP) support on account of the country's ongoing default on the large (US$10 billion+) external

---

[20] From 15 member states during the Cotonou Agreement to 20 countries when the EPA negotiations with the ACP configurations started, to now 27 member states.

debt. Since that default began at the end of the 1990s, both the ZANU (PF) (2000-2009) and GNU (2009-2013) administrations failed to unlock financial and technical resources from the international community. Attempts in mid-2016 were foiled by the simple failure of Zimbabwe to find sufficient hard currency to make a $1.8 billion down payment; at the time it could not even pay its soldiers, police and civil servants on time.

Meanwhile, the EU and its corporate allies mobilised vast human, financial and technical resources to gain the best possible deal in the iEPA negotiations with Africa. In contrast, Zimbabwe's elites were extremely divided and there was very little attention paid to civil society concerns. The EU used its commercial unity to negotiate favourable international trade agreements, and all member states together defended the process (Meunier, 2000) that for Zimbabwe was made even thornier by the EU's relatively unified position on political (personal) sanctions against ZANU (PF) leaders.

Zimbabwe performed poorly in these negotiations, as a result. Could Harare's delegation have been stronger? This book provides details about conflictual relationships between the negotiating parties, and between government and other key stakeholders (civil society groups and sections of the business community). The EU's 'smart sanctions'[21] against the ZANU (PF) leadership and associated companies together with its public funding of civil society groups working against the government on non-trade and development issues such as electoral, governance, and human rights problems, together exacerbated the extreme political polarisation between the MDC and ZANU (PF) with corresponding alliances forming in civil society and the mass movements. This in turn undermined social cohesion, inclusiveness, trust, confidence and cooperation in economic management and economic policy making, including the EPA debate. Whether intended or not, the EU funding served as a policy instrument that contributed to an iEPA that was against Zimbabwe's interests, for it enhanced the competitiveness of EU entrepreneurs to maximise trade benefits over the long term.

---

[21] The imposition of smart sanctions was triggered by the expulsion of the EU election observer team and its head in 2002, the escalation of political violence and Zimbabwe's worsening human rights record.

The dominance of corporations in this round of EU-Zimbabwe trade negotiations was amplified by adverse financial conditions (capital deinvestments) which put added pressure on Harare to conclude a deal. The EU's competitiveness against Zimbabwe grew, as the latter's very low industrial productive capacity (often below 10 percent during the 2000s) prevented achievement of economies of scale and export competitiveness, even for primary and unprocessed commodities. The anticipated inward foreign direct investment (FDI) and technology flows did not arrive during the GNU period. As a result, Zimbabwe's new indigenous economic empowerment entrepreneurs, including new farmers, faced very stiff trade competition from the EU, as well as from the regional powerhouse South Africa and the East Asian economies, whose products flooded into Zimbabwe during the post-independence era. Given the adverse balance of power, the question arises of why the Zimbabwe authorities opted to be among the first African countries to sign an iEPA with the EU. This is an especially interesting question, given the antagonistic relationship between the two, and the state of the Zimbabwean economy.

Throughout the period since Independence, Zimbabwe lacked broader industrialisation strategies, and trade policy[22] was ad-hoc and often incoherent (ZCTU, 1996; Chizema and Masiiwa, 2011). Bargaining from a position of weakness, ZANU (PF) elites had mobilised their rhetorical energies against western countries which opposed land reform, but they relaxed this hostility during the EPA negotiating process. The dysfunctional GNU administration failed to respect many crucial GPA provisions that would have increased unity and a sense of purpose, and hence there were sharp economic policy contradictions, especially when it came to the new trade regime with Europe. This reflects a more general problem during the period 2009-2013: the state's failure to depoliticise public policy and to prioritise resource allocation and collective energies for industrialisation, export diversification, research and skills development and technological advancement in the country.

---

[22] Zimbabwe only launched formal industrial and trade policies in 2012.

Failure by both ZANU (PF) and the GNU administrations to embrace unifying macro-economic policies and to revamp economic production across the economy undermined Zimbabwe's prospects of competing with European products. By denying Zimbabwe access to EDF resources (especially the 'development assistance envelope') given to all EPA economies, the EU ensured that Harare suffered from an adverse negotiating capacity. For example, as discussed further below, one of the most important sites where limited technical competence affected the Zimbabwe negotiators was in sanitary and phytosanitary issues with respect to live animals and beef products and cut-flowers. Failure to build competences to negotiate effectively in the above areas left Zimbabwe in a disadvantageous position to benefit from European markets in the short to medium term under this iEPA trade regime. The EU negotiators also benefited from Zimbabwe's lack of capital outlays for overdue infrastructural investment; much lower technological capabilities; and failure to acquire economic, financial and technical assistance during the GNU era. As illustrated in the box below, Zimbabwe, like most other regional economies, is failing to use trade as a tool to contribute towards economic growth and social development.

Box 1.1   Zimbabwe's trade and development related problems (seen from the Commonwealth's perspective)

Limited institutional capacity to formulate and implement trade and industrial policies necessary to exploit opportunities associated with globalisation.

Limited technical analytical capacity to identify areas of concerns and points of leverage during bilateral and multilateral trade negotiations within the context of multi-layered regional integration initiatives.

Poor institutional infrastructure coupled with low technical capacities among trade officials and other relevant stakeholders to engage in trade policy design and trade negotiations.

Poor multi-stakeholder relationships, especially during trade negotiations and economic frameworks.

Source: Commonwealth Secretariat Hub and Spokes Project (2012)

As a result, the new trade regime between the EU and Zimbabwe guaranteed an expanded African market for EU products in the short to medium term, given the state of Zimbabwe's own weak industrial capacities, and presented no competitive risk to the EU given Zimbabwe's weak exports, leaving only hard currency shortages, over-indebtedness and trade finance boycotts as barriers to total EU dominance. As Tadeus Chifamba[23], Zimbabwe's chief EPA negotiator in 2012 claimed, "the goal of negotiating an EPA with the EU was meant to secure a predictable future trade regime" but this was not achieved. Zimbabwe was unprepared in this round, especially given deficiencies in state-stakeholder relationships. One aspect was the Harare negotiators' apparent desperation to agree to a deal in order to secure Zimbabwe's future market, regardless of the prevailing macro-economic environment, as Angelica Katuruza[24] claims:

> The main objective to negotiate an EPA with the EU – in spite of tense bilateral relationships heightened by the imposition of sanctions including travel prohibition to enter the capital city of the EU – was largely informed by the country's future needs in the EU market in particular and the global economy in general.

Yet as Chizema and Masiiwa (2011) argue, trade liberalisation under iEPA will result in the de-industrialisation of inefficient sectors as a result of trade with the EU. This will not only confirm the EU's self-interested strategy but also undermine any further progress by the ZANU (PF) government on land rights and other economic empowerment programmes. The withdrawal of Britain from the EU – 'Brexit' – makes matters even more complex, especially in the event that the EU economy declines (limiting potential Zimbabwe imports) and British exporters will naturally become more aggressive in seeking new (non-EU) markets, with Zimbabwe's traditional neo-colonial relations with British firms; a major factor in London's

---

[23] Interview discussion with Tadeus Chifamba, Harare, Zimbabwe, 14 September 2012.

[24] Interview discussion with Angelica Katuruza, Johannesburg, South Africa, 28 May 2012.

choice of new trade negotiating partners. This brings to the fore economic uncertainty with potential local market volatility, resulting in slower economic growth given the dominance of agricultural and mineral commodities. However, The Brexit's impact on trade with Zimbabwe in particular and Africa in general was not easy to predict as this book went to press. This calls for a separate enquiry on how Zimbabwe has to negotiate its way with UK separately from the EU at the end of exit process within 2 years and the implication thereafter.

The challenge ahead for Zimbabwe's producers, large and small, is to withstand Europe's most adverse influences and divisive strategies, as European (and British) firms pursue short to medium term commercial interests. To do so will require the kind of re-engaged civil society that was not permitted into the negotiating process under the GNU, yet many of the leading civil society groups – especially those associated with labour and anti-debt constituencies – have also been ambivalent about working with the ZANU (PF) administration, a condition likely to prevail even after Mugabe's departure from the presidency[25]. Whether any reconciliation can occur in the period ahead is a critical question, given the failure of civil society advocacy in the past.

Zimbabwe remains an opaque society in which to draw conclusions, and Zimbabwe-European relations are no exception, especially in terms of trade policy. The study that forms the basis for this book was conducted, using surveys of trade-related government portfolios, CSOs, and private sector umbrella bodies. Given Zimbabwe's politically charged environment, my previous professional fieldwork and research experiences allowed me to source what is normally hidden information, especially from senior chief negotiators and politically insecure junior officials.

The enquiry has focused on EU-Zimbabwe trade relations; the state of play of the EPA process; and state shortcomings and civil society advocacy. It coincided with the 2012 trade and industrial policies of the GNU that came up short given the ongoing economic

---

[25] Lack of clear succession plan in the governing party constantly exposes crude and stubborn character assassination politics devoid of reaching out to broader civil society formations and other opposition political parties.

crisis. The research encompassed the GNU period's strong disagreements in ideologies and state-society conflictual relations.

Towards the end of the research for this book, the EU and Zimbabwe government together commissioned work[26] on i-EPA. The book therefore grapples with a wide variety of rapidly-shifting interests in Zimbabwe during a period that included tumultuous events: global economic crisis (2008-09); a discredited presidential election and follow-up negotiations for the GNU (2008); the GNU's brief shift to more market-oriented strategies (2009-13); the zig-zag return of Mugabe's economic dirigisme (2013-15); the crash of platinum prices as the Chinese-related commodities import boom faded (2011-16); the decline in the volume and value of world trade (2014-16); a major shake-up within ZANU (PF) as vice president Joyce Majuru (the leading contender to replace Mugabe) was unseated mainly by Mugabe's wife, Grace (2014-15); public allegations by Mugabe that the relationship his military enjoyed with Chinese diamond purchasers had caused a revenue shortfall of $15 billion that should have come from the Marange fields (2016); an import ban on various basic products from South Africa during a severe cash crisis, generating major protests by small traders whose livelihoods had become dependent on street-side commerce (2016); and the British 'Brexit' retreat from the European Union (2016). Together, these forces appear to be gathering for some sort of transitional process, but given the importance of the military in Zimbabwe and the bureaucratic hostility to change, it is not yet clear whether a post July 2013 ZANU (PF) government will be more friendly to western interests and open to the drastic austerity measures – for example vast cuts in the civil service and extensive privatisation – that will be demanded by international financiers in exchange for a bailout. Trade with the EU will continue, but will it.

Besides the above chapter, the book comprises six chapters. In this respect, Chapter two provides the theoretical background by way of comprehensively reviewing relevant literature as well as identifying specific issues and debates in three key areas of interest in the context of EU-Zimbabwe EPA negotiations debate, namely, the theories and

---

[26] I was a member of the consultant team, whose work was in two-phases: July-August 2015 and June 2016.

models underpinning trade negotiations; the nexus between FTA and trade negotiations; and past inspirations of civil society advocacy and trade negotiations. This exploration better situates the EU-Zimbabwe EPA negotiation process in the contemporary intellectual discourse, highlighting aspects that require attention.

Chapter three chronicles and demonstrates how the EU-Zimbabwe[27] trade relations have evolved since the latter's independence in 1980 and underscores the important links between the Zimbabwean economy and its trade performance. This navigation not only highlights the dominance and influence of the EU in the process at ACP, configuration and national levels, but also analyses related technical and ideological issues in the context of balance of power between the negotiating parties.

Chapter four explores and discusses the state of play in the EPA process by assessing institutional and structural dynamics in the negotiation process; critiquing state-stakeholder relationships in the context of inclusiveness and transparency in handling the economic trade agenda, particularly ongoing trade negotiations; and exploring the link between EPA ideology and seemingly guerrilla negotiation strategies and tactics on the one hand and the formulation of Zimbabwean interests, positions, and offers on the other.

Chapter five examines the nexus of Zimbabwe's state shortcomings and civil society advocacy by navigating the contours of state-stakeholder relationships, and in the process, summarises the available evidence and interpretations of emerging EPA-related fears, implications, and policy options.

Chapter six interrogates the unfolding bilateral re-engagement within the context of implementing iEPA regime in Zimbabwe. This further not only highlights trade flaws between negotiating parties, essential features of the new trade regime, and key re-engagement milestones and macroeconomic policies, but also explores ways in which Zimbabwe can reap benefits from implementing iEPA regime.

---

[27] On 4 November 1980, Zimbabwe signed the agreement to accede to the second Lome II Convention in Luxembourg, in the presence of the Foreign Ministers of the nine European Community member states and the European Commission representatives.

Chapter seven concludes the study by discussing theory versus benefits of bilateral trade relations as well as summarising major lessons which the research holds for trade negotiations in the context of hostile bilateral relationships between the negotiating parties, conflictual state-civil society relationships and political polarisation. The chapter also highlights related policy recommendations; contributions which the study may offer to future regional, bilateral and multilateral trade negotiations; and potential topics for future research. Further, the chapter ends by questioning if Zimbabwe is ready to make progress?

Chapter Two

The Basis of Negotiations

Most trade talks are integrative in nature; negotiating countries or regions enter into the process primarily because of 'expectations to derive some commercial, social, and political benefits' (Kramer and Messick, 1995: 13). Thus, the EPA objectives listed in the box below features throughout the process not only between EU and ESA configuration negotiations, but also between the former and the rest of other ACP EPA groups.

Box 2.1   EPA objectives
EPAs are conceptualised as capable of promoting deeper integration among ACP countries and act as a stepping stone for further integration into the global economy - taking into account geographical, historical, and economic factors;
EPAs outcomes must be economically meaningful, politically sustainable and socially acceptable in order to foster an economic growth and developmental trajectory that leads to reduction in poverty and inequalities;
EPAs outcomes must progressively abolish all trade restrictions, thereby making them WTO-compatible; and
EPAs must take into account the different levels of development of contracting parties by providing sufficient scope for flexibility, special and differential treatment and asymmetry, especially with regard to the LDCs, small and vulnerable economies, landlocked and small island countries.

Source: Deve (2006) and Kamidza (2007)

The joint ESA-EC roadmap promises that 'no country in the configuration would be worse off' (Kamidza 2008: 2) as the negotiations somehow assume a win-win scenario between negotiating parties that are both economically and politically unequal with huge developmental differences between them – as well as within the group (ESA) itself. While it is debatable that outcomes of

21

the EU-Zimbabwe trade negotiations will achieve the above objectives and promises, Kachingwe (2004), Deve (2006) and Kamidza (2008) are of the view that EPAs are essentially Free Trade Area (FTA) negotiated between unequal[28] parties, both in political and economic terms. Goodison (2007) adds that the EPA process perpetuates asymmetrical power relations between the EU and the respective configuration countries.

Trade negotiation is a framework that seeks to define trade and development cooperation between and among nations as informed by relative factor distributional effects[29]. This is supported by Stolper and Samuelson (1941) who favours the distributional effects of trade by arguing that free trade benefits factors of production that are relatively abundant compared to locally scarce ones. Such a comparison accurately describes the EU-Zimbabwe trade and development cooperation relationship. This is in accord with the Ricardian theory of comparative advantage, which argues that countries specialise in producing goods and services relative to production cost differences (Stephen and Chang-Tai, 2002). Thus, differences in production costs among countries as well as different levels of productive and export efficiency are at the heart of international trade. When production efficiency is stimulated, countries realise increased trade flows and maximise consumer welfare, firms' profits and national wealth. Robinson (1998) observes that in the contemporary world economy, trade flows, capital movements, inward and outward FDI and technology flows, are components that sustain the dominance of TNCs and MCs thereby giving them competitive advantage in the global trade arena. This explains why countries with a greater presence of TNCs and MCs tend to enjoy not only market competiveness for their products and services, but also determine the pace and framework of trade negotiations. Todaro (1990) argues that the principal benefits of world trade accrue disproportionately to rich and poor nations. This explains why industrialised economies are scrambling for commercial

---

[28] EU and ACP countries.

[29] Since the focus is on the EU-Zimbabwe trade talks, no analysis, reflection and interrogation has been made with respect to the factor endowment or factor distributional effects of the negotiating parties.

markets of their goods and services in poor countries through multilateral (WTO) and bilateral (such as EPAs) trade agreements. The EU is an industrialised economic powerhouse with a huge presence of TNCs and MCs, whose influence filters directly to developing economies through policy prescriptions of the global financial institutions (GFIs) (see Figure 3.1).

Negotiation conduct, practices and outcomes explain why some regions such as the EU succeed in negotiating international trade agreements as a single entity in spite of diverging preferences. Indeed, European member-states have since 1957 accepted the principle of a single external voice in trade, that is, a common position in which they all defend with a single voice (Meunier, 2000) at both the bilateral and multilateral levels. European countries always adopt at the onset the lowest common denominator position which prevents negotiators from making innovative proposals, especially by submitting numerous offers to opponents. By this means, the bloc is able to not only guide their negotiators during the bargaining process, but also to provide the necessary human, financial, technical and moral support in order to obtain the best possible deal from the opponent, while conceding the least. The theory also guides the bloc in articulating offensive and defensive strategies and tactics in line with the assumed position of lowest common denominator in trade talks. Meanwhile, Meunier (Ibid) argues that negotiation theories allow member-states to collectively allocate and utilise resources in ways that not only create a large market, but also attract foreign trading interests. Thus, regions such as the EU, on the wisdom of this theory, are home to TNCs and MCs, a development that gives the negotiating bloc greater international leverage over its counterparts, particularly in ACP regions.

It is difficult for developing countries, and particularly Zimbabwe, to balance the outcomes of negotiations with the social development question. The two parties (Zimbabwe and EU) must manage the flow of events that surround the negotiation process, as well as opportunistic behaviour. This supports rule-based trade negotiations though the outcomes may not necessarily redress social developmental challenges such as poverty, underdevelopment and inequalities, in developing countries such as Zimbabwe. This reality of developing countries contradicts Crump (2006), who notes that multilateral negotiations are based on evolving rules that are non-discriminatory, while bilateral and regional negotiations reduce trade barriers on a reciprocal and preferential basis. This resonates with the natural interaction of the two trading systems as well as the inherent challenges and opportunities for developing trade and regional integration policies. Thus, the EPA negotiation process is tied to a fixed WTO-related time frame. Indeed, Crump (2005) argues that negotiation theory, although it provides substantial understanding about negotiation processes and outcomes, fails to adequately consider the social context in which the negotiations take place. This means that the EU-Zimbabwe trade talks should have broadly been conducted within a social context including historical, cultural, political, economic and organisational forces. It is thus possible when a negotiation is under way that other events can influence negotiation process and outcome via this shared social context. This view is in line with those of Sebenius (1996) and Watkins and Passow (1996) who argue that negotiations are not conducted in a vacuum. This is further supported by Kramer and Messick (1995) and Menkel-Meadow (2001) who observe that negotiations are not only complex and dynamic, but also require isolating parties, goals, interactions and outcomes from the social context in which they are embedded. While these views emphasise the necessity for the negotiating parties to have considered the prevailing social and economic developmental challenges in Zimbabwe during the negotiations process, the political hostilities and polarisation, state-civil society conflictual relationships, and poor EU-Zimbabwe diplomatic relationships make it difficult to implement the above wisdom.

Hammouda and Osakwe (2008) argue that trade negotiation is a bargaining game in which power relations among countries and the availability of information influence their strategic behaviour during the negotiation process, which in turn affects the outcome. Harrison and Rutström (1991) link the bargaining strength of trade negotiators to their ability to draw a positive balance sheet of concessions from their counterparts. Each party aims to extract maximum benefits from their respective opponent(s). Sometimes, both parties conclude the process without any acrimony. In other instances, parties misjudge each other's intentions while assuming an irrational approach to the process.

Kahler and Odell (2004) argue that developing countries require sufficient economic power to create or threaten an important economic interest in a sharp and immediate manner during the negotiations. However, as Rothstein (1979) argues, negotiating groups such as ESA lack procedural cohesion and substantive unity which diminishes the possibility of achieving viable settlements, while the EU bloc maintains a unity which is based on ideological principles and the sum total of the group's demands compared with those of its counterparts' level of ambitions. The emphasis is on the importance of first-mover advantages in negotiations and the extent to which big countries or regions control the manner in which negotiations are conducted (Myerson, 1991; Brander and Spencer, 1992), and how big countries or groups such as the US and the EU are in a better position to influence the agendas and pace of negotiations, even though this has serious implications for the ability of weak African nations to protect their own interests (Osakwe, 2007). It is, therefore, necessary to evaluate the impediments and surprises such as dirty tactics and divide and rule strategies, embedded in trade talks.

Within the context of public choice theory, trade negotiation is seen as a process of interaction between competing interests, and sometimes parties agree to trade off variables against one another to maximise their respective socio-economic welfares. But in trade-related institutional frameworks, and in particular the WTO and the EU, there are no spaces for civil society to effectively and directly participate in the negotiation process. CSOs are not welcome at the preparation platforms[30] or in the negotiation rooms. At the national level, whether CSOs become involved in trade talks depends on governmental institutions, political climate and operational capacity. Das (2004) argues that institutional interaction has the potential to generate full confidence among the various interest groups, particularly economic operators, producers, exporters and the public in general in the trade policy and trade regime of the country. Basevi

---

[30] Unless CSOs' representatives participate as members of a government delegation, in which case their views automatically become that of the government.

(2008) observes that governments set up their trade policies and act as if they care more about the interests of various constituencies (producers, importers and exporters) than they do about consumers. This is illustratable by government's decision to ban the importation of genetically modified organism products from South Africa, the regional main trading partner, and other economies including the EU.

Within the context of the game-theory models, negotiation or bargaining is recognised as a strategic interaction between competing parties and lobbying groups, which take into account possible trade-offs and the efforts of other groups and/or countries. This interaction includes not only the parties, but also the game-like negotiations between government and various actors in the country. Rege (2004) observes that actors have differing self-interests which they pursue rationally and systematically in ways that maximise the country's economic benefits and commercial interests, taking into account the political, institutional and other constraints under which they operate. However, these actors are not always fully informed about all the aspects of the issues, positions and interests under consideration. This is due to lack of information because the parties deliberately attempt to obscure available facts and ignore the predictions and commitments of their counterparts. This underscores the need for assessing the strategic importance of various constituencies[31] in the process.

Goodison and Stoneman (2005: 40) warn that "it would be an act of foolish optimism to expect integrity or honesty in the EU's trade policy towards southern Africa in particular and the wider ACP group in general." Their opinion is largely informed by the dominance and influence of the EU in previous bilateral trade agreements with the ACP region, and a similar approach by its Directorate General for Trade, whose mandate is to secure European prosperity at the expense of social and economic development of latter. The founder and former SEATINI trade expert, Tandon (2004), notes that trade-related issues are usually framed in technical language which is difficult for many people to understand, despite

---

[31] Such as producers, exporters, civil society groups, political leaders, and negotiators.

the fact that it affects their livelihoods in very significant ways. He further deplores not only GFIs' (the World Bank, and the IMF) support to the former imperial region, but also their undemocratic practices, which *inter alia,* undermine institutional and state-society relationships, and effective policy structures and systems. Kamidza (2007) argues that the EU misleads negotiators of vulnerable and poverty-stricken countries into thinking that any negotiated trade regime guarantees sustainable industrial and/or sectoral growth, development and export competitiveness and diversification, as well as social development which includes human capital formation and poverty alleviation. Zimbabwe is thus a classical case in which the trade negotiation with the EU were concluded and ratified notwithstanding perennial weak and vulnerable industrial and export capacities coupled with other political and social challenges.

Thus, the process and outcome of any trade and cooperation agreement with the EU sometimes produces unintended challenges, such as structural and institutional capacity limitations. Bond (2007) argues that the outcome is likely to resemble the Doha agreement which amplified the free-trade agenda that had generated intense unevenness, inequality, eco-destruction and women's suffering over previous decades. In essence, the process in Zimbabwe has undermined social cohesion, equity, inclusiveness, trust, confidence and cooperation and promoted an atmosphere of suspicion, paranoia, and deceit. This mirrors the Angola-EU and Mozambique-EU fisheries agreements (FA) that were characterised by poor consultative relationship between negotiators and diverse stakeholders, weak monitoring capacity in the agreement's legal provisions and a lack of institutional memory to dictate possibilities of reopening negotiations on previously agreed provisions (Kamidza, 2008). By tabling fishing compensation payments, the EU concluded FA frameworks with respective governments' negotiators without the knowledge and participation of key constituencies such as the general population – the people[32], the fisher folk and the private sector. They also overlooked post-trade pact challenges, including fish stealing by European high-tech fishing vessels in the respective

---

[32] People sector refers to civil society groups whose programme interventions are a response to the collective needs of communities and/or citizens.

countries' waters, unfair fishing competition against local fishing folk who use old technologies and a weak review process of the compensation fees in line with national developmental goals. This illustrates the impact of unintended consequences in trade and development cooperation agreements between unequal parties in terms of both economic and political standards. It is certain that the potential for unintended consequences in the EU-Zimbabwe trade talks is very high on account of the tense government-CSO relationship and the business sector's mistrust of government. For instance, the business sector could not submit a comprehensive list of sensitive products to government negotiators (see Table 5.3). The outcome of the process is also unpredictable due to GPA related political tensions and the economic policies and programmes, posturing and contradictions within the GNU.

Linder (1961) explains why trade occurs between countries that have similar demand preferences and produce the same goods and services. It means that the countries' production varieties are not primarily determined by domestic demand, but also by trade with countries with similar demand patterns. More importantly, this is the basis for bilateral and multilateral trade negotiations and, as such, emphasises the WTO's role in developing and shaping rule-based international trade regimes. The WTO negotiation framework provides guidelines for bilateral trade negotiations, such as ongoing EPAs between the EU and ACP countries. As Ralph (2008) argues, EPA negotiations have been based on the WTO's principles of reciprocity and non-discrimination. In many instances, rule-based trade and development cooperation has become potentially more conflictual since economic gains or outcomes are translated into political utilities at the country level. This is also the basis of Europe-Zimbabwe trade talks where, to some degree, similar products are in demand in both economies (although huge gaps in technical, financial and productive capacities, and institutional support will translate into an outcome that reflects the socio-economic and political realities of both parties). Indeed, the EU is demanding market openings despite Zimbabwe's current inability to produce market competitive products, to build technical and analytical capacities in trade negotiations, to generate fiscal revenues or to develop and implement sustainable pro-poor and pro-development policies. Revival of the Zimbabwean economy was hampered by political rhetoric and posturing on fundamental economic processes, both prior to and post the GNU administration. This justifies not only an assessment of the implications of the EPA outcome for the economy's future in the context of regional and global market integration, but also of the negotiators' information dissemination strategies.

The EU has established negotiating institutions, divisions, structures and systems (See Chapter 4) that are not only invisible to their counterparts, but also deprive them of certainty in the process. Putnam (1988) agrees that domestic institutions, divisions and structures are bargaining assets in international trade negotiations, a constraint which the ACP in general and Zimbabwe in particular face in the ongoing EPAs negotiations. For instance, the EU negotiators always employ the 'Schelling conjecture' strategy to obtain leverage in the process (Meunier, 2000): their counterparts are reminded of the likelihood that the deal under negotiation may be rejected by the member-states or the European Parliament, or as in the case with EPAs, that other regions may have already agreed on some process(es) or position(s) (João Machado[33]). This explains why Zartman (1991) defines negotiation as a process of combining conflicting positions into a common position while the power game theory broadly defines negotiations as successive stages, namely, pre-negotiation, stalemate and settlement.

Sequentially, the negotiation process starts with a pre-negotiation phase in which parties identify and agree which issues to focus on (the joint road-map), after which neither party can refuse to negotiate. The second phase is the actual conduct of negotiations on substantive issues, interests, positions and offers during which concessions are made and details hammered out. Theoretically, however, negotiating parties, especially at the bilateral level, may withdraw from the negotiations (although in practice this often depends on the strengths of the negotiating parties and the level of their ambitions). This is supported by Garfield and Knudsen (1997)

---

[33] Observation made during the joint EU-SADC EPA countries negotiations, Johannesburg, 20-22 March 2013.

who explain how international relations theories seek to develop multi-disciplinary models of trade policy behaviour, which allows a protectionist mentality to influence the course and outcome of the negotiations. This means that negotiating parties endowed with human, financial and technical resources naturally control both the process and outcome. In many instances, the road to rule-based trade cooperation is potentially conflictual because economic gains or outcomes are translated into political utilities at the country level. The trade regime as prescribed by international bodies is not sufficient to guarantee fair trade, particularly in strategic industries of weaker economies. For instance, in Seattle both the USA and South Africa failed to co-opt the former Zimbabwean Minister of Industry and Trade, Nathan Shamuyarira, the leader of a group of African delegations who persuaded the Organisation of African Unity caucus to issue a statement withdrawing consensus, claiming "there is no transparency in the proceedings and African countries are being marginalised" (Tandon, 1999: 18). As a result, they (USA and South Africa), flexed their international trading power by imposing ever-tougher anti-dumping penalties against impoverished trading partners such as Zimbabwe (Bond, 2006a and 2007; and Bond and Manyanya, 2002).

The foreign relations theory of realism (Gideon, 1998) argues that states, as primary actors in world affairs, treat all other states as autonomous, self-interested and animated by the single desire to pursue power. This is supported by regime theorists who uphold the right of states to pursue wealth, political stability and domestic distributional objectives. In this context, Shell (1995) advises states to balance the interests of groups who seek protection from foreign imports against the interests of exporters and others who prefer to expand free trade, mainly on account of creating jobs and incomes. The Wise Men's Report (2005) to the WTO Director-General notes that many firms in poor nations that are currently struggling to find a small niche market in a tough global economy require some positive discrimination to exploit small comparative advantages born of a preference. This provides insight not only into the conduct of multilateral and bilateral trade negotiations between countries or regions, but also how negotiations on a given issue cannot be examined separately from other issues. Trade talks require competence from negotiators in terms of flexibility, autonomy and authority.

The standard trade theory defines Free Trade Areas (FTAs) as a designated group of countries that agree to eliminate tariffs, quotas and preferences on most (if not all) goods between them. This makes FTA superior to all other trade policies, though there are usually a few administrative delays[34] (Balchin and Kamidza, 2008). Kahuika *et al.* (2003) note that FTAs embody the Ricardian theory of comparative advantage[35] (Stephen and Chang-Tai, 2002) which mean that countries that engage in trade specialise in producing goods relative to the production cost differences. Dunn (2009) argues that in practice free trade has almost always been a question of degree since all states maintain some restrictions but few practice complete autarchy, and that the degree of openness or closure bears little or no relation to overall economic performance. However, as Chang (2007) illustrates, governments nurture and protect strategic, infant and important industries until they are ready to compete in regional and global marketplaces. This is contrary to the views of free trade economists, particularly from global institutions such as the IMF, the WB and the WTO who prescribe rapid large-scale trade liberalisation in developing countries[36] despite the fact that their local producers are still at a developmental stage in terms of production (Hartmann, 2008). This view is supported by the former WTO Director-General, Lamy (2010), who argues that trade openness delivers efficiencies, generates wealth and lifts millions of people out of poverty.

The second best theory suggests that free trade may not be efficient or welfare-enhancing in the presence of other distortions in the economy. The trading system sometimes restricts or discriminates against "low cost" suppliers (Raghavan, 2004) in the sense that an importing country decides on the quantities and prices

---

[34] As goods pass freely from one country to another.

[35] A country has a comparative advantage in producing a good if the opportunity cost of producing that good in terms of other goods is lower in that country than it is in other countries.

[36] Developing countries are obliged by the WTO national treatment to extend policies aimed at boosting their own national industries, such as tax breaks, to other foreign companies in the same industry.

of imported products to be sold in its domestic market. As a result, tariffs and residual quantitative restrictions as well as discriminatory non-tariff measures, though gradually liberalised, are still unevenly distributed, thereby hurting the major suppliers from third world countries. As a result, the system undermines potential imports from developing countries which also have to cope with stringent trade distorting measures such as countervailing duties and subsidies, particularly in the agricultural sector.

Irwin (1996) argues that the international market share is reminiscent of mercantilism, and that the volume of world trade is fixed and divided among a few countries. This notion treats trade as a zero-sum game in which no consideration is given to consumers' welfare. By demonstrating a 'strong correlation between firm size and international trade', Valodia and Veila (2006) argue that larger firms have been more successful at integrating their manufacturing activities into the global chains of production leading to increases in exports, competition, and volatility of local economies. Reimer *et al.* (2006), argue that while many international food and agricultural markets are oligopolistic in nature, government interventions result in relatively small price-cost mark-ups and modest potential trade gains.

In the case of EU-Zimbabwe trade relations, the former demands asymmetrical market openings while the latter experiences huge socio-economic deficits and industrial and productive capacity constraints which hinder the implementation of sustainable, equitable, and people-centered development programmes including the current the Zimbabwe Agenda for Sustainable Socio-Economic Transformation (Zim-Asset) national blueprint (2013-2018). However, the Zimbabwe government's intervention[37] in the agricultural sector - an attempt to ameliorate the abovementioned weaknesses - has yet to produce positive outcomes. At the same time, the GNU's economic transition has made little progress on account of the failure of the GPA's framework (belligerent parties and SADC and African Union (AU) leadership), to secure the withdrawal of sanctions against the ZANU (PF) leadership and its associated

---

[37] Intervention in terms of fast-track land redistribution and inputs (seeds, fertilisers, tillage, and fuel) to farmers.

companies, from the EU in particular, and the international community (western governments) in general. As a result, the necessary investment has not been forthcoming. As a result, efforts to implement the critical interventions in building technical and analytical capacity in trade negotiations, supporting industrial structures and restoring confidence in the economy are undermined. Also undermined are efforts to improve trust and cooperation between the state and the business community and inclusive and constructive collaborations between the state and CSOs on economic policy making including trade negotiations.

The question whether or not 'free trade' is automatically associated with superior growth and employment performance has attracted a great deal of debate (Chizema and Masiiwa, 2011). The debate supports the Bretton Woods Institutions (the IMF and the World Bank) trade liberalisation agenda, and has in recent years influenced approaches, strategies and tactics in bilateral and multilateral trade negotiations processes. In this respect, Bretton Woods Institutions argue that countries with more open markets achieve higher levels of economic growth, development and employment. In particular, the EU (1999), while explaining its approach to the WTO Millennium Round Conference, argues that trade liberalisation and strengthened multilateral trade system rules have resulted in significant contributions to global prosperity, development and poverty alleviation. A study by the Organisation for Economic Cooperation and Development (OECD) (1999) agrees that more open and outward-oriented economies not only consistently outperform countries with restrictive trade and foreign investment regulations, but also foster innovation and the development of an information economy. This is further supported by Chizema and Masiiwa (Ibid) who observe that trade liberalisation contracts inefficient sectors by realigning domestic prices of tradable goods with world prices, while expanding new and efficient productive structures. This supports the argument by Rodrik (1990) that political sensitivities and considerations sometimes compel governments to protect infant industries and inefficient sectors from trade taxes. The above sustain the scholars' arguments of anti-trade liberalisation for continued state intervention in directing the flow of foreign trade. Change theory, which evaluates the effectiveness of foreign policy advocacy efforts, that is, how the actions of civic bodies influence changes in policy, attitude, or public will in ways that lead to desired outcomes, has been employed to evaluate civil society practices in terms of engagements, lobbying, and building synergies and coalitions in support of bilateral trade and development cooperation negotiations between the EU and Zimbabwe. In particular, CSOs' advocacy on trade and development co-operation agreements invites actors to combine resources with a view to building synergies and deepening strategic networking and engagement in order to build greater leverage during negotiation processes. This forms the genesis of strategic consultative engagement between CSOs and other relevant stakeholders working on trade and development issues. However, the strategic consultative engagements that take place between CSOs and government are often acrimonious.

Keet (2007) supports the above observation by noting how the division between African negotiators and civil society activists worsened during the WTO Ministerial Summit in Doha in 2001, and decries Pretoria's failure to use its political or moral weight and democratic reputation to actively prioritise real institutional reforms as an essential pre-condition for any other WTO trade related discussions, an intervention that could have offered lessons for the on-going ACP-EPAs negotiations. In particular, Keet (Ibid) accused South Africa's former Trade minister, Alec Erwin, of accepting a controversial 'friend of the chair' position, which made him responsible for negotiating WTO rules, but in the process, disappointing observers and civil society critics. In spite of the coordinated civil society advocacy at Doha, Keet maintains that WTO ministerial conferences are characterised by flagrantly inequitable, manipulative and undemocratic practices including the appointment of 'friends of the chair' in informal working groups, an outcome that institutionalises undemocratic decisions on key issues. Keet further argues that Africa's strategic alliance suffered a setback when Pretoria dumped traditional allies including the Nigerian, Tanzanian, Ugandan, Kenyan, and Zimbabwean delegations, rejected NGO advisors to African governments, and carefully advanced a pro-WTO position in favour of a 'new round' or 'broad-based agenda'. However, a demonstrated unity in civil society advocacy, coupled with the ambitions of some African delegations, led to the articulation of extreme basic positions aimed at pro-poor development outcomes (CIDSE[38] Discussion Paper, 2000). Strategic networking and synergy building is further highlighted by Bond (2007) who quotes Keet's claims:

> What is amazing, and inspiring, is that the many colourful banners and placards, flags and chants, songs and drumming, each with their distinctive cultural characteristics, all carry similar messages against the WTO, against the unjust and destructive economic system it is being used for, against the damages to the world environment, to livelihoods and lives - as expressed dramatically in the symbolic suicide of the Korean farmer, Lee Kyung Hae… With our distinctive black and green t-shirts and banner proclaiming that 'Africa is Not for Sale', the African people's organisations in Cancun are sending a clear message to the WTO and African governments that we are here to demand that the needs and rights of our people are not sold off by our governments (Keet, 2003: 1).

As argued elsewhere in this book, trade talks at the WTO level, in terms of strategies and tactics influences, to some extent, the bilateral negotiation processes. This means that the experiences of past WTO ministerial conferences could directly or indirectly have a positive influence on the ongoing EU-Zimbabwe trade and development cooperation negotiations. Unfortunately, the strength of the strategic alliance between civic groups and African governments in general, and Zimbabwe in particular, has been uncoordinated, discredited, suspect and weaker compared to the advocacy activities around past WTO events. The Zimbabwean EPA process has been characterised by lack of social cohesion, equity, inclusiveness, trust, confidence and cooperation in an atmosphere of suspicion, paranoia and deceit (Kamidza, 2007). This is supported by

---

[38] CIDSE (International Cooperation for Development and Solidarity) is a coalition of 15 Catholic development organisations in Europe and North America working with two thousand partner organisations in developing countries.

SEATINI (2004), who observes that the RNF meetings' communiqués, draft texts, proposals and timeliness were not shared with other constituencies to inform and share wisdom on the process, particularly at the national level. Further, the ESA configuration - where Zimbabwe belongs - shut the door on civil society representation in its RNF meetings in December 2004, thereby undermining the 'inside-outside advocacy approach' (Tandon, 2004) in terms of pursuing and/or linking specific issues with specific government delegations. Critics argue that this created a vast gulf in understanding the sticking points and issues as well as prohibited the sharing of experiences between negotiators and civil society groups. Indeed, frustration in advocacy work sustains CSOs' perceptions that ESA governments were/are 'selling out their countries and people to European capitalism' (Deve, 2006: 4).

Throughout the process, the CSOs have been irked by anecdotal evidence which reveals that sub-Saharan Africa-EU trade flows declined from 3.2% to less than 1.4% between 1985 and 2006 in spite of the series of Lomé Conventions (1975–2000) that provided 'comparative advantage' of ACP products to European markets through trade preferences such as duty-free and quota-free (DFQF) market access, and the Everything-but-Arms (EBA) initiatives. They have been equally disappointed that ACP countries are failing to access the EDF envelopes designed to improve ACP countries' industrial capacities, institutional technical capacities and supply-side bottlenecks to global markets before the conclusion of EPAs. The CSOs have also been frustrated by the fact that the ACP countries opened up their economies to EU competitive products through iEPA signatures without corresponding improvements in their respective limited industrial capabilities and export competitiveness. Further, they have been worried by the seeming lack of desire to protect strategic, infant and sensitive sectors of the economy for various socio-economic and political reasons. In the Zimbabwean case, while the state has been directly involved in the economy through contested politically motivated programmes, particularly fast-track land reform and indigenisation, and its economic empowerment policy, that trajectory has not been robustly defended during the negotiations. As a result, CSOs' advocacy constantly highlighted negative perceptions about the process against the backdrop of the EU's failure to adequately redress supply-related bottlenecks and improve industrial and export diversification and competitiveness as promised by the EDF's developmental assistance envelopes since 1975 (Draper, 2007).

Nalunga (2004) observes that CSOs have been suffering from limited resources to finance both EPA-related programmes and activities and the EC's existing aid portfolio in ACP countries. CSOs have therefore been lobbying various EU institutions to honour past promises with respect to EDF resources, claiming that by dangling the 'development aid envelope' the EU has split 89 ACP countries into six EPA regions (the Caribbean Forum (CARIFORUM), the Pacific, the Economic Community of West African States (ECOWAS), the Economic and Monetary Community of Central Africa (CEMAC), the ESA and the SADC EPA as they prepared to negotiate a new trade regime with the EU. Lobbying EU institutions also explicitly justifies the need for more allocations under the 10th EDF financial window covering the period 2008 to 2013 to adequately support most ACP countries, particularly Zimbabwe, which has been experiencing perennial negative economic growth, especially between 2000 and 2009[39], with a view to improving industrial production structures, export diversification and competiveness, as well as attracting domestic and foreign investors.

Advocacy has been focusing on the negative implications of EPA frameworks for existing regional integration projects in Africa in general and southern and eastern Africa in particular. This means the focus has been on the implementation challenges with respect to aligning liberalisation schedules and commitments in iEPAs with those agreed on at regional levels as part of regional integration commitments. In this respect, Oxfam (2002) observes that three decades of structurally adjusting their economies according to neo-liberal precepts, especially trade liberalisation, have left many African economies more open and integrated into the global economy than their European counterparts. This revelation from a pro-trade

---

[39] The economy experienced positive growth following the GNU's introduction of dollarisation, that is, legal replacement of local currency with multi-currency for the purchase of goods and services.

liberalisation lobbyist contradicts the anti-EPAs advocacy which argues that the scope, structure, format and terms of EPA negotiations were entirely EU member states-driven in the context of donor-recipient relationships between ACP countries and their former colonies (Christian Aid, 2003; 2004). This further favours liberal civil society advocacy groups which criticise the Lomé Conventions for failing to provide adequate development aid assistance as well as to increase and diversify production and trade in Africa. The weakness of four generations of Lomé Convention provides a sufficient basis for CSOs to anchor their advocacy work. In the case of Zimbabwe, anchoring advocacy on Lomé Conventions' shortcomings would have created all the necessary scope and space for CSOs to link the current total liberalisation with the economy's economic recovery agenda within the context of EPA negotiations.

Christian Aid (2005) warns that over 20 years of advocacy for trade liberalisation in developing countries has proved disastrous for poor people and poor producers. From this study and the Stop unfair trade campaign[40] (2007), the following testimonies were captured:

> Our economies will not be able to withstand the pressures associated with liberalisation as prescribed by the WTO, and that as partners, we need to ensure that the EPAs outcome does not leave the ACP countries more vulnerable to the vagaries of globalisation and liberalisation, thus further marginalising our economies (Festus Mogae, former President of Botswana, May 2004: 4).

> We express our profound disappointment at the stance taken by negotiators in the European Commission (EC) insofar as it does not adequately address the development concerns that must be the basis of relations with Africa. We urge our negotiating partners to clearly demonstrate the development content of the proposed agreements (AU Trade Ministers Declaration on EPAs, 14 April 2006).

---

[40] Stop unfair trade campaign aims to stop trade deals between Europe and ACP countries

It has become quite clear from our frank discussions that the two years of regional negotiations have generated very little tangible outputs, particularly as related to the two areas of critical interest to the ACP regions and countries, namely, the development dimension of EPAs and the support for regional integration processes (John Kaputin, ACP Secretary General, October 2005).

Europe's aim is a new framework, where neighbours work together to benefit from freer trade while we offer assistance to integrate them into the world trading system (Peter Mandelson, EU Trade Commissioner, December 2004: 2).

EU imports of frozen chicken wings destroyed the local market...EPAs are free trade agreements, and as such, they will bring poverty to Africa. ... If EPAs carry through, African countries will have to kiss goodbye to their industrialisation efforts (Tetteh Hormeku, programmes director of ATN, April 2005: 6).

The above is supported by the 'Anti-EPAs' campaigners such as Christian Aid, Oxfam GB, ATN[41], and the Third World Network who observe that no African government has ever proposed the voluntary opening of its market to EU imports as part of a national development or industrialisation strategy. Liberal critics view EPAs as an opportunity to negotiate better deals from the EU in formal regional negotiations rather than relying on the goodwill of European governments to grant them preferential schemes. While the above suggests grey areas for CSOs in ACP countries to intervene with specific advocacy activities, limited resources do not allow them to undertake research analyses that inform issues, interests, positions, and offers.

Advocacy activities highlight the failure of past trade preferences to stimulate industrialisation, diversification of exports and market competitiveness in the ACP countries. Kamidza (2007: 9) supports the above argument by noting:

---

[41] SEATINI, MWENGO, ZIMCODD and Trade Centres are affiliated members of ATN.

Unprocessed commodities (such as diamonds, petroleum oils, sugar and tobacco) continue to make up the bulk of ACP's exports to the EU. This means that countries are yet to develop and diversify their production structures and exports; add value to their exports; and increase their market share in line with the imperatives of globalisation. In particular, given the narrow industrial bases that characterise the SADC and ESA configurations, EPAs are likely to provide only limited options for increased exports into the EU (Kamidza (2007: 9).

Thus, CSO activism focused on growing fears about the outcomes of EPAs. Firstly, CSOs have been arguing that EPAs would limit the policy space needed for the development and protection of national infant industries. Secondly, they have argued that the outcome of the EPAs will either slow down the growth of infant industries or destroy their potential altogether, resulting in unemployment and social dislocation of families, households and communities. Thirdly, they have been expressing fears that EPAs may intensify and entrench the liberalisation of national and regional economies to an even greater degree than the structural adjustment programmes of the 1980s and 1990s. Fourthly, they have been expressing the fear that further trade liberalisation will flood local markets with cheap imports from Europe and other global competitors. Lastly, they have been worried that the outcome of the EPAs may have the potential to dampen the ability of countries to create opportunities for human development in terms of skills training, innovation, research and development.

The advocacy literature has assisted in evaluating the contribution of Zimbabwean civic groups who generally have had poor relationships with ruling elites but closed ranks with the EU on matters of governance, pluralistic democratic processes and human and property rights (Kamidza, 2009c). This provides difficult terrain for civil society advocacy on EPA processes in the context of glaring state shortcomings, frosty Zimbabwe-EU diplomatic relations, a conflict-ridden GNU and limited resources to engage the EU's constituencies[42]. All this undermines the elucidation of advocacy

---

[42] This includes negotiators, parliamentarians, institutions (DG Trade and DG Development) and a rotating presidency.

activities, especially with respect to forewarning negotiators of the dangers of locking the Zimbabwean economy into a pre-determined pattern of liberalisation.

This poor state-civil society relationship continued under the GNU while the signatory parties, especially ZANU (PF), which has consistently displayed a non-committal attitude to GPA provisions intended to support the country's political and economic transitions, particularly the unlocking of funding support from the international community. This disregard of GPA provisions was a constant frustration to western governments, donors, and broad sections of civil society, hence their collective resolve to demand 'clear and practical evidence of power-sharing' (Kamidza, 2009a: 4) before committing financial resources and technical assistance to the country's socio-economic transition. Kamidza (ibid) notes that the above alliance had, prior to the signing of GPA, developed a set of benchmarks[43] to evaluate the GNU's commitment to political and economic transitional processes. In fact, this strategic activism was intended to unlock the necessary financial resources from the international community in support of projects, technical assistance, and budgetary expenditures. Unfortunately there has been no evidence of support in the ongoing EPA trade negotiations.

In fact, lack of funding denied many civic bodies the opportunity to become part of government delegations to RNF and joint ESA-EU meetings which were held in the region and in Brussels. The process thus lacked monitoring from within. The plea for fair and just EPA outcomes remains largely unheard, which further weakens the advocacy of civic bodies who (Deve, 2006) have had no discernible impact on the unbalanced and heavily biased match between a vulnerable Zimbabwean economy in meltdown and an economically powerful European region.

---

[43] These include full and equal access to humanitarian assistance; development of macro-economic stabilisation policies; restoration of the rule of law, judiciary and respect for property rights; releasing of all political prisoners as well as an end to political violence; respecting media plurality, democratic process, human rights standards, freedom of expression and assembly; and timely elections to be held in accordance with international standards. They are also demanding 'no cherry picking', meaning that 'all the principales' should be treated with equal importance as stipulated by the GPA framework.

Since 2000, the trade debate in Zimbabwe has been partisan and tense due to state-society relations, cold state-EU relations, politically induced social polarisation and economic policy contradictions. Indeed, the economic policy environment, including trade, has greatly compromised relevant stakeholders' constructive and collective consultations and engagements; the strategic synergy building and networking of stakeholders; and the advocacy of CSOs on the EPA process. The enquiry that forms the basis of this book was motivated by the following:

The 1990s trade liberalisation policy de-industrialised much of the Zimbabwean manufacturing sector. By the late 1990s, the stage was thereby set for civil society opposition to state and/or donor-led trade policies, in conjunction with a world trade movement that emerged at the Seattle WTO summit.

The ZANU (PF) government was instrumental in both liberalising trade and (in the 2000s) defaulting on debt obligations and imposing new financial and trade controls, until January 2009 when the currency collapsed.

The ZANU (PF) government's revolutionary credentials (epitomised by guerrilla tactics and unorthodox reclamation of land and mining rights from erstwhile colonialists), could not match the EU's influence, dominance and divisive strategies and tactics in pursuit of short to medium term offensive commercial interests in the Zimbabwean economy.

Civil society experienced a conflict between a democratic and a redistributive standpoint, and although several economic justice organisations such as the Alternative to Neo-liberalism in Southern Africa (ANSA), the Labour and Economic Development Research Institute of Zimbabwe (LEDRIZ), SEATINI, the TRADES Centre, and ZIMCODD straddle these two views, their first opportunity to influence both the ZANU (PF) government and the GNU on trade, did not have the desired impact.

Chapter Three

Bilateral Trade Relations

Introduction

After independence in 1980, Zimbabwe became a signatory to the four generations of Lomé Convention which since 1975 has been the basic framework for economic cooperation between the EU and 71 ACP countries (FAO Report, 2003[44]). Through the various Conventions, the EU's bilateral trade cooperation regime with ACP countries was characterised by non-reciprocal clauses, which entailed a range of trade preferences under DFQF market access that also guaranteed better market prices for goods originating from the ACP countries. Subsequently, Zimbabwe became a signatory of the Conotou Agreement, the successor to the Lomé Conventions, which in its turn is set to be replaced by the EPAs. Thus, the Europe-Zimbabwe bilateral relationship has been based on a predictable trade regime guided by negotiated trade and development cooperation principles and parameters of both the Lomé Conventions and the Cotonou Agreement.

The Conventions acknowledge different levels of economic development in the two parties, and within the framework of the ACP-Europe economic and political relationship in particular. This also meant that the trade regime reflected the geopolitical times during which the European Economic Commission (EEC), under the influence of the MCs' and TNCs' capitalistic commercial interests, pursued a trade regime characterised by access to cheap raw materials in agriculture and the extractive sectors rather than access to products produced in Zimbabwean and other ACP markets. Europe thus assumed explicit 'benign' control over the trade and developmental agenda of all the ACP countries, but implicitly continued to set conditions that facilitated the

---

[44] Study prepared for FAO by Tekere Moses with assistance from James Hurungo and Masiiwa Rusare, TRADES Centre, Harare.

entrenchment of MCs' and TNCs' capitalistic expansion, exploitative commercial tendencies and hegemonic influence over local domestic producers, exporters and, to a certain degree, the political leadership as well. It can be argued in the Zimbabwean case that its former coloniser (the United Kingdom) and other EU member states, through this bilateral trade relationship, maintained its dominance over the economy in ways that impacted on future trade and development cooperation negotiations and/or relationships. In particular, Anglo-Zimbabwe relations adversely affected the economy, resulting in a 68% drop in the latter's exports to the former (Chigora, 2006: 20).

For Zimbabwe, the preferential market access has generally been positive. The FAO Report for 2003 noted that for four consecutive years from 1994, the country enjoyed a balance of trade surplus with the EU. In this regard, Zimbabwe's agriculture, manufacturing and mining export commodities to the EU covered both traditional and non-traditional product lines - as reflected in Table 3.1 below. From the table, it is clear that agriculture has been central to all EU-Zimbabwe bilateral trade cooperation agreements.

Table 3.1   Zimbabwe exportable commodities to the EU, 1980-2000

Sector	Characteristics and remarks
Agriculture	The preferential tariff quota under the Convention's 'Beef Protocol' that allowed Zimbabwe to export 9,100 tonnes of beef annually into the EU market up to 2011.
	The sugar protocol under the ACP-EU Cotonou Agreement that facilitated both refined sugar and raw sugar on two arrangements: the normal ACP-EU duty-free annual quota and the special preferred sugar arrangement. The protocol also benefited from Zimbabwe's economic structural adjustment programmes (ESAP) trade liberalisation policy and the enlargement of the EU market, both of which

	significantly improved the commodity's market access situation in Europe.
	Horticulture: cut flowers, floriculture, fresh produce (mostly vegetables), herbs and spices, citrus and subtropical and deciduous fruits, whose combined total export value jumped from US$6 million in the 1986/1987 season to an estimated US$103 million in the 1996/1997 season. The horticulture industry enjoyed better production conditions including low costs, good climate, vast availability of suitable land, export processing zone status and a number of airlines servicing the industry.
	High-quality hand-picked cotton with very long fibres whose exports rose from 18,797 tonnes in 1993 to 92,769 tonnes in 1997 before falling to 79,671 tonnes in 1998. Of the total cotton export, raw gin and fabric account for approximately 80% and 5% respectively.
	About half of Zimbabwe's tobacco crop, especially flue-cured tobacco, enjoys access to the EU market. However, tobacco production, which dropped from 237 million kilogrammes in 2000 to 47 million kilogrammes by 2008, has since recovered to about 140 million kilogrammes by 2011.
	Processed tea and coffee
Manufacturing	Beverages, leather and textile articles.
Mining	Precious or semi-precious metal, scrap/stones, nickel and ferro alloys.

Source: Food and Agricultural Organisation (2003c)

Notwithstanding the STABEX fund that sought to support export earnings due to a decline in prices of commodity exports, Zimbabwean export levels of most commodities gradually declined due to a combination of factors: suppressed global prices in the late 1990s, the 2000 fast-track land redistribution programme, increasingly volatile political environment, the ongoing diplomatic row between Harare and the EU, and exchange rate policy inconsistency between policy and practice (that is, linking prices of goods and services with the parallel exchange rate rather than the official rate). In particular, after 2000 horticulture suffered from the withdrawal of major airlines that normally transported these products to the European markets, falling global demand in flower markets and prices, and the introduction of exchange rate controls. All the above significantly depressed production, and export volumes to the EU region.

Meanwhile, the EU, by excluding non-ACP WTO member countries from DFQF market access, violated the WTO principle of non-discrimination in global trade thereby paving the way for a time-bound[45] EPA process between the EU and ACP configurations, whose outcome would determine the future industrialisation thrust of the latter, and in particular weak and vulnerable economies such as Zimbabwe. The outcome would also determine the former's ability to protect its industries, producers, exporters, investors, farmers and consumers through negotiated tariff liberalisation and commitments on trade-related issues. Masiiwa and Chizema (2011) warn that the EU's demands for the inclusion of WTO-plus intellectual-property rules would make it difficult for Zimbabwe's producers, exporters, and investors to access the knowledge and technology necessary for industrialisation and enhanced agricultural production. Such a development would only guarantee short to medium term markets for European products.

This chapter interrogates current EU-Zimbabwe relations, which are being negotiated in a hostile political and economic environment. It starts by reviewing the socio-economic and political crises of 1997–2008, focusing on the agricultural and manufacturing sectors whose products would be most likely to compete with those from Europe in both the EU and local markets. The chapter also describes the pre-crisis context under each sector before discussing the transitional period under the inclusive government (2009-2012). It reviews the EU-Zimbabwe negotiation processes, analysing the EU's dominance and influence on the process through its economic and political

---

[45] Initially, EPA negotiations between the EU and the ACP configurations were to be concluded by 31 December 2007.

leverage - not only within the context of the ACP and the ESA group, but also during the iEPA signing ceremony. The chapter concludes by examining related ideological and technical issues that have dominated the EPA process.

The crisis period, 1997 – 2008

Since the late 1990s, the Zimbabwean economy has suffered stop-gap economic management policies coupled with incoherent trade policy implementation. In particular, the government became increasingly hesitant to wholeheartedly embrace neo-liberal policies and trade liberalisation. Chitambara (2011) argues that rising hardship-induced discontent and civil society activity, impelled government to introduce irrational controls, inconsistences and reversals, populist and knee-jerk implementation of policies, including:

> A penchant for unbudgeted expenditures in the late 1990s: once off gratuity (US$4,167) and monthly pension (US$140) awards to each of the 50,000 war veterans of the liberation struggle at the end of 1997; military intervention in the DRC war estimated at US$33 million a month in August 1998; and between 69-90% salary increase for civil servants in January 2000 (Chitambara, 2011: 40)

The above, coupled with disrespect for property and human rights and the rule of law and deficiencies in governance and democratisation, worsened the relationship between Zimbabwe and its international development partners to a degree that the country earned itself a high-risk profile that amounted to pariah status (Kanyenze, *et al.*, 2011). In response, donors and investors deserted the economy en masse, while by 1989 the country was no longer able to access BOP support from the IMF. Further, slow export growth, a surge in imports and dwindling external financing and investment saw not only the overall BOP worsening from about US$200 million to an all-time low of about US$1.9 billion in 2009, but also accumulated arrears on foreign-debt repayment, which rose to US$1.3 billion by December 2002 and about US$6 billion by

December 2009 (Chitambara, 2011). As a result, the economy experienced an acute shortage of foreign currency, and a thriving parallel market emerged.

The Zimbabwe Programme for Economic and Social Transformation (ZIMPREST) adopted in 1998, reflects the divergence between official policy and practice with Structural Adjustment Programme Review Initiative Network (SAPRIN) (2004: 45-6) observing policy contradictions with respect to 1998 tariff rationalisation, 2000 tariff mid-loading (application of tariff lines midway through the agreed time-frame) under the SADC FTA, and the removal of several tariff exemptions on the one hand and proposed reintroduction of price controls on the other. This is supported by Masiiwa and Chizema (2011) who maintain that under both ZIMPREST (1998-2000) and the Millennium Economic Recovery Programme (MERP) (2000-2001), the official position on trade was to increase liberalisation, yet in practice the government has taken several measures that indicated a reversal of this trade policy. Kamidza and Mazingi (2011) observe that the Zimbabwean economic environment has suffered from perennial poor economic performance despite formulating five economic blueprints between 2000 and 2007 which were poorly implemented (see Table 5.4). The IMF Report (2011: 5) argues that the ZANU (PF) leadership presided over an unprecedented melt-down of the economy between 1998 and 2008 through its economic mismanagement, resulting in large industrial and sectoral output losses and culminating in a hyperinflationary environment and a country-wide humanitarian crisis in 2008. This reflects the dismal failure of both fiscal and monetary policies to stimulate an economic turnaround. In particular, extensive controls and regulations, especially with regard to the exchange rate that was fixed by the central bank at a highly overvalued Zimbabwe dollar, resulting in price distortions since the determinant of prices of goods and services was the parallel exchange rate.

Kamidza (2002) highlights the limited choices policy makers had for dealing with high price instability and persistent inflationary pressures, declining business/investor confidence amid complete withdrawal of donor support, dwindling export competitiveness, resulting in chronic shortages of foreign currency and an erratic supply of fuel in an environment in which the prevailing political competition[46] created conditions for populist short-term policies and/or policy interventions focused only on winning elections. The policy makers were motivated by the political contestation between the former ruling ZANU (PF) and the opposition MDC formations. This highly polarised political environment further triggered politically motivated social and economic policies and/or programmes, and public finance management that was entirely partisan. This resulted in conflictual bilateral relations between the negotiating parties and between the state and other stakeholders. This affected the EPA process which became associated with gross violation of human and property rights and disregard of the rule of law, all of which undermined the economic export value of most sectors of the economy, especially in regard to agriculture and manufacturing.

The ZANU (PF) government used sanctions as their main excuse for the non-performance of the economy, particularly in agriculture, and it was also a convenient cover-up for inadequacies and corrupt activities in the diamond fields of Chiadzwa. The sanctions excuse was used to cover up glaring weaknesses in economic policies and programmes, including the ongoing trade negotiations with Europe, while the economy continued to suffer from unpredictable policies, lack of clear political direction and the associated potential ramifications as well as huge challenges in social development.

The manufacturing sector

The major constraint on Zimbabwean economic growth from the late 1970s to the early 1990s was industrial investment, which affected manufacturing production and capacity utilisation (Bond, 1998). The import-substitution policy was only effective in textiles, metals and paper products, and hence exports remained insignificant, apart from textiles and metals. Meanwhile, domestic market expansion was driven by transport, beverages and tobacco

---

[46] The country's intense electoral contestation included presidential (2002), parliamentary (2005), by-elections and mayoral and/or council elections.

processing, construction materials and pharmaceutical products and foodstuffs. While the manufacturing sector stagnated, numerous erratic and significant devaluations of the local currency negatively affected exports since production depended on imported raw materials, intermediate production-related goods and capital equipment and machinery. As a result, the country's BOP problems worsened, making it difficult to attract multi-national corporate investment.

At independence in 1980, Zimbabwe inherited a relatively developed and diversified manufacturing sector, consisting of some 1,260 separate economic units producing about 7,000 different products (Doroh, 2011). Independent Zimbabwe's re-entry into the international community paved the way for access to new markets not only at the regional level (COMESA and SADC), but also under the four generations of Lomé Convention (which provided preferential entry for agro-exports into the EEC markets). Tekere (2001) notes that the Rhodesia-South Africa and Lomé Convention trade arrangements and a guaranteed domestic market not only protected the sector from global competition, but also resulted in some firms becoming increasingly uncompetitive, especially on account of limited value addition and innovation. Manufacturing has since been a central key driver of economic growth, contributing significantly to GDP, export receipts and employment creation. It also developed strong backward and forward linkages with other key sectors of the economy, particularly agriculture (See Box 2.1) and mining.

In the mid to late 1980s, the government replaced its import-substitution industrialisation strategy with a trade policy that protected local industrial development and the diversification of domestic markets through import restrictions and foreign-exchange controls (Rattso and Torvik, 1998). Doroh (2011) argues that the deliberate policy of compressing imports in order to manage the BOP situation left capital stock in an obsolete and depleted state. The new policy failed to support sustainable economic growth, as the industrial and export capabilities could not compete with global products. Hence, by the late 1980s, investment was significantly depressed and resulted in stunted economic growth, foreign currency shortages, limited productive sector expansion and increased unemployment.

In response, the country adopted the World Bank and IMF supervised and sponsored neo-liberal trade liberalisation policy, which removed export incentives and import-license restrictions, resulting in sluggish performance from manufactured exports. Some domestic firms de-industrialised or scaled down their productive investments, due to a surge in competition from imported products. Doroh (2011) blames the weak response of non-traditional exports to price incentives generated by exchange rate depreciation while Tekere (2001) laments the poor performance of both traditional and high-tech[47] industries. Kapoor (1995) bemoans the lack of any measures to upgrade export infrastructure, provide export financing and develop market intelligence in support of exchange rate depreciation to achieve a structural shift towards exports between 1991 and 1996. But a high degree of political and economic uncertainty and extensive government restrictions discouraged any new investment in the economy. Thus, instead of resulting in export-led growth, ESAP prescriptions contributed to export-led decline across key productive sectors, particularly manufacturing and agriculture.

The manufacturing sector was hardest hit by the trade liberalisation and market-led policy prescriptions imposed under ESAP in the 1990s. Hitherto protected, it now had to face up to new business conditions. As a result, the unlocking of GFI funding could not sustain the growth and development of this sector in particular and the economy in general. According to Rattso and Torvik (1989), the new approach was due to increase political pressure to join the international trend of implementing liberal economic reforms, and assurances from the Bretton Woods Institutions that liberalisation would unlock funding (Chizema and Masiiwa, 2011. The sector suffered further from the consequences of the unfolding politically-driven economic empowerment policies and programmes. Manufacturing almost came to a halt, due to a combination of factors, including scarce domestic production inputs; a lack of

---

[47] This includes machinery, electrical goods and transport.

foreign currency to import production inputs and to replace aging tools, machinery and equipment; and a highly politicised operational environment characterised by threats to property rights, and macro-economic policy contradictions and uncertainty.

In particular, the sector suffered from the withdrawal of investors (both domestic and foreign) and donor confidence, and the subsequent sudden and massive abdication of investors (both domestic and foreign) and donors, who preferred the neighbouring countries of Botswana, Mozambique, South Africa and Zambia. Manufacturing was also a major casualty of price distortions between 2000 and 2008, especially the pegging of the exchange rate at a highly overvalued rate at a time when the country's industries were net consumers of imported inputs (raw materials, machinery, spare parts and equipment and intermediate goods).

Kramarenko *et al.* (2010) blame the fast-track land reform for triggering the inevitable collapse of the manufacturing sector, leading to a corresponding sharp decline in export earnings. The sector's interdependence with agriculture through strong backward and forward linkages (see Box 2:1) resulted in a drastic fall in its total contribution to foreign currency earnings from US$815 million in 2000 to US$210.3 million in 2008 (Doroh, 2011), amid a significant surge in foreign competition on the domestic market. The combination of a slump in manufacturing production and export capacity also resulted in foreign exchange rate instability and subsequent BOP pressures. This forced the country to default on many of its external obligations with the IMF and the World Bank, thereby accumulating further debt. In an effort to ameliorate the situation, the then Reserve Bank Governor, Gideon Gono, introduced multiple exchange rates, that is, a fixed exchange rate, a managed two-tier exchange rate and a foreign exchange auction, all of which failed - as aptly summarised by Kramarenko *et al.* (2010) thus:

> Zimbabwe performs poorly in terms of competitiveness, whether it is measured by governance (including rule of law, property rights and corruption), investment climate (including enforcement of property

rights and infrastructure) or price indicators (Kramarenko *et al.*, 2010: 31).

The Confederation of Zimbabwe Industries (CZI) Reports of 2008 and 2009 support the above, citing limited competitive export markets, high cost of production, low capacity utilisation, lack of foreign currency and working capital as the main constraints on the sector. This is further supported by Kanyenze *et al.* (2011) who blame policy inconsistencies and reversals, volatility and unpredictability of the exchange-rate system, lack of secure and predictable property rights, degradation and collapse of infrastructure, severe human resources deficits emanating from out-migration, serious governance deficits, a hostile investment climate and severe shortages of essential inputs (fuel, raw materials and intermediate inputs).

Furthermore, the economy in general and the manufacturing sector in particular suffered from price distortions owing to the introduction of price controls (especially, between 2000 and 2008) that deliberately ignored the fact that the sector was obliged to source scarce foreign currency, mainly from a parallel market, to import the necessary inputs. Ultimately, industrial capacity utilisation and competitiveness plummeted, triggering a subsequent drastic fall in export receipts. The above contributed to the sector's production and export capabilities falling to their lowest ebb in the country's living memory[48]. Sibanda (2012) observes that Zimbabwe's manufacturing exports to South Africa, the main regional trading partner, declined from 30% to 12%. Manufacturing became not only a shadow of its past well-diversified industrial and export base in terms of regional and global links, but was also unable to compete with the EU under the proposed new trade regime.

Agriculture

Land is at the heart of development in Zimbabwe because the economy is agro-based, and it has also been an influential factor in the country's political development since colonial times. At

---

[48] See section 1.1 in which Nyakazeya (2009) estimated 4 and 10% industrial capacity utilisation.

independence, ZANU (PF) inherited a highly developed, sophisticated and largely commercially driven agricultural sector (Matondi, 2011). The sector had a relatively developed infrastructure and farming capacity that attracted significant levels of confidence and investment. The sector was supported by prudent government policies, and complemented by the Lancaster House Agreement's 'willing seller-willing buyer' constitutional clause, which successfully ring-fenced the sector as the anchor of the economy. Agricultural exports in real value increased from Z$409.2 billion in 1981 to Z$1.1 billion in 1988, with tobacco, cotton and sugar accounting for about 75% of the total income generated (Matondi, 2011). The 1990s also witnessed strong intensification of production and export of commercial crops including cotton, maize, tobacco and wheat as well as diversification into horticulture and other new income streams (including ostrich-farming and game-ranching).

In the late 1990s, ZANU (PF)'s rapidly waning public support in the face of the swiftly increasing popularity of a new opposition political party – the MDC – caused its leadership, in league with former freedom fighters and some villagers, to call upon the ideals that had underpinned mass mobilisation during the liberation struggle. White commercial farmers were violently removed from their land. The unorthodox guerilla-type strategies that were used disregarded the country's rule of law and bi-lateral protection guarantees. The distribution of the acquired land was largely partisan[49], populist and politically motivated. This unfolding process disregarded the sector's historical importance as the backbone of the economy and main source of livelihood for most people. This is shown by the African Development Bank (AfDB) (2011) in Box below. These actions also disregarded the importance of farm management abilities, skills training, experience in agricultural production and the motivation and commitment to agriculture as a business.

---

[49] Including cabinet ministers, ZANU PF parliamentarians, war veterans, army generals and senior civil servants.

Box 3.1	Linkages between agriculture and manufacturing

The manufacturing sector has always had strong linkages with the agricultural sector, with agriculture sourcing from it over half of intermediate goods - including insecticides, stock feeds and fertiliser - while half of agricultural produce is supplied to the manufacturing sector. The performance of the two sectors has historically been closely correlated. Therefore, the collapse of agricultural activities associated with the implementation of the fast track land reform programme by the ZANU (PF) government had a devastating impact on the manufacturing sector, which experienced a cumulative decline of 92% between 1999 and 2008.

Source: African Development Bank (2011: 4)

Agricultural production suffered across the range of commercial commodities. New Agriculturalist (June 2011) confirms a significant reduction in coffee production from 10,000 tonnes in 2002 to 300 tonnes in 2010 following the new farmers' diversification to maize. Further, Zimbabwe (which by end of 2000 had been the world's third-largest producer of flue-cured tobacco), recorded a 56% reduction in both the area put to the crop and the corresponding production in the 2001/2002 season, compared with the 1990s (Matondi, 2011). The overall reduction of area, yield and output of the traditional major foreign-currency earners, tobacco and cotton, are reflected in Table 3.2 below. Although new farmers seem to have shown resilience in cotton production, the global price fall is forcing them to diversify to tobacco, whose production levels are significantly lower than that of the commercial farmers before 2000. Meanwhile, the EU's efforts to rejuvenate the declining sugar cane production with an estimated €45 million in funding support between 2008 and 2013 towards rehabilitating abandoned cane fields and improved infrastructure has failed to increase production from 300,000 tonnes in 2009 to the projected 1 million tonnes by 2013.

Thus, across all the commodities (commercial and non-commercial), the sector's productive and export performance fell to its lowest in living memory in terms of providing food security and food sovereignty, ensuring forward and backward linkages with other sectors of the economy; and generating foreign currency, job opportunities, incomes and livelihoods. As a result, the displacement of former commercial farmers who opted to go to neighbouring countries (mainly Mozambique and Zambia) and beyond (Nigeria) not only caused a collapse in agricultural activities, but also significantly distressed the manufacturing sector. Subsequently, agricultural exports were overtaken by minerals and unprocessed industrial raw materials as the country's leading exports, even though the volumes exported had contracted (Kaminski and Ng 2011).

Table 3.2   Cotton and tobacco production trends, 2000-2009

Growing season	Cotton			Tobacco		
	Area	Yield (kg/ha)	Production (mt)	Area	Yield (kg/ha)	Production (mt)
1999/2000	415,000	850	353,000	85,000	2,770	236,000
2000/2001	397,000	840	337,000	76,000	2,650	202,000
2001/2002	229,000	850	195,000	71,000	2,330	166,000
2002/2003	282,000	850	240,000	54,000	1,510	82,000
2003/2004	389,000	850	331,000	41,000	1,580	65,000
2004/2005	350,000	560	198,000	56,000	1,330	75,000
2005/2006	300,000	860	258,000	27,000	2,030	55,000
2006/2007	354,000	840	300,000	53,000	2,160	79,000
2007/2008	431,000	520	226,000	62,000	1,100	70,000
2008/2009	338,000	730	247,000	48,000	1,330	64,000

Source: Adapted from Matondi (2011: 102)

The above is supported by Coorey *et al.* (2007) who argue that the chaotic seizure of commercial farms and unresolved property rights issues relating to security of land tenure fueled the country's hyperinflationary environment and an estimated 30% contraction of the economy since 1999. Coorey *et al.* (Ibid) further note that the country's commercial banks find it difficult to provide finance to new farmers under existing 99-year lease arrangements that do not provide adequate security of land tenure. The fast-track land reform programme not only triggered a loss of confidence[50], but also paralysed the backbone of the economy by weakening forward and backward linkages with socio-economic sectors of the economy. In particular, the sector's linkages with the rest of the economy both qualitatively and quantitatively weakened after 2000, as was evident in the cessation of downstream agro-processing industries and other agricultural-related economic activities. This severely compromised the capacity to produce agricultural commodities that would feed into agro-processing industrial capabilities and the export drive into the EU market in the short to medium term. Current poor agricultural outputs and exports reflect the lack of business acumen and commitment on the part of most new farmers. Indeed, the sector's capacity to generate foreign currency through cash crops such as cotton, sugar and tobacco scaled down significantly in both volume and value. For instance tobacco, once the main earner of foreign currency in the country, is still struggling to improve the quality of its gold leaf. Further, country-wide disruption in the beef sub-sector due to foot and mouth disease cost the country its previously guaranteed and uncontested market share of beef in European cities.

The above is supported by Sandrey and Vink (2011: 18) who argue that "Zimbabwe, once regarded as the bread-basket of Africa, is a tragic example of the consequences of economic mismanagement of the sector", quoting Food and Agricultural Organisation (FAO) data showing an average annual decline of about 0.7% in agricultural production between 1990 and 2007. This mirrors the decline in foreign currency earned by tobacco and cotton from US$566 million and US$174 million in 2000 to US$245 million and US$95 million in 2007, respectively. Dismal trade performances in tobacco and cotton are reflected in a production decline estimated at two-thirds and a third respectively over the same period. Sandrey and Vink (2011) further argue that commercial farms are now largely occupied by people who are unable and unwilling to make productive use of the land. Since 2000, all categories of farmers (A1 Model, A2 Model and

---

[50] Donors and investors (both foreign and domestic) significantly withdrew from the economy.

peasant) have failed to produce enough agricultural-related quantities of foodstuffs and products to feed the nation and its industrial economic activities. As a result, Zimbabwe has become a perennial recipient of humanitarian food assistance or parcels, which ironically come from the EU and other western governments and donors.

In recognition of the sector's importance, the government adopted supportive mechanisms in the form of agricultural schemes including seeds, fertilisers, all types of fuel, chemicals, and ploughs and tractors, administered by the former Zimbabwe Central Bank Governor, Gideon Gono. These quasi-fiscal interventions by Gono reflected a high degree of encroachment into the policy jurisdiction of the Ministry of Finance, and an equally high degree of poor governance in public finance management. The inputs only benefited those farmers who were aligned to the ZANU (PF) party, regardless of their commitment and capacity to utilise the land to the level that had existed under the previous owners. Since then, the sector has continued to struggle to approach pre-2000 performance levels in terms of production and productivity, despite the new farmers having access to and control of the best soils and vast tracts of land. This shows that direct financial support from the government over the decade was not the answer to the revival of the sector. Such a revival calls for additional interventions including the development of capacity in business acumen and farm management as well as the depoliticisation of the sector.

Despite the production and export-related challenges, under the new trade regime the weak agricultural sector is supposed to compete with EU farmers who are protected by the Common Agriculture Policy (CAP) from external competitors through direct subsidies. The EU observes that its support for the agricultural sector is WTO compatible. Goodison (2007) argues that EPA-related outcomes and implications have the potential to undermine government revenues (loss of state revenues generated from tariffs) as well as efforts to promote national exploitation of economic resources. This is supported by Bilal and Rampa (2006) who point to the EU's unfulfilled promise to assist ACP countries, not only to develop new sources of government revenue to replace the tariffs that were removed, but also to improve the competitiveness of the productive sector in order to face off cheaper imports. An EPA-led tariff phase-down in this sector compromises its contribution to fiscal revenue generation, and consequently support for agricultural related production capacity initiatives, including research and development. Already, a combination of low agricultural production and social and humanitarian crises have triggered a surge in agricultural imports from Europe and other emerging economies such as Brazil, ranging from poultry to dairy, cereals and other processed agricultural products. However, the increase in imports cannot at this stage be linked to the signing and ratification of the iEPA. This development accelerates and sustains de-industrialisation as well as discouraging first-stage processing of agricultural commodities before export. This means that cutting trade barriers and opening markets alone does not necessarily generate development, especially in developing countries and particularly in Zimbabwe.

The transitional period, 2009 – 2013

The 2011 IMF Report on Zimbabwe notes that economic growth, which started from a low base, was concentrated in primary commodity sectors such as mining and agriculture, both of which are sensitive to exogenous shocks. The economy showed encouraging signs of being on the path to macroeconomic stabilisation following its de facto adoption of the US dollar as legal tender as a result of the implementation of its multi-currency system in February 2009. However, the strong post-hyperinflation period rebound has been slowing down, with GDP growth falling from 10.9% in 2011 to 3% in 2014 (SADC Secretariat, 2015; See also graph 3:1 below) largely due to poor agricultural output, extensive power shortages and the slow pace of economic reforms (SADC Secretariat, 2015 and EU-Republic of Zimbabwe Report, 2015). The above macroeconomic stabilisation sign was simultaneously complemented with a stronger fiscal discipline by the GNU administration, resulting in renewed capital inflows, an accommodative external environment and economic growth of 9.0% and 5.5% by 2010 and 2011 respectively (IMF, 2011;2012). Inflation has since remained in the low single digits, though marginally rising, as reflected in the diagram below.

From the graph, estimates for 2014 indicate an increase, which is likely to remain, unless the international community open their wallets to the ZANU (PF) government.

Graph 3.1 Zimbabwe's annual GDP growth rates and inflation rates, 2009 - 2014

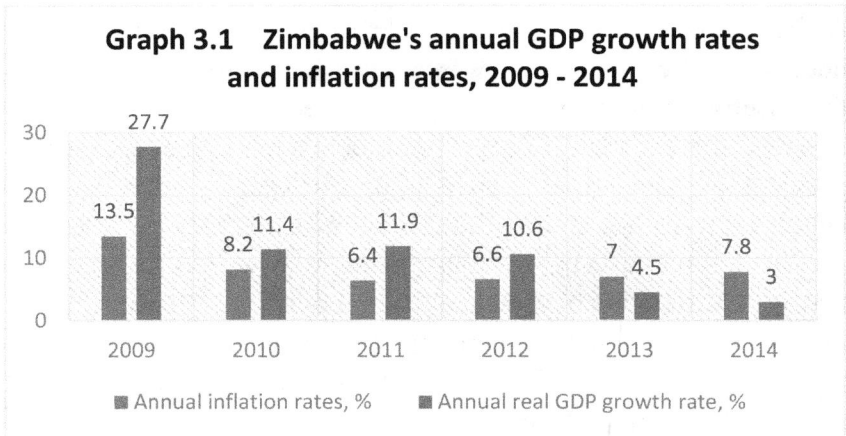

Source: SADC Secretariat, 2015

For example, over the past decade, the Zimbabwean economy has continued not only to experience widespread deterioration of the physical infrastructure, especially roads and railway networks, and energy and water utilities due to years of poor maintenance, but also widespread electricity and water cuts - two essential inputs into the industrial production process. Furthermore, challenges persist that poison the economic climate, especially with regard to much needed investment. Since the birth of the GNU, investors (both domestic and foreign) continue to sit on the fence. The fragility of the economy is reflected in the high unemployment rate, estimated at around 90% and depleted international reserves. The graph below further provides evidence of this fragility with external debt jumping from US$6,289 million in 2009 to US$8,934 million in 2013 (SADC Secretariat, 2015) including a major accrual of arrears. The graph also projects a worsening situation for 2014 (US$10,646 million), and a likely scenario for 2015 and 2016 if the re-engagement with western governments and GFIs fails to materialise. This has not only undermined the business environment, but also has a negative impact on and implications for the country's economic performance and social development.

Graph 3.2   Zimbabwe's total external debt, US$ Million

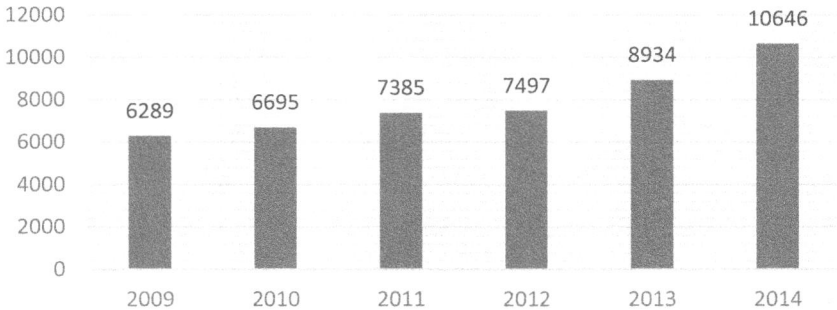

Year	Value
2009	6289
2010	6695
2011	7385
2012	7497
2013	8934
2014	10646

Source: SADC Secretariat, 2015

The overview of Zimbabwe's total external debt as at 31 December 2014 amounted to US$10,8 billion, of which US$6,8 million and US$4,0 billion was public sector debt and private sector external debt, respectively. As shown in table 3.3 below, the public sector debt is not performing compared to the public sector one. Further, the table shows that the country publicly guaranteed external debt mainly to state-owned enterprises, estimated at US$3,6 billion and US$2,6 billion is owed to bilateral creditors and multilateral creditors, respectively. The above arrears status to the multilateral creditors has rendered the country ineligible to access funding from these institutions (Republic of Zimbabwe, 2015).

Table 3.3: Zimbabwe's total external debt as at 31 December 2014 (US$ Million)

	Debt outstanding disbursed	Principal arrears	Interest arrears	Penalties	Total
Total public external debt	**1,214**	**3,271**	**1,262**	**1,023**	**6,768**
Bilateral creditors	260	1,101	313	771	2,445
-Paris Club	156	1,040	308	759	2,264
-Non-Paris Club	103	61	5	11	180
Multilateral creditors	380	1,028	670	-	2,078
-AfDB	0	250	262	-	512
-AfDF	38	12	4	-	54
-IBRD	-	325	288	-	613
-IDA	317	165	53	-	534
-IMF	-	97	23	-	120
-Other	252	179	40	-	245
External debt (Publicly Guaranteed Parastatal Debt)	**574**	**1,143**	**280**	**251**	**2,248**
Bilateral creditors	574	297	87	197	1,155
-Paris Club	98	297	87	197	679
-Non-Paris club	476	-	-	-	476
Multilateral creditors	-	279	194	54	527
-AFDB	-	37	36	-	73
-IBRD	-	139	144	-	283
Other Multilateral creditors	-	103	14	54	171
Other external debt	-	566	-	-	566
Private sector external debt	**4,069**	**-**	**-**	**-**	**4,069**
Total External Debt	**5,283**	**3,271**	**1,262**	**1,023**	**10,837**

Source: Republic of Zimbabwe, 2015

Other challenges include: macro-economic policy setbacks, contradictions and uncertainties; political tensions within the governing coalition parties on account of pre-31 July 2013 election debates and the implementation of GPA provisions; recent announcements of fast-track indigenisation and economic empowerment programmes[51] of the mining sector (Government of Zimbabwe, 2011); and structural bottlenecks including rigid labour market legislation, lack of security of land tenure and poor governance in the diamond sector. Unclear strategies for redressing these challenges and structural bottlenecks continue not only to cloud short to medium term economic prospects, but also export performance[52] that has fallen well short of its potential to drive the economy to higher rates of economic growth and development.

These setbacks expose the vulnerability of the industrial sectors in particular and the economy in general. Structural impediments continue to weigh heavily on manufacturing and utilities, which were in the past engines of economic growth and development and employment creation. Zimbabwe's manufacturing sector is relatively large and well-diversified, but is yet to record steady progress in terms of restructuring and improvements in export industries. Since the rebound of the economy, the manufacturing sector has failed to provide firm direct linkages with the other sectors of the economy, particularly agriculture to which it previously supplied 50% of its output in the form of fertilisers, feed-stock and insecticides.

Manufacturing faces challenges due to lack of financing, working capital and relatively high production costs owing to its outdated plants and equipment, unreliable supplies and exorbitant tariffs of

---

[51] Indigenous is defined as a person who before 18 April 1980 was disadvantaged by unfair discrimination on the grounds of his or her race, and any descendant of such person, and includes any company, association, syndicate or partnership of which indigenous Zimbabweans form the majority of the members holding the controlling interests. In other words, this refers to indigenous black Zimbabweans. 'Ownership requirements under the indigenisation programme stipulate that 51% of equity of companies with assets exceeding US$500,000 belong to indigenous Zimbabweans. While there is broad agreement in the government on the policy in general, there exist significant differences of opinion regarding pace and modalities of the policy.'

[52] Since 1980, increases in exports have been positively associated with increases in national income.

key utilities, especially electricity, water, fuel, and coal. The above is supported by a recent survey carried out by the CZI that has found that local products continue to struggle to compete in national, regional, and global markets due to a combination of factors including a shortage of working capital to meet orders, high costs of production and failure to identify potential external markets. The sector further continues to experience other restrictive trade policy measures including high import duties and charges, duty drawback and inward processing rebate schemes, import and export licensing, and tariff and tax concessions on various imported inputs and capital goods. To ameliorate the situation, SADC secretariat (2000) reports that the country launched industrial policy pledges to remove controls in interest and exchange rates as well as to liberalise foreign currency in order to buttress the sector's performance as the new engine of economic growth. Though the country is surrounded by fast-growing regional economies, it is yet to benefit from such growth. In the mining sector, all inputs are imported while nearly all outputs are exported without processing or value addition.

In many instances, the GNU failed to develop and implement practical implementable and inclusive stabilisation policies and programmes. The inclusive government has also ignored calls for a conducive economic and political environment anchored in comprehensive structural reforms, predictable policies, recapitalisation programmes covering all industries, inclusive broad-based land reform and indigenisation and economic empowerment programmes. Such policies would have restored investor and donor confidence much sooner, and unlocked international financial and technical resources which would have assisted in the recapitalisation of the industrial and export sectors, thereby expanding the economy, creating jobs and ensuring development and pro-poor EPA outcomes.

As the manufacturing sector remained under severe stress and small to medium enterprises (SMEs) struggled to emerge from a decade-long economic slumber while economic units and consumers relied increasingly on informal cross-border imports. The GNU administration did not make a difference to the former ZANU (PF) government's economic operational environment since the rate of recapitalisation of the sector remains very slow due to resource constraints, in addition to unpredictable and uncertain policies and economic empowerment programmes such as the indigenisation programme. The economy's high dependence on imports including food items is illustrated by the former Industry and Commerce minister, Welshman Ncube, who says: "Brazilian chickens are finding their way on the local market disguised as South African products." (The Herald, 5 March 2010). Former CZI president, Joseph Kanyekanye claims that "Zimbabwe has opened her market too much to foreign players. How do you justify importing canned food?" (Bhebhe, 2012: 1).

Zimbabwe's agricultural sector struggles to shake off the negative effects of irrational and unorthodox policies and the partisan distribution of land and agricultural support inputs. The sector, also struggles to have a multiplier effect on the economy on account of its comparatively modest contribution to GDP. Further, the sector is no longer the principal source of employment. Notwithstanding the sector being heavily protected and supported through high tariffs and a price band system, its development remains hampered by numerous factors including erratic weather (repeated droughts), limited access to and high costs of financing, and infrastructure bottlenecks. As a result, the nation continues to depend on humanitarian assistance to a large degree, which means that the sector no longer contributes to socio-economic development (through tariff revenues), employment creation, livelihoods, sustenance (food security), foreign currency generation and backward and forward linkages with other economic and social sectors. Even though the GNU administration has acknowledged the importance of agriculture in socio-economic transformation, there are visible signs of politicking. Resources and capacity to add value to agricultural products through agro-processing activities targeting mainly crops and livestock products remain limited. The country continues to experience food insecurity and limited agricultural input into other sectors, which casts doubt on the ability and capacity of new farmers to compete with EU farmers under the new trade regime in both EU and local markets. Both new and smallholder farmers are threatened by the EPA outcomes, judging by the list of sensitive products, including agricultural products, submitted to the EU. This list is not only narrow but is also unambitious, clearly indicating the negotiators' failure to adequately contextualise them. This confirms this book's argument that the negotiation process suffered from a lack of input from farmer organisations, which have been dysfunctional since 2000. This confirms that Zimbabwe has not sufficiently protected its agricultural interests in both the EU and local markets, a development that has serious implications for the economic prospects of the new farmers. The country should have articulated its commercial interests and long-term agricultural vision for growth and expansion in the EU and other global markets. Agriculture should have been the compelling pressure point for Zimbabwean negotiators to aim for more concessions for the sector, which has huge potential, despite sour relations with the EU.

Notwithstanding the decade-long economic challenges, the Zimbabwean services sector remains relatively diversified, accounting for approximately half of the economy's GDP. The most prominent sub-sectors include tourism and transportation. For instance, the dominance of transportation services is a reflection of the remoteness of the economy from key markets and sea ports (in Mozambique, Namibia, Tanzania and South Africa). Furthermore, the services are provided (*de facto* or *de jure*) exclusively by state-owned enterprises. The harsh economic conditions of the past decade continue to militate against efforts to restructure and recapitalise the state-owned companies, making the supply of key goods and services inefficient and costly. However, financial services (insurance and insurance-related services, banking and other financial services) that struggled during the economic crisis are slowly recovering.

Europe's dominance in the EPA process

The dominance of the EU is driven by MCs and TNCs, which are ready to exploit every market opportunity in Zimbabwe to advance their own modes of production, usually represented by outward expansion of the production frontier (See Figure 3.2), that is, continued increase in the supply of goods and services. Under the EPA framework this is an expanding search for markets in ACP countries in general and Zimbabwe in particular in order to sustain overproduction or high productivity of goods in Europe as well as employment opportunities and profit margins (see Figure 3.2). According to the FAO Report (2003), EU dominance is increased by the MCs' and TNCs' agribusiness companies which have privileged access to crucial market information that very few other constituencies (including most developing governments) can aspire to.

The mutual relationship between the EU, and MCs and TNCs in ongoing EPA negotiations is reflected in Figure 3.1 below, illustrating that their respective powers are multi-faceted, ranging from concentrating on marketing environments to influencing global economic policy making processes and frameworks, including bilateral and multi-lateral trade negotiations. In this respect, MCs and TNCs businesses pursued skewed EPA outcomes by extensively and consistently lobbying European institutions, the EU Commission, the European Parliament and EU member states, to simultaneously deliver a new trade regime that opens new sustainable markets in Zimbabwe while limiting import surges from European markets. It can also be argued that the EU's imposition of smart sanctions and travel bans on the ZANU (PF) leadership and associated companies were in sympathy with the former government's total disregard for MCs' and TNCs' commercial interests, especially in the agricultural sector. The MCs and TNCs have the leverage to lobby the Bretton Woods Institutions (the IMF and the World Bank) in support of market-led policies and trade liberalisation agendas in the developing economies to levels that resonate with the EPA process. The Zimbabwean trade liberalisation agenda in the 1990s was a case in point. Linked with the above are the MCs' and TNCs' lobbying efforts directed at bilateral and multilateral donors such as the EU, the IMF, and the World Bank. This resulted in the suspension of critical aid from the IMF and World Bank at the peak of Zimbabwe's shortages in foreign currency to support industrial productive capacities, export competitiveness and fulfillments of debt obligations. It can further be argued that the MCs and TNCs successfully exerted pressure on the EU thereby contributing to the lack of movement during the WTO Doha Development Round

(WDDR) in order for the bloc to first secure EPA markets in ACP economies. This was done in the knowledge that most weak and vulnerable countries, including Zimbabwe, have limited financial and human resources to simultaneously negotiate both EPA and WDDR processes in ways that provide meaningful resistance to future commercial interests from both the EU market and countries where they have a commercial presence.

Figure 3.1   EU - Zimbabwe Trade Negotiations Structures

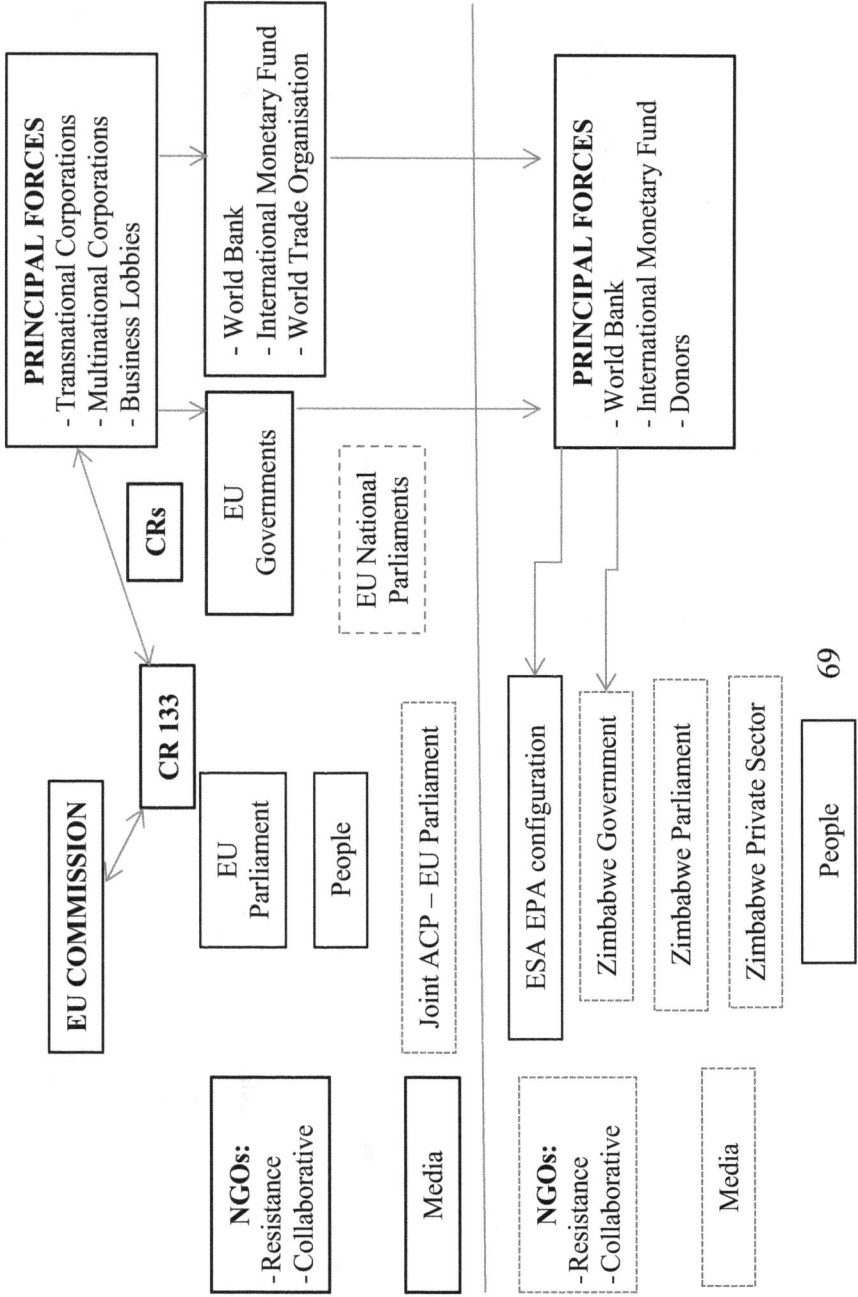

Legend Notes

1. *Zimbabwe government in particular and ESA EPA group governments are under pressure from both EU governments and principals (World Bank, IMF and donors);*

2. *Dotted lines represent weak structure: Zimbabwe (government, legislature, business, Non-Governmental Organisations (NGOs) and media); and EU (national legislatures and joint ACP-EU parliament);*

3. *Continuous line represents powerful structure: Zimbabwe (people through Parliament); and EU (national governments, EU legislature, people, NGOs and media);*

4. *Resistance: Zimbabwean anti-EPA focused NGOs were not funded by EU compared to collaborative and adaptive counterparts working on governance, democratisation, human rights and humanitarian assistance;*

5. *Media in Zimbabwe has been weak because it focused more on unfolding political developments than the EPA process;*

6. *CR stands for Committee Room(s)*

Source: Author's compilation

Figure 3.1 shows Zimbabwe's weak and uncooperative private sector and a divided media accused of being anti-ZANU (PF) government, and little interest on EPA process. For instance, a continued economic downward spiral coupled with visible signs of mistrust between the state and the private sector generally undermines the latter's participation in the ongoing trade talks. The figure also reflects resistant CSOs, most of which have an uneasy relationship with the government. While the diagram reflects the importance of the people, the process has failed to involve them through representation in parliament. Indeed, owing to her weak and vulnerable economic position, Zimbabwe could not financially support the participation of the national parliament through the Trade and Development Committee (TDC) membership. Politically, the composition of members of parliament (MPs) in the TDC reflects two distinct groups, namely the anti-EU section and those whose party has been supportive of the EU's economic and political measures against the former governing party. These financial limitations and political polarisation vis-à-vis the EU undermines the Zimbabwean parliament's ability to proactively resource their participation and involvement in the EPA process, as was the case in previous economic programmes such as ESAP and ZIMPREST. During the ESAP and ZIMPREST process and implementation, Zimbabwean MPs actively engaged other relevant stakeholders. However, the above shows that the EPA process favoured the anti-Zimbabwe camp's commercial and political interests.

The FAO (2003) further observes that TNCs' agribusiness firms have access to enormous sums of capital necessary to cover the futures marketing contracts of some agricultural commodities, thereby influencing the prices at which trade-policy-mediated domestic support and export subsidies are set. Such interventions obviously benefit TNC firms and reflect how the global nature of the TNCs' and MCs' operations give them political and economic leverage. It also allows them to be the dominant and manipulative presence in dozens of weak and vulnerable countries, thereby creating a powerful force to influence economic policies in support of their own commercial interests. In this regard, it is possible that

MCs and TNCs, through their close relationship with the national political leadership may influence the adoption of a trade regime that limits competition by creating barriers to entry into the market in which they enjoy a monopoly. Although the MCs and TNCs currently have no monopoly in Zimbabwe (having been displaced by the ZANU (PF) regime), their influence and dominance in the process would open future commercial opportunities in the country. This would result in a market-led onslaught on the Zimbabwean economy in the short to medium term.

The Zimbabwean economy has been dominated by MCs and TNCs since the colonial era. They are the cornerstone of Europe's capitalist expansion, ensuring economic integration with the industrial process in Zimbabwe through the EPA regime. Europe has remained Zimbabwe's leading trade partner despite the strained bilateral trade and development relationships that coincided with EPA negotiations. These conflictual relationships have largely been influenced by the EU's imposition of smart sanctions on the ruling elite and their associated companies on account of ZANU (PF)'s serious deficiencies in governance and democratisation practices. The EPA process is potentially an onslaught on the Zimbabwean economy in the short to medium term, as reflected in the following two scenarios:

> Firstly, the EU blames the former Zimbabwean government's poor record of governance, democratic values, human rights, electoral processes and selective application of law for directly undermining stakeholder consultative engagement and transparency in the participatory processes. However, such public grandstanding on the part of the EU has from the outset been designed to shield its institutions and structures, as well as its member states, from public judgment and condemnation if the EPA fails to satisfy well-known pro-poor and pro-development objectives, especially those of a developmental nature. It would lead those constituencies that are fighting for a new Zimbabwe to absolve the EC from responsibility for any negative EPA outcome, and rather blame the shortcomings of the state. Given the slow pace of political transition to a pluralistic and constitutional democracy, the civil society voice that is ready to protect the EU from any wrongdoing

continues to be justified. This means that a significant proportion of the population has not yet, and might not in the future, understand and acknowledge the contribution of the EU to an EPA outcome that may not necessarily support a sustainable social and economic development process.

Secondly, the ZANU (PF) government accuses the EU of meddling in the political processes of the sovereign state by supporting CSOs that have been strong allies of MDC formations; that have always been vocal against state-led macro-economic policies and programmes (especially the indigenisation economic programme) and macro-economic transformation (fast-track land reform); and that have been lobbying for the imposition of smart sanctions against the ZANU (PF) leadership and associated companies. This has sustained the anti-colonial agenda (especially the economic emancipation project) which portrayed the EU as a predatory negotiating counterpart ready to exploit internal consultative weaknesses to ring-fence the commercial interests of member states in the proposed EPA deal.

All Zimbabwean economic sectors - including agro-processing, mining, manufacturing and services - are vertically linked to EU industrial processes. In particular, services such as banks and insurance perpetuate the reproduction of capitalist modes of production by facilitating the extraction and exploitation of the country's natural resources, and exportation of the country's commodities to the EU market and other developed economies at predetermined international prices. Economic dominance has ensured that Europe, and particularly the United Kingdom, remains a major Zimbabwean trading partner, despite the rhetoric linking economic performance with the sanctions imposed on ZANU (PF). The United Kingdom is also the largest development aid donor to Zimbabwe via the Department for International Development, which increased assistance from £12 million in 2000 to £18 million in 2001 and to £23 million in 2002 (Chigora, 2006).

Table 3.4 Zimbabwe's trade with main partners, 2011

Rank	Import	€Mn	%	Export	€Mn	%	Trade	€Mn	%
1	South Africa	2,045.7	55.5	**EU (27)**	**419.0**	**22.3**	South Africa	2,373.1	42.7
2	China	336.6	9.1	South Africa	327.5	17.5	**EU (27)**	**661.8**	**11.9**
3	**EU (27)**	**242.9**	**6.6**	China	318.0	17.0	China	654.7	11.8
4	Zambia	127.4	3.5	DRC	220.5	11.8	Botswana	315.4	5.7
5	India	120.7	3.3	Botswana	196.8	10.5	DRC	263.9	4.7

Source: Adapted from European Commission, DG Trade Statistics and EUROSTAT, 2012

Note: *Mn = Million*

As seen in Table 3.4[1], the ranking of five major Zimbabwean sources of imports, major destinations of exports and trading partners reveals a healthy EU-Zimbabwe trading relationship: the second major overall trading partner is the 27 EU member states as a bloc; the leading major exporter of goods and services and third major consumer of Zimbabwean products. ZimTrade (2015) data shows that the trade between the two countries has since risen from a total value of about US$661.8 million in 2011 to about US$800 million in 2013. Over the past decade, Zimbabwean exports have increasingly become concentrated in primary commodities and resource based manufactures, with their associated vulnerability to global fluctuations in prices.

This is shown in table 3.5 below, showing the real value of the main EU-Zimbabwe products traded between 2007 and 2011, a period that mirrors 2000 and 2006. The table shows that Zimbabwe's main exports to the EU continue to be dominated by vegetable products, prepared foodstuffs, beverages, spirits, vinegar, tobacco, mineral products, base metals, and articles of base metal. Conversely, the country's imports over this period were and still are dominated

---

[1] Since ZANU (PF)'s rhetoric on EU economic sanctions has not changed, the table data for 2011 is used as a proxy for 2000-2008, the period prior to the formation of the Government of National Unity.

by machinery and mechanical appliances, electrical equipment, vehicles, aircraft, vessels and associated transport equipment and products of chemical and allied industries. The table further shows the negative impact of disruptions in the agricultural sector with respect to trade flows of beef-related products (animal or vegetable fats and oils and their cleavage products, footwear, headgear, umbrellas, sun umbrellas and walking-sticks) owing to the country-wide outbreak of foot and mouth disease[2], resulting in the cancellation of the Zimbabwean 9,100 beef quota[3] to the EU market in 2001. The fast-track land reform greatly undermined Zimbabwean capacity to supply most agriculture-related products, including beef, sugar, cotton lint, textile articles and clothing, as well as horticultural products that, prior to 2000, were competing favourably on the EU market. The table also confirms the EU ban on the trade of arms and ammunition, parts and accessories thereof. Thus, at the current level of industrial and export development, economic integration over the past decade means that the country derives low value added and decreasing returns from export commodities to the EU markets compared to high value added increasing returns on imported products and services from the same market. Zimbabwe has little or no say in the regulation of external trade affairs, particularly with its former colonial master whose capital base has direct and indirect links with companies or firms that were operating in the country prior to the fast-track land reform-induced political tensions.

---

[2] The fast-track land reform caused a laxity in the control of the mingling of domestic animals (cattle, sheep, goats and pigs) with wild animals (water buffalo, antelope, deer, bison, and elephants), resulting in a country-wide outbreak of foot and mouth disease.

[3] Madambi (2013) reports that Zimbabwe is one of the largest suppliers of beef to the EU. This despite the fact that the country's beef quota is still not authorised by the bloc because other internal regulations of the European market require Harare to comply with all sorts of stringent measures which Zimbabwe could not satisfy, particularly controlling the movement of cattle from one zone to another and technical provisions in several areas: animal health, general hygiene residue monitoring and organisation of official controls to these areas. While the EU institutions are yet to certify Zimbabwe's improvements in these areas, drought, destocking by commercial farmers uncertain about land tenure, shortage of breeding stock, high in-put costs and the deregulation of slaughterhouses are hindering the rebuilding of the national herd.

Table 3.5   EU trade with Zimbabwe, 2007 – 2011, € Million

Product\Year	Imports					Exports				
	2007	2008	2009	2010	2011	2007	2008	2009	2010	2011
Total	**358**	**314**	**226**	**299**	**444**	**148**	**130**	**108**	**189**	**232**
Live animals and animal products	3	3	2	1	2	2	1	1	7	2
Vegetable products	60	40	35	46	33	1	6	0	3	1
Animal or vegetables fats and oils and their cleavage products	0	0	0	0	0	0	0	0	0	0
Prepared foodstuffs, beverages, spirits and vinegar, tobacco	77	73	98	75	185	1	2	4	4	3
Mineral products	43	35	19	16	16	0	0	0	0	0
Products of chemical industries	1	0	0	0	0	24	10	10	12	18
Plastics and articles thereof, rubber and articles thereof	0	0	0	0	0	6	5	6	3	4
Raw hides and skins, leather, fur skins and articles thereof	8	11	8	12	18	0	0	0	0	0

Category										
Wood and articles of wood, wood charcoal, cork and articles of cork	0	0	0	0	0	0	0	0	0	0
Pulp of wood or of other fibrous cellulosic material, paper or paperboard	0	0	0	0	0	10	12	2	3	4
Textiles and textile articles	16	12	11	13	15	2	2	2	4	5
Footwear, headgear, umbrellas, sun umbrellas, walking-sticks	0	0	0	0	0	0	0	0	0	0
Articles of stone, plaster, cement, asbestos, mica or similar material	0	0	0	0	1	1	1	0	1	1
Natural or cultured pearls, precious or semi-precious stones	13	20	15	26	23	2	3	1	0	1
Base metals and articles of base metal	126	115	43	106	142	6	3	2	5	6
Machinery and mechanical appliances, electrical equipment	4	0	1	1	1	68	62	60	112	126
Vehicles, aircraft, vessels and associated transport equipment	0	0	0	0	0	13	15	8	22	45
Optical, photographic, cinematographic, measuring, checking, precision products	0	0	0	0	0	2	3	6	6	9

Arms and ammunition, parts and accessories thereof	1	0	0	0	0	0	0	0	0	0
Miscellaneous manufactured articles	1	1	1	1	0	0	1	1	1	2
Works of art, collectors pieces and antiques	1	1	1	1	1	1	0	0	0	0
Other	4	2	3	2	7	7	4	4	5	3

Source: Adapted from European Commission, DG Trade Statistics and EUROSTAT, 2012

This table further highlights the correlation between economic sanctions and the access to and control of the means of production under the economic empowerment dispensation. It also brings to the fore the logic of the theories which underpin the sanctions arguments and the necessity for a rational debate and assessment of why targeted sanctions and travel bans became punitive measures that harmed the entire economy.

According to Zimbabwe's chief negotiators, Angelina Katuruza[1] and Tedious Chifamba[2], the dominance of the EU in trade direction and flow largely influenced the decision to negotiate the proposed new trade regime with Europe despite the ZANU (PF) leadership's rhetoric of anti-colonialism and anti-imperialism. Zimbabwe's chief negotiators and government officials saw this decision as a means of survival that would guarantee the country a viable, predictable and sustained future trade regime able to withstand politically motivated bi-lateral tribulations. The rationale to negotiate with the EU (despite the fallout in bi-lateral political relations) was based on economic linkages forged in colonial times.

---

[1] Interview discussion with Angelica Katuruza, Johannesburg, South Africa, 28 May 2012.

[2] Interview discussion with Tedious Chifamba, Harare, Zimbabwe, 14 September 2012.

Graph 3.3 EU merchandise trade flows with Zimbabwe, percentages, 2005 – 2010

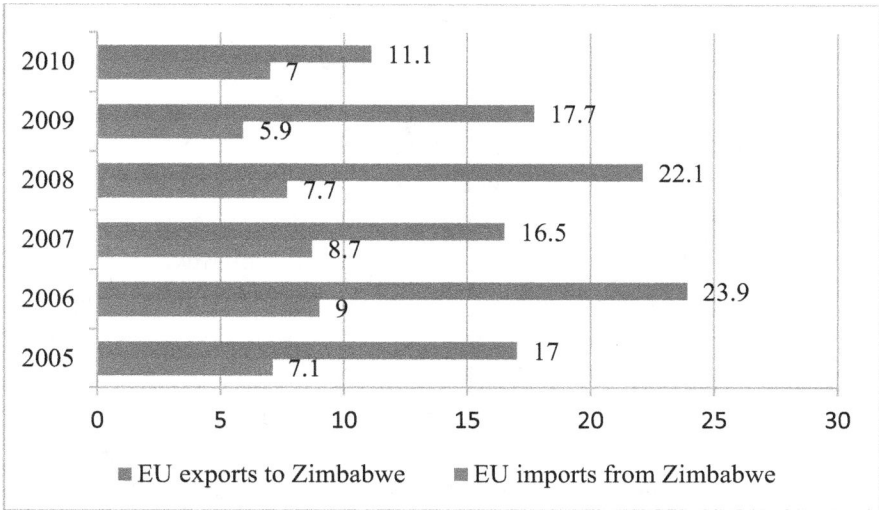

Source: Adapted from European Commission, DG Trade Statistics and
EUROSTAT, 2012

The figure above not only illustrates the historical importance of
Europe for the Zimbabwean economy, but also vindicates the
argument of both Angelina Katuruza and Tedious Chifamba, the past
and present chief EPA negotiators, that "the decision to negotiate an
EPA is the only guaranteed way to secure a future and predictable
market for the country's products while allowing imported EU
products into the country in the post-conflictual EU-Zimbabwe bilateral political and economic development cooperation as espoused
in the Conotou Agreement"[3]. It is the only realistic option for
generating the much needed foreign currency to meet growing
national import demands, ranging from fuel - the lifeline of any
industrial and commercial activity - to basic consumable
commodities. Indeed, in spite of dwindling exports to European
markets in volumes and value terms, the latter has increasingly
become the only viable and predictable option for generating foreign
currency, following the decision by the IMF and the World Bank to

---

[3] Interview discussion with Angelica Katuruza and Tedious Chifamba on 28
May 2012 and 14 September 2012, respectively.

suspend Zimbabwe, and the withdrawal of both foreign investors and donors from the economy. However, continued dwindling of the total volume and value of Zimbabwean exports destined for the European market translates into low foreign currency in-flows to support industrial development, industrial production and export and market competitiveness.

It seems that Zimbabwe's fractured economy, owing largely to the body political delusions and economic mismanagement, is set to continue facing challenges relating to weak industrial productive capacities across all sectors and export competitiveness in the European market. There is also a strong possibility that the dominance of MCs and TNCs - coupled by relentless pressure from global institutions (the IMF, the World Bank, and the WTO) - will guarantee strict implementation of iEPA outcomes in order to ensure trade openness. The country already has memories of how the MCs and TNCs benefited from the dominance of the Bretton Wood institutions' 'one-size-fits all' neo-liberal policies, including trade liberalisation, imposed and implemented without thorough analysis of the political ramifications. The ongoing EPA process is firmly premised on a neo-liberal paradigm that seeks to entrench global and commercial institutions in Zimbabwe through a trade liberalisation agenda informed by agreed tariff liberalisation schedules and commitments. Zimbabwe's economy has, since 2000, suffered from a poor state-civil society relationship, resulting in automatic opposition to any economic policy and programme proposed by the ZANU (PF) government. The economy has further been constantly subjected to a highly politicised national body politic and tense bilateral relations with the negotiating partner. As a result, it is feared that the outcome may not necessarily improve industrial and export capacities in the short – to medium term even though the EPA objective of a 'win-win' outcome suggests potential market opportunities between negotiating partners. It is further feared that the overall outcome is likely to have painful short to long term consequences in most sectors of the economy and indeed for the economy as a whole.

EU's influence in the EPA process

The EU influences the EPA process on three levels - ACP, configuration, and respective country - with each stage producing a desired outcome aimed at delivering a better deal for the EU member states. The nature and extent of this influence, with specific reference to Zimbabwe, is discussed below.

The ACP level

Since the Lomé Conventions, the EU has provided development assistance financial packages to ACP countries aimed at redressing production and export-related constraints, including supply-side bottlenecks. Such benign partnership support from the EU to ACP countries has been extended through the EDF development envelope window that covers a period of five years. At the conclusion of each round of trade negotiations with ACP countries, the EU always announces the total allocations within the EDF window, which has since reflected incremental nominal values, to be available for those countries with bankable projects. In this respect, the total allocations for the 4th to 9th EDF allocation cycle are reflected in the table below, which shows, contrary to development wisdom, that all the ACP economies have absorbed less than 43% of the total allocations per each five-year cycle window since 1975. The table also shows that the accessibility trend continued to decline since the 6th EDF allocation window, reaching 20% of total resources of the 8th EDF allocation before a marginal improvement to 28% in the following funding cycle. From the above, it can be inferred that the EU refers to development aid allocations without necessarily having the actual amounts ready for disbursements to deserving ACP countries. It can further be inferred that the EDF allocations are a function of improved EU trade in value terms, within the ACP region.

Table 3.6 Funds allocated versus funds spent during each five-year EDF financing cycle, € million

EDF assistance package	Total funds allocated (nominal value)	Real value of envelope (1975 base year)	Total disbursements (nominal value)	Percentage of total allocation disbursed in the 5 years to which it was allocated
4th EDF (1975-1980)	3 390	2 696	1 454,5	43
5th EDF (1980-1985)	5 227	2 586	2 041,0	39
6th EDF (1985-1990)	8 400	3 264	3 341,6	40
7th EDF (1990-1995)	12 000	3 514	4 417,9	37
8th EDF (1995-2000)	14 625	3 463	2 921,6	20
9th EDF (2000-2007)	15 200	3 131	4 239,0	28

Source: Adapted from Grynberg and Clarke (2006).

The table shows that since the introduction of the EDF financial window, ACP countries have experienced challenges with respect to accessing promised resources intended to improve their respective productive capacities, export competiveness and supply-side bottlenecks. This is supported by Draper (2007), who comments on the EU institutions and respective government's complex bureaucratic requirements or demands associated with the approval of ACP member states' requests for industrial and supply-side related projects to be financed through EDF development envelopes. Kamidza (2007) maintains that the ACP countries continue to encounter numerous difficulties including unreasonable administrative requirements of both EC and the EU member states that preclude or restrict them from accessing promised EDF funds. Thus, most ACP economies fail to significantly exploit non-reciprocal trade preferences including EBA and DFQF market access. Indeed, given the prevailing industrial and supply-side constraints and the surge in concluding bi-lateral and multi-lateral trade negotiations in most ACP economies, the availability of such a large funding window could have triggered a corresponding appetite to develop bankable projects. While it is true that some countries might have a dearth of technical expertise and/or capacity to develop acceptable project proposals, it could also be argued that such developments would have equally inspired the solicitation of technical assistance from other development partners.

The EU continues to dangle the same bait during each negotiation round. While the allocations shown in the table above were meant to support all ACP countries under the EPA process, the EU has proposed an EDF funding window totaling €1.783 billion which is further split into six allocations covering six years (as shown in the figure below), which illustrates that ESA has the largest share of the funding followed by ECOWAS, CEMAC and CARIFORUM, SADC, and the PACIFIC.

Graph 3.4 Indicative 10th EDFprogramme 2008-2011, € Million

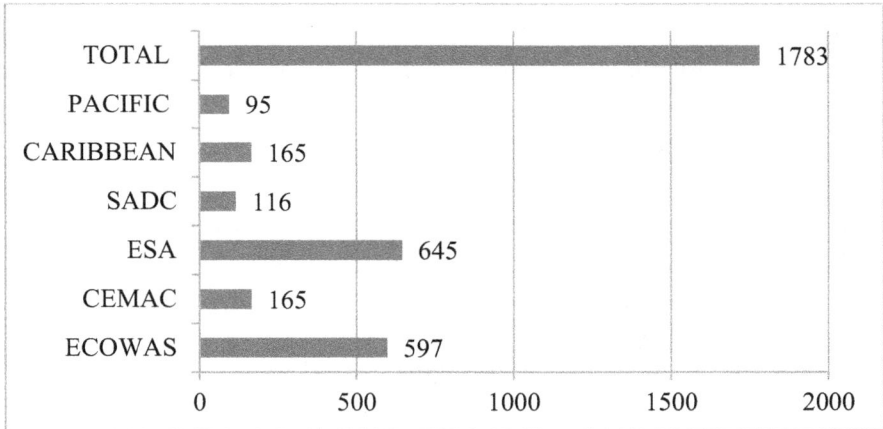

	€ Million
TOTAL	1783
PACIFIC	95
CARIBBEAN	165
SADC	116
ESA	645
CEMAC	165
ECOWAS	597

Source: Adapted from EC Staff Working Paper (2011)

The EC Staff Working Paper (2011) describes the 10th EDF financial window as supporting mainly a regional economic integration agenda including broad-based support for economic integration and trade policies, structural reforms, infrastructural development, food security and the environment. This is expected to sufficiently improve the coherence between regional and national development plans or activities within the context of overlapping memberships, that is, sub-regional countries belonging to various Regional Economic Communities (RECs) with similar mandates. It is argued here that all sub-regional RECs have expressed commitment to improve intra-regional markets with a view to improving economic diversification and creating complementarities between national economies thereby reducing over-dependence on a small number of export commodities. The allocations to regional infrastructural developments are also expected to improve interconnections, thereby reducing excessively high costs for intra-regional transport and utilities. Furthermore, the funding is expected to improve ownership and institutional capacity at regional and national levels by redressing challenges relating to inadequate mandates, the absence of legal and political tools for effective policy implementation and insufficient ownership by stakeholders, particularly civil society and national administrations.

By agreeing to engage with fragmented African configurations that are outside existing regional integration mandates, the EU demonstrates a certain strategic craftiness. As in previous EDF allocations to the ACP region, the 10th EDF attempts to identify specific areas of support, but there are possibilities that some deserving economies may fail to access the announced resources. In addition, the fact that configuration indicative allocations are publicised before the conclusion of the EPA process reflects direct EU influence on the process and outcome and points to potential challenges with respect to linking allocations with the particular needs of the group. While the EU uses the publicised allocations to prove its benevolence towards weak, vulnerable and fragmented configurations, memories of their dismal failure to access previous allocations are still fresh in the minds of all the stakeholders. Furthermore, while African countries have been insisting that any EPA should be accompanied by a robust development package that can support countries in coping with the negative effects of implementing the new trade regime, the EU has never wanted to bind these commitments beyond the 10th EDF five-year cycle. South Centre (March 2010) observed that the EU does not provide new sources of funds that are binding and permanent, despite the fact that

African countries in bi-lateral and multi-lateral trade negotiations end up making permanent binding liberalisation commitments. Civil society groups in their advocacy consistently point out that there is no new money from the EU, but rather a re-allocation of existing budgets (Tandon 2004).

The ICCO Study (2008) observes a key rhetorical feature of the EU's negotiations with the ACP states, claiming that EPAs support existing regional integration initiatives and that regionalism is a development strategy that essentially assists the integration of ACP countries with the EU market. It is on this basis that the EC's Council reiterated in May 2007 that:

> EPAs should primarily build upon, foster and support ACP regional integration processes by recognising existing political and economic realities and regional integration processes, thus providing flexibility (ICCO Study, September, 2008 8).

The above is supported by promises of development aid funds only to those regions or groups of countries ready to negotiate with an enlarged, economically powerful counterpart. Indeed, by dangling development aid envelopes, the EU has facilitated the following:

a split of ACP regions into six configurations;

a split of Africa into four groups;

a split of the SADC region by allowing the DRC to negotiate under the CEMAC group, seven countries[4] to negotiate under the ESA group and seven countries[5] to negotiate under the SADC configuration;

---

[4] Madagascar, Malawi, Mauritius, Seychelles, Tanzania, Zambia and Zimbabwe
[5] Angola, Botswana, Lesotho, Mozambique, Namibia, South Africa and Swaziland

a split of ESA by allowing the East African Community (EAC) countries to continue negotiating as a bloc while other group countries[6] presented iEPA market access offers as individuals.

This funding window thus highlights the challenges associated with regional overlapping memberships and the divisive EPA process that has created configurations outside existing regional initiatives in southern Africa in particular. The above demonstrates the success of a 'divide and conquer' approach and merciless manipulation by an economically powerful negotiating partner.

At the regional level

The EU's strategy of dangling a development assistance envelope reflects that its political and economic commitment to fund and advance the regional integration agenda in the ESA sub-region, was largely intended to secure a better deal with a configuration that is diverse but still offers huge economic opportunities. Through its economic influence, the EU, despite adopting a joint roadmap with the ESA group in Mauritius in February 2004, continued to allow configured member states to realign with other configurations for the purposes of EPA negotiations. The EU argues that it is a sovereign decision for a country to choose configurations for the purposes of negotiating EPAs. It further 'sweetens' ESA group countries by financing impact assessment studies that inform them during the negotiations, developing the terms of reference to guide the studies, and presiding over the selection of technical institutions through an open tender system. The EU is aware that the ESA group comprising of countries from various RECs[7] - some of which have no or limited common historical political, economic, and social bonds[8] - has natural fault-lines, which, given the fast-pace of the process, would likely cause divisions and eventually split the configuration thereby undermining the integration of these economies with Europe. This strategy was vindicated when in 2005 the DRC pulled out of the

---

[6] Madagascar, Mauritius, Seychelles and Zimbabwe
[7] COMESA, EAC, the Indian Ocean Community (IOC), the Inter-Governmental Authority for Development (IGAD) and SADC
[8] Especially between some IOC, IGAD and southern African countries.

group to join CEMAC while Tanzania, a former member of the SADC EPA configuration, joined the EAC group. In addition, towards the end of 2007, the ESA group split into two. The first group comprised the EAC countries, which failed to initial and sign an iEPA with the EU though they continued to negotiate a comprehensive EPA as a bloc. The other group constitutes the ESA configuration, of which four economies[9] individually signed iEPA market access offers with the EU in 2009. The iEPA economies are now integrated into the European market under different trade liberalisation commitments that are not in line with regional integration commitments.

Thus, the EU, by means of funding, influences the creation of another layer of overlapping regional EPA integration membership with distinct commitments only to itself as the dominant negotiating partner. In this regard, the SADC Secretariat (2011) reports that the 10th EDF financial window supports mainly regional economic integration agendas. The SADC secretariat study (2012) allocated €92.8 million of the €116 million to support regional economic integration within the SADC EPA group as follows: SADC EPA member states (€52.8 million), regional economic integration (€20 million) and regional infrastructure development programmes (€20 million). Configurations through these allocations are expected to redress challenges relating to both regional and national institutional, productive and export capacities. This 10th EDF regional integration financial window is a separate initiative from the general EU funding for existing regional integration initiatives[10] in the sub-region, a development that exerts more pressure on existing limited institutional capacities. However, agreed different levels of iEPA trade liberalisation may fail to facilitate regional integration of configured economies in spite of the above clear financial allocations for that purpose. While it is unclear why the EU is sacrificing the very regional integration initiatives that it has since its inception been bankrolling, it is clear that de-legitimising existing regional integration agendas satisfies its desire to exploit EPA-related short to medium term commercial interests in the sub-region, particularly in vulnerable

---

[9] Madagascar, Mauritius, Seychelles and Zimbabwe
[10] COMESA, EAC and SADC.

economies such as Zimbabwe, which is still struggling to rejuvenate its fragile economy.

While the EU has for several decades demonstrated unwavering commitment to bankrolling sub-regional regional integration schemes, it has ironically signed iEPAs with four individual countries, a development that points to a hasty conclusion without necessarily matching agreed tariff schedule liberalisations with existing regional integration initiatives commitments. As a result, the tariff scheduling and liberalisation commitments of individual member states have the potential to undermine the agreed targets of various regional integration schemes. This confirms the divisive character of the EPA process that has the potential to derail prospects for greater economic growth and development in many regional economies. In the case of Zimbabwe, this suppresses economic recovery to pre-2000 levels, when the country's products were competitive in the national, regional and EU markets.

The above demonstrates how the EU, using its influence as a donor has created weaker and more vulnerable configurations for negotiating a WTO-compatible new trade regime with Europe. It also ensures that the new trade regime framework is superior to existing regional economic integration initiatives, hence no effort was made to ensure that the iEPA corresponds with any commitments of the RECs. This has resulted in creating weaker and more vulnerable configurations with equally weaker institutions and structures in terms of the technical capacities and skills to square up with an enlarged Europe - with its massive financial, human, and technical resources. Ultimately, Europe's commercial interests through MCs and TNCs are secured, especially in vulnerable economies such as Zimbabwe.

At the national level

Since independence, Europe's economic influence in Zimbabwe has been sustained by its benevolent, philanthropic and developmental aid assistance to all three pillars of the state[11], as well as the private sector and civil society groups. This support was made

---

[11] The Executive (government), the Legislature and the Judiciary.

possible by a series of EDF financing windows as well as other funding options based on a mutually beneficial relationship between Zimbabwe and the EU as a bloc, as well as with individual EU countries. Indeed, over the years, the EU has been a leading bi-lateral donor complementing government fiscal spending and financing government-related projects; bankrolling broad sections of civil society activities focusing on economic policy (including trade negotiations) and financing business sector initiatives.

However, owing largely to questions about pluralistic democratic and governance values and economic policies and programmes, Zimbabwe between 2000–2013 was no longer a recipient of any funding from either the EU bloc or EU countries. In fact, the EU and other western governments suspended all forms of direct developmental funding assistance to the ZANU (PF) administration, a decision that also denies funding to private sector initiatives. This reflects the foreign policy principles of the states of the Global North and international financial institutions via their respective FDI policies and loan extensions. While ideologically the EU cannot exclude Zimbabwe from the 10th EDF funding cycle designed to benefit all ACP countries, the European Council adopted appropriate measures under Article 96 of the revised Cotonou Agreement by Council Decision 2002/148/EC, covering the period 2002-2010 which re-oriented financing towards the social sectors (health, education and food security), democratisation including GPA-related reforms, respect for human rights, and the rule of law. The above interventions were channeled through national CSOs, international NGOs and multilateral organisations. For instance, under the GNU administration, FAO Zimbabwe implemented programmes in the food security sector covering in particular smallholder agricultural activities as reflected in Table 3.7 below. Similarly, national CSOs were supported through a project-based approach, that is, projects funded by various thematic budget lines[12].

This decision maintained funding relationships with broader sections of civil society that have been traditional allies of the MDC

---

[12] European Instrument for Democracy and Human Rights, Non-State Actors and Local Authorities, Instrument for Stability.

formations. In this respect, the key provisions of the council decision are:

Financial support for all projects is suspended except those in support of the population, in particular in social sectors and those in support of the reforms contained in the GPA. Financing shall be re-oriented in support of the population, in particular in social sectors and in support of the stabilisation process of the country, in particular with regard to democratisation, respect for human rights and the rule of law (EC Staff Working Paper, 2011: 44)

Table 3.7 EU Interventions in Zimbabwe implemented by FAO between 2009 and 2012

Contract title	Contract period	Planned amount	Action location
Promotion of Conservation Agriculture and Coordination of Agricultural Activities in Zimbabwe	2009–2012	€9,173,043	Zimbabwe - National
Regional "Food Facility, EC-FAO 1". Zimbabwe: "Agricultural Input Assistance to Vulnerable Smallholder Farmers in Zimbabwe and the Coordination and Monitoring of Agricultural Emergency Interventions"	2009–2013	€15,400,000	Zimbabwe - National
Support to smallholder farmers in Zimbabwe through improved agricultural productivity and market-based interventions	2010–2012	€6,777,224	Zimbabwe – National
Improved livelihoods, food, nutrition and income security of smallholder farmers in Zimbabwe through provision of agricultural inputs, market linkages and extension support	2012–2014	€5,424,425	Zimbabwe – All provinces
Streamlined Coordination mechanisms in agriculture to increase productivity and income generation in the smallholder sector	2012-2014	€2,000,000	Zimbabwe - National

Source: EU-Republic of Zimbabwe ToR (2015)

Bi-lateral tension between the negotiating parties caused aid delivery to Zimbabwe to become even more uncertain. As a donor, the EU has the final say over 10th EDF development aid delivery to the country, which it claims still lacks credible governance and democratic values and practices. Indeed, the EU has continued to deny funding to the GNU administration in general. It only allows funding based on annually formulated comprehensive short-term strategies in support of food security, rural development, social sectors and governance and human rights activities. The above funded areas fall under the portfolios of the MDC formations. The EU continues to provide humanitarian assistance to poverty stricken people through NGOs, a decision that not only infuriates the ZANU (PF) leadership and its allies, but also fuels suspicions about a regime change agenda through NGO distribution of donated material goods, including food. The EU and other western governments' decision to continue significantly funding anti-ZANU (PF) civil society groups, especially those implementing pluralistic democratic and governance activities, fuels the tensions between Harare and Brussels. Even though Zimbabwe was the fourth country to sign the iEPA, the levels of suspicion remain high owing to the continued imposition of smart sanctions and travel bans on Mugabe and his inner circle and associated firms relating to charges of human rights abuses. The above shows how funding developments since 2000 have sustained EU-ZANU (PF) leadership tensions, compelling the latter to sustain a regime change mantra at the expense of collectively rallying resources and energies for a better EPA outcome. Also excluded from funding are CSOs working on trade and development (including the EPA process), in spite the fact that trade negotiations is an integral component of Zimbabwe's economic policy. This means that the six-year 10th EDF financing window will continue denying resources to EPA-related activities. All of this illustrates how EU leverage in the process closes off all possible flows of funding towards adequate preparations for trade negotiations in an environment that is well known for its state–NSA conflictual and suspicious relationship.

Counter-intuitively, in spite of the bilateral stand-off epitomised by the imposition of smart sanctions and travel bans on the ZANU

(PF) leadership, the EU has provided financial resources that facilitated the participation of government officials in all EPA-related RNF and joint ESA-EU meetings held in the region and in Brussels. Because the EU had a special interest in the outcome, travel ban rules were ignored in all instances that demanded the presence of the former minister of Industry and International Trade, Samuel Mumbengegwi[13], at EPA meetings in Brussels prior to the formation of the GNU in February 2009. While financial support was made available for a private sector representative to participate in all EPA-related regional and Brussels meetings, in some instances the support ended up being given to a government official. The EU also bankrolled Zimbabwe's EPA negotiation preparatory processes, including financing impact assessment studies, and EPA related stakeholder workshops held in Harare and Bulawayo.

According to Benoliel and Hua (2009), EU negotiators invest in building good relationships with counterparts in order to 'oil' the negotiation process and make it appear mutually beneficial. In this regard, the EU has supported the relationship with ACP countries by financially backing up all EPA-related activities. Though this benign donor-recipient relationship is appreciated, in some instances it allows the dominant party to impose its negotiating issues, interests, and options on the weaker. For instance, the EU financially supports development projects in sub-regional member states that not only buttress existing regional integration efforts, but are also linked to national economic projects and programmes. Even though this has enabled other EPA negotiating countries to access capacity and skills development support, Zimbabwe has unfortunately not been a recipient of this regional funding window owing to its strained bilateral relations with Europe. This means that Zimbabwean negotiators and government officials have not been able to benefit from EU-funded trade negotiations training programmes offered within the context of existing SADC or COMESA frameworks. As a result, Zimbabwean government negotiators and officials have

---

[13] Following the imposing of EU travel bans on ZANU (PF) top leadership and government officials on 26 July 2002, the former Industry and International Trade minister, Samuel Mumbengegwi was allowed to participate in Brussels EPA meetings on 28 September 2002, 16 May 2003, and 19 August 2004.

missed out on opportunities to exchange ideas, experiences and best practices with colleagues in the SADC and COMESA regional blocs, as well as to develop innovative negotiation skills, styles, strategies and tactics to improve the country's bargaining position in the on-going negotiation process. This further undermines the authorities' efforts to support not only regional integration efforts in the country's favour, but also the economic transition of a decade-long economic meltdown.

In spite of its institutional and technical inadequacies, the ESA group in general and Zimbabwe in particular, have continued to engage with a financially well-resourced EC that has layers of technical, legal, social, economic, and political experts backing up a pool of competent, knowledgeable and seasoned negotiators and officials. The EC also has well-established and competent technical institutions whose research findings and outcomes either directly strengthen Europe's negotiating positions, strategies and tactics or provide insights into the ESA economies in general and Zimbabwe in particular. According to Medicine Masiiwa[14], a former lecturer at the University of Zimbabwe and now coordinator of SADC Regional Economic Integration Support programme, who led a delegation of four CSO representatives on a lobbying mission to EU institutions, various EC directorates[15] and the EU presidency and parliament, the EU revealed that "due to its technical and financial capacity, it has been able to undertake 50-year focus studies on each ESA participating country". This is instructive because it reflects the EU's capacity to know its negotiating counterparts' strengths and weaknesses, which can then be exploited during the negotiation process.

Throughout the negotiating process the EC has had access to information and research findings on Zimbabwe's shortcomings, including the conflictual state-civil society relationship, uncooperative private sector and a bullying government bent on crushing dissent in political and economic discourse. As a result, the EU negotiators have been better prepared and therefore able to out-

---

[14] Interview discussion with Medicine Masiiwa, Gaborone, Botswana, 25 August 20012.

[15] Director – General Trade and Director-General Development.

manoeuvre their Zimbabwean counterparts at every stage of the negotiations. The EU has been able to ensure that the imposition of travel bans on top ZANU (PF) officials, coupled with no formal direct contact with Zimbabwe senior officials, has secured uncontested short to medium-term market access. It is a fact that Zimbabwean products (currently composed of largely unprocessed and mineral related commodities) are uncompetitive vis-à-vis European products in both markets (the EU and local).

EPA technical and ideological issues

Negotiations for an EPA with Europe lock ESA countries in general and Zimbabwe in particular into an unhealthy post-colonial dependence on Europe for development aid, fiscal support and market access. It also has a direct bearing on sensitive sectors and infant industries that need protection from intense competition in an environment dominated by powerful producers and investors, including MCs and TNCs. In particular, Zimbabwean agricultural producers and exporters require protection if they are to graduate to the level of commercial farmers. Figure 3.2 illustrates how Europe is ideologically set to solve its twin crises of over-production and profitability by indirectly opening up more markets for its products in the ACP regions, targeting mainly weak and vulnerable economies like Zimbabwe. This guarantees a significant proportion of European products easy access to the Zimbabwean economy. It offers a solution to the on-going Eurozone crisis by potentially linking European investors, producers and exporters with Zimbabwe's consumers and industries and confirms the EPA process as essentially 'FTAs' between economically unequal partners (Burnett and Manji, 2005; Deve, 2006; Kamidza, 2007). The EPA process is also a reminder of the trade liberalisation policy of the 1990s, which forced Zimbabwe to open her market to competitive products in the region and beyond, resulting in the closure of some productive sectors, with consequent unemployment and state-society tensions.

Through this ideological framework, EU-Zimbabwe trade relations, which were non-reciprocal for several decades, are set to be confined within the reciprocity principle, thereby risking the removal of any pro-development value to the EPA process. For instance, one of the EPA's objectives is essentially to replace past special preferences of DFQF market access and EBA initiatives with WTO-compliant and competitive clauses. For instance, having noticed individual iEPA signatories' reluctance to sign while still negotiating a full EPA, the EU's three[16] political structures in early 2012 unanimously agreed to withdraw the Market Access Regulation[17] (MAR) 1528 of 2007 that was unilaterally put in place to allow trading between the two parties while negotiating a WTO compatible trade regime by 1 October 2014. Given that the EU remained Zimbabwe's major trading partner (Table 2.3) despite the public disagreements, the country signed up to it in September 2009. This resonates with a body that is becoming increasingly sensitive to the demands of new member states that are reluctant to be tied to a trade regime with ACP countries on the basis of past colonial relationships (Kamidza, 2008).

On the basis of the implementation of iEPA, Europe is fortifying its vertical links with Zimbabwe in particular and the ESA region in general in the context of EPA negotiations. This has led to a rapprochement between many Zimbabwean CSOs, who are infuriated by the fact that the EPA process has failed to take into account differences in industrial production, import and export capabilities, resources and technological capacities, as well as socio-political conditions. While the outcome guarantees economic integration with Europe, it is unlikely to facilitate industrial productive innovation, export diversification or competitiveness and social transformation and development in Zimbabwe.

Makanza (2007: 4), addressing SADC MPs in the TDC during their annual meeting on regional integration and trade, argued that "the EU's push for EPAs is inextricably linked to the WTO's political processes, where decisions are based on a one-country, one-vote consensus." So, EPA agreements coupled with EPA-related assistance create the conditions for a strategic alliance between the EU and signatories of the new trade regime. This development assists the EU in fostering a community of interest between itself and ACP countries in future WTO negotiations. This means that the ACP-

---

[16] The European Parliament, the EC and the European Council of Ministers.
[17] This is a unilateral scheme put in place by the EU with no contractual basis.

EPA negotiations with the EU provide an ideal political framework for the latter (EU) to neutralise any potential opposition to its future agendas in WTO ministerial dialogue sessions. This argument is based on the fact that of the 157 WTO member[18] countries, 116 belong to the ACP region (89) and the EU (27). Assuming that the EPAs processes and outcomes generate bilateral consensus on trade and development-related issues between the negotiating regions, Europe as a developed region will have enough allies to neutralise any potential opposition to its agendas at the level of multi-lateral trade negotiations. This has the potential to assist the EU politically by fostering a long-term trade and development bond based on a vertical economic integration with its former colonies[19] in future WTO negotiations at the expense of those countries' sustainable social and economic development. This has led to negative political ramifications in Zimbabwe that have not only resulted in further conflict between the state and civil society, but also poisoned the economic policy-making environment.

It seems as though the dominant negotiating partner does not have the political will to defend a pro-ACP position in the multi-lateral trade and development platforms. Tandon (2004) describes the plethora of EPA configurations across Africa as being worse than the 1884 Berlin Conference which carved the continent into small, weak and vulnerable and therefore controllable states solely for the benefit of Europe:

> This is an integral and active part of a new scramble for Africa, in which the EU competes with the US and emerging economies such as China to gain access to and/or secure control over markets and resources for their own interests (Tandon, 2004: 18).

The ongoing EPA negotiations are taking place in the context of a skewed economic relationship between Africa and Europe that is already blamed for hindering socio-economic development

---

[18] WTO now has 157 member countries following the entry of Russia and Vanuatu in 2012.

[19] All ACP countries are former colonies of the majority of the current EU Member States.

prospects, and indirectly fermenting tensions between state structures, civil society groups and the business community. Such a situation can be seen in Zimbabwean stakeholder relationships over the period under review. Kamidza (2005) predicts a victory for the EU in this round of negotiations, arguing that the dominant partner has ensured that the process reflects its commercial and political interests. As Europe fortifies its vertical economic and trade links with Zimbabwe through the iEPA tariff liberalisation scheduling and commitment, the outcome is unlikely to facilitate industrial development or export competitiveness in Zimbabwe in the short to medium term. This outcome has to be measured against the spread and severity of the country's social and economic distress due to the political dynamics (tension, suspicions, and lack of cooperation between the main political parties), the melting down of the economy and the ZANU (PF) government's isolation from the EU and other western governments and donors. Thus, the pursuit of an asymmetrical power relationship causes a politically undesirable, economically unsustainable and socially unjustifiable process that is likely to produce an unequal trade and development partnership while being inimical to poverty alleviation strategies embedded in a rational and mutual pro-development trade regime. The EU is exploiting its superior bilateral bargaining power to push for an EPA outcome that maximises the commercial interests of its investors, exporters, and producers.

While government negotiators argue that engaging the EU has enabled the country to secure a future trade regime along with the rest of the ACP countries, some studies have shown that the TNCs currently facing a profitability crisis[20] in Europe have over the last decade been intensifying their search for alternative and sustainable markets in poor and vulnerable economies. The Zimbabwean economy offers just such a market. Currently, economic and political developments - characterised by unpredictable economic policies, lack of cooperation between the state and other stakeholders and a body-politic in conflict with itself - all point to a stalling of the

---

[20] This is evidenced by a vicious cycle of falling demand and a scaling down of industrial production leading to growing unemployment, and domestic and external borrowing.

economic recovery - a development that suits EU commercial interests. Alongside politically motivated public policies and programmes, and intolerance towards civil society activism and advocacy in general, the GNU has failed to generate confidence in the new commercial farmers' ability to compete with the heavily subsidised European farmers who are actively looking for markets in poor and vulnerable economies such as Zimbabwe. Indeed, Zimbabwe's productive agricultural capacity has yet to show signs of improvement since the fast-track land reform programme was implemented. This means that in the short to medium term, the country continues to rely on food products and other agricultural consumables imported from the EU and other trading partners.

While the countries in the configuration have mostly been concerned about how to access the promised 'developmental assistance resource envelope' Europe has been busy prioritising issues within the six clusters (development, agriculture, services, trade-related issues, fisheries, and market access) to be negotiated. In particular, the EU has been working hard to restore WTO ministerial issues rejected at Singapore, including: competition policy; services and investment; public procurement; protection of intellectual property; taxation (tax governance) and sustainable development. For instance, during the joint EU-SADC EPA member states negotiations held in Johannesburg, South Africa, in March 2013, the EU commission's deputy director general of trade and the chief negotiator, João Aguiar Machado, argued:

> ... negotiating sustainable development is a standard requirement by the European Parliament which eventually approves the new trade regime, and this delegation insists on negotiation clauses of this important area in the EU's interests despite your lack of political mandate to so ..... Machado, during the joint EU-SADC EPA member states negotiations, Johannesburg, South Africa, 20-22 March 2013).

Conclusion

This chapter traced the trajectory of the conflictual EU-Zimbabwe bilateral trade relations in the context of the country's internal political dynamics. While the negotiating parties publicly blame each other for political developments in the country, bringing complexities of governance and pluralistic democratic values to the economic and trade debate, the economy continues to underperform in all respects and has a record of more than eight years of negative growth, despite adopting five economic blueprints within seven years (Table 6.4). Focus and energies have been expended on costly and elusive political questions under the supervision of the SADC region, with support from the AU.

It is not surprising therefore that since 2000, Zimbabwe has failed to implement any industrialisation, diversification of productive and export structures, value addition[21] processes or establish downstream industries. This reflects not only an uncooperative government–business relationship but, more importantly, a lack of resources (financial and technical) and investment in industrial innovation and development. Current EU-Zimbabwe trade relations have changed since 2000. The deteriorating EU-Zimbabwe bilateral relations mirror the state-NSA relationship, juxtaposed with the EU's dominance in pursuit of its own commercial interests.

Zimbabwe's level of ambition in this round of negotiations has been undermined by the persistence of limited economic activity. As a result, throughout the negotiation process the economy has continued to suffer from dwindling revenue flows, thereby dashing hopes of any industrial development to anchor forward-looking innovations, production and/or export diversification and market competiveness, as well as a revival of industrial capacity utilisation, and sustainable modernisation programmes. These limitations have been linked to the sectoral interests of agriculture and manufacturing which in the short to medium term are set to interface with the onslaught of EU products in the local market.

---

[21] New Agriculturalist (June 2011) claims that "with very few agro-processing facilities, there is little value addition in the agricultural sector".

The chapter further interrogated the EU's dominance and influence on state-stakeholder relationships which have made it difficult to collectively and proactively develop strategic interventions in the economy with a view to building confidence in the business community and broader sections of civil society. The chapter also analysed EU dominance and influence at the level of the ACP region, the ESA configuration and Zimbabwe. The analysis also illustrated Zimbabwe's challenges in terms of identifying economic activities and/or sectors with potentially strong domestic and export value chains in the short to medium term. Equally elusive has been a constructive effort to promote an institutional framework and/or policy intervention to revive the country's industrial capacity utilisation and/or market competitiveness.

EU-Zimbabwe bilateral relations in the context of the EU's dominance and influence in the process illustrates how the nexus between politics and economic development since 1998 has remained unresolved. For instance, prior to 2008 the country's economic and social crisis was a function of internal political contestation, while current agricultural and industrial capacity utilisation levels are a function of GPA commitment - which unfortunately has not been implemented in full. Similarly, the implementation of the 2012 ratified iEPA prior to 31 July 2013 remains largely a function of the forthcoming electoral contest between the belligerent parties. While it is probable that there will be little commitment to the iEPA against a backdrop of an economy struggling to recover from many years of stagnation, failure to compete with European products on the local market in the short to medium term is a certainty.

Chapter Four

State of Play in Negotiations

Introduction

Zimbabwe opted to negotiate EPA under the ESA, a configuration of countries seemingly randomly grouped, with few common social, economic, political or historical features. Since February 2004 the ESA-EU has been negotiating an EPA that initially focused on six sectors, namely: agriculture, development co-operation issues, fisheries, market access, services and trade. As the process progressed, avoidance and settlement of disputes as well as institutional and final provisions were included for negotiation. These negotiations seek to enhance the respective countries' economic performance, competitiveness and value chains, leading to economic transformation, sustainable development and meaningful integration, both individually and collectively, into the global economy. In addition, the negotiations seek to ensure that EPA outcomes are not only compatible with WTO rules, but also take into account the different needs and levels of development of ESA countries vis-à-vis those of the EU.

Aside from belonging to COMESA, the ESA group of countries (including Zimbabwe) which are negotiating with the EU do not have legal status or formal structure as a bloc. Within the configuration, there are four secretariats of regional economic communities: COMESA, the EAC, IGAD and IOC. The COMESA secretariat is the leading institution driving the EPA process, with support from the other three secretariats. In this respect, the EPA became a key Result Area of COMESA Regional Integrated Support Programmes: Regional Integration Support Programme (RISP)1[22], RISP2[23] and

---

[22] The first Contribution Agreement (CA) worth €33 million was signed between the EU and COMESA Secretariat in 2005 to support the implementation of RISP1.

[23] CA supported the implementation of RISP2 with €50 million.

RISP3[24] funded through a Contribution Agreement signed between the EU and the COMESA Secretariat. The COMESA secretariat thus plays a coordinating role in the process.

Of the 16 ESA countries, the EAC initialed the iEPA as a bloc while four individual countries, namely Madagascar, Mauritius, Seychelles and Zimbabwe signed the iEPA that has since been ratified and entered into force from May 2012. This has assured the aforementioned countries access to European markets following a unanimous decision by the three[25] political structures of the EU in early 2012 to withdraw MAR 1528 of 2007 by 1 October 2014. This allowed trading between the EU and ACP countries while negotiating to conclude a WTO compatible trade regime. The signing ensures that individual iEPA member states remain locked in an unhealthy post-colonial dependence on EU institutions and individual EU member states for fiscal projects and/or programmes in terms of financial and technical support as well as funding for human capital development, public policy design and implementation, entrepreneurial modernisation initiatives and supply-side improvement - all of which facilitates better access to the European market while improving the level of competitiveness in the domestic market. Other ESA countries, which are LDCs, are not under pressure to sign the iEPA since they are assured of access to the European market under the EBA regime (See Table 3.2). For instance, Malawi's Trade Director, Christina Zakeyo Chatima[26] notes that the country is yet to review its market access offer for onward submission to the EU for consideration and finality of the process. All ESA countries are committed to negotiating a full EPA[27] which is expected to be concluded before the withdrawal of MAR by 1 October 2014. In order to give impetus to the process, Moses Tekere, EPA unit Chief Technical Advisor (CTA) at the COMESA secretariat observes that:

---

[24] CA supported the implementation of RISP3 with only €7.4 million, resulting in drastic reduction of programme and administration staff at the COMESA Secretariat from 70 to 11.

[25] The European Parliament, the EC and the European Council of Ministers.

[26] Interview discussion with Christina Zakeyo Chatima, Lilongwe, 24 November 2016

[27] This is sometimes referred to as "comprehensive or inclusive EPA".

…. The 17th ESA Council held in Kampala, Uganda in November 2012 underscored the need for sustained continuous and robust engagement with EU at all levels that EPA negotiations supporting regional integration and development be concluded timeously. …. the Council further underscored the need to dedicate technical and financial support mainly to support formulation of country and regional positions and facilitate negotiations (Tekere, 2013: 2).

The above process has been guided by the ESA-EPA roadmap which endorsed two levels of 'negotiating institutions and structures', as stipulated by the Cotonou Agreement. The roadmap agreed on the composition of stakeholder participation subject to the discretion of specific countries. Key stakeholders in this instance include government officials, NSA[28] representatives and officials from COMESA, who manage the process with support from the EAC, IOC and IGAD secretariats. The roadmap also agreed that the negotiating institutions and structures at the national level would be undertaken by the National Development Trade Policy Forum (NDTPF) and at the regional level by the Regional Negotiation Forum (RNF).

During the process, Katuruza (2012[29]) observes that 'the EU has legal status supported by institutional structures including the Council of Ministers and the European Parliament'. It is further observed that the EU has a powerful functioning bureaucracy based in Brussels that is staffed by a large team of skilled negotiators and a host of experts under the authority of a single negotiator, the EC Trade Commissioner. This gives the EU negotiating team a mandate to navigate and balance existing and potential contradictions and divisions amongst EU member states before their chief negotiator, the trade commissioner, faces negotiating counterparts (the outside world) with a single voice as the Box on EU step by step trade negotiations explains.

---

[28] The private sector, CSOs/NGOs, media, community based organisations, religious organisations and trade unions.

[29] Interview discussion with Angelica Katuruza, Johannesburg, 28 May 2012.

Box 4.1   EU step by step trade negotiations

Who negotiates EPA agreement?

The EU's trade policy empowers the EC to negotiate EPA with Zimbabwe on behalf of individual bloc countries. However, the EC closely cooperates through regular contact with the Council of the EU and European parliament, which ultimately approve the overall agreement.

How did EC prepare for negotiations?

The EC conducted impact assessment studies including holding public consultations on the content and options for the proposed EPA. The Council then gave the EC negotiating directives, spelling out general objectives to be achieved, which would be shared with the EU Parliament.

What were the contents of the negotiations and level of ambition?

Opening new markets for goods and services.

Increasing investment opportunities and protection of investments.

Making trade faster by facilitating transit through customs and setting common rules on technical and phytosanitary standards.

Making the policy environment more predictable by undertaking joint commitments on areas that affect trade including intellectual property rights, competition rules and public procurement.

Supporting sustainable development by fostering cooperation, transparency and dialogue with partners on social and environmental issues.

The level of ambition depended on the development and capacities of ESA group or Zimbabwe and offer flexibilities as determined by ESA group or Zimbabwe needs and capacities.

What was the negotiation process?

Chief negotiator, usually director general (DG) Trade, leads negotiating teams including experts covering all different topics under negotiation drawn from across the commission.

Chief negotiators (EU and ESA group (not Zimbabwe) are expected to regularly contact each other including meeting outside formal negotiation rounds.

Negotiations were based on a policy of 'negotiation is not over until everything is agreed', that is, draft negotiations texts were not made public during the process even when certain chapters (or topics) were closed.

When negotiations reached technical finalisation stage, the EC immediately informed the European parliament and the Council, after which finalised texts were sent to both institutions.

Source: European Commission (June 2013)

On the other hand, Zimbabwe trade negotiations are headed by a government chief negotiator without the experience, skills or capacities to match the EU counterpart. The government chief negotiator also lacks institutional memory of previously agreed or contestable issues and positions. In addition, the government chief negotiator engaged without a clearly articulated mandate[30] from both cabinet and parliament based on informed scoping research analysis in line with national developmental goals, or public opinion through consultation on the content and options of the proposed new trade deal on the economy prior to the engagement. Consulting a wide variety of stakeholders contributes positively towards a more realistic and innovative methodology geared to finding common positions and offers, and to creating mechanisms for engaging citizens in general in the process (Roux, 2008). Furthermore, the country has a huge deficit of seasoned and experienced teams, as is evident from the high rate of staff turnover in government, especially during the period under review. For instance, since the EPA process started in February 2004, the country has recorded three different chief negotiators, two of whom were recalled and deployed to Embassies in Pretoria and Lusaka. Senior trade officials from the Trade and Industry ministry (now Industry and Commerce) left government for the private sector and there were changes in ministerial portfolios[31] and ambassadorial postings in Brussels. The domestic process also suffered from a lack of serious technical support from business as

---

[30] Discussion with chief negotiators reveal that the negotiations process was not guided by a minimum threshold beyond which the team could consider walking out of the negotiating room.

[31] Welshman Ncube of the smaller of the two MDC formations, took over the Trade and Industry ministry from Samuel Mumbengegwi, ZANU (PF) in the GNU.

well as an absence of economic intelligence gathering and surveillance, as Elijah Munyuki notes:

> Government was very late to realise that economic intelligence gathering is a critical in-put in trade negotiations. For instance, the Office of the President Cabinet - where most intelligence operations are based - was completely out of direct involvement in terms of gathering key economic information that would have empowered technocrats from the relevant trade-related ministries. As a result, negotiators lacked crucial information about their EC counterparts including composition of negotiating team, character and attitude of negotiators and other crucial negotiating secrets of the EC negotiating team. Elijah Munyuki, interview in Gaborone, Botswana, 25 August 2012

In addition, Zimbabwean MPs in the TDC, who are responsible for constitutionally handling issues of trade and trade agreements, have not been involved in the process with a view to preparing them for eventual ratification should there be an agreement. Excluding MPs in the TDC from the process confirms that the legislative body has not given the process national strategic direction, based on a shared national ethos and imperatives in line with the redistribution of economic resources through land reform and economic empowerment programmes. The non-participation of MPs in the process was further complicated by the fact that, since 2000, the political contestation and dynamics in the country resulted in changes in the composition of TDC membership at each legislative electoral period. Meanwhile, fiscal constraints and the lack of donor funding means that the MPs could not benefit from related trade negotiations and international agreements' capacity building activities or programmes.

The section below discusses national and regional institutions and/or structures that have not only guided the EU-ESA negotiations process - culminating in some non-LDCs, including Zimbabwe, individually initialing and eventually signing the iEPA with the EU - but are still guiding the on-going 'comprehensive[32] EPA' process, expected to be concluded by December 2016.

National development trade policy forum[33]

Zimbabwe negotiated EPA with the EU within the ESA configuration. The negotiations, which focused on six clusters[34], were initiated in February 2004. The joint EPA roadmap directed every ESA member state to establish an NDTPF comprising all the relevant stakeholders including government officials from the trade-related ministries, and representatives from the business community, civil society and labour. In line with this, the Zimbabwe ministry of Trade and Commerce established NDTPF in 2004 as a strategic structure that would provide an environment for constructive and inclusive engagement in any subsequent EPA-related preparatory work. This platform is meant to facilitate multi-stakeholder discussions on the country's research including impact assessment findings that can subsequently feed into the national perspectives during RNF and joint ESA-EU meetings held in the region and in Brussels. The NDTPF's main function has been assumed to be that of developing national positions and offers for subsequent discussions at RNF meetings as well as coordinating the country's trade policy.

As a cluster-inclusive and multi-sectoral structure, the NDTPF was expected to ensure wider and deeper consultations and involvement of all the relevant stakeholders, individual constituencies and citizens. This suggests that the NDTP has been providing an interactive platform for all the relevant stakeholders to effectively participate in all EPA-related national dialogue sessions (conferences, seminars, and workshops) convened to review EPA-related research methodologies and the findings of sustainable impact assessments

---

[32] This is sometimes referred to as "full and inclusive EPA".

[33] This is now called the "EPA committee", and is made of stakeholders from the "economic ministries"; parastatal organizations; and representatives of the private sector and civil society.

[34] Agriculture, development issues, fisheries, market access, services and trade-related issues.

and other related sectoral studies. It implies that the NDTPF, as a preparatory negotiations platform, has been facilitating stakeholder consultations on EPA issues, interests, positions and offers. National stakeholders, through this platform, have been expected to collectively strategise and produce progress reports detailing both offensive and defensive positions and offers within the context of national economic and political (industrial transformation and broad-based economic empowerment) interests while building networks, coalitions and synergies prior to subsequent RNF and joint ESA-EU meetings in the region and in Brussels.

In line with the above, the Trade and Industry ministry appointed an officer to coordinate all related activities of the NDTPF. The figure below represents the two-way interaction between the NDTPF and trade related ministries, between the NDTPF and the Brussels-based ambassador, and between the NDTPF and the private sector. The structure has been interacting with the cabinet through the Minister of Trade and Industry. The figure also shows minimal interaction between the NDTPF and the sections of civil society working on trade and development, as well as between the NDTPF and research and academic institutions. In this respect, most CSO representatives, while noting requests from the structure for interactions prior to trade-related meetings at the RNF and Brussels levels, decried the lack of rigour in the engagements and inputs. Similarly, some academic institutions with previous undisputed track records[35] of interrogating fundamental macro-economic processes such as the implementation weaknesses of the ESAP paradigm, including trade liberalisation policy, have not engaged the structure and the responsible ministry with a view to contributing towards a better trade deal. Another weakness shown here is the limited two-way interaction between NDTPF and MPs, whose constitutional function entails ratifying and monitoring the implementation of the new trade regime by the executive. In addition, a lack of shared reports on proceedings makes it difficult to verify the true functionality of the structure in terms of harnessing stakeholders' input into the process.

---

[35] Such as publications and public dialogue sessions on the policy process and impacts thereof

Figure 4.1   Zimbabwe EPA negotiation stakeholders

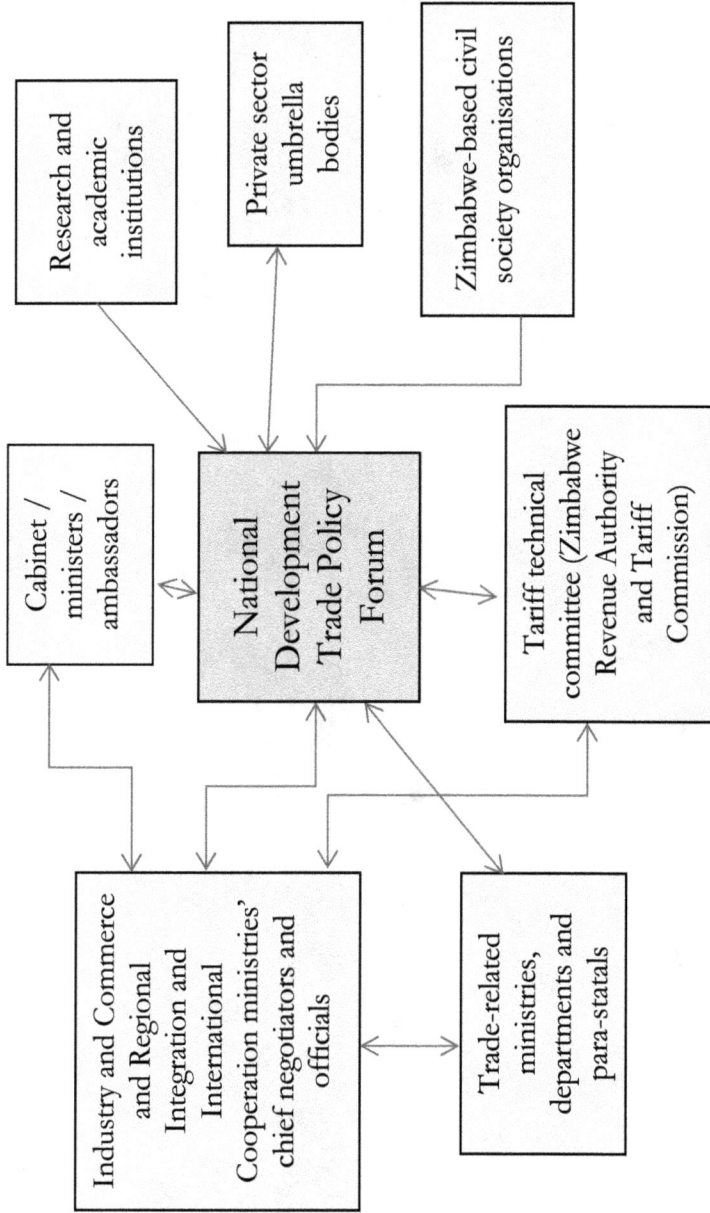

Source: Author's compilation based on various sources

However, some critical voices are excluded from interacting with other stakeholders at all levels. This means that the NDTPF structure has suffered from limited democratic space to potentially amplify pro-poor and pro-development voices during the preparatory stages of the EPA negotiations. Furthermore, some civil society representatives question the inclusiveness of all the relevant stakeholders working on the EPA process in the NDTPF platform. The exclusion of critical voices is supported by the sampled civil society groups and research scholars who confirm that the country's NDTPF suffers from lack of wide and deep consultation as well as the involvement of all relevant stakeholders and citizens, including poor constituencies. The exclusion of critical voices further compromises collective articulation of strategies, tactics, synergy building, coalition formations and options as well as chances of securing a just and fair EPA outcome.

As a result, some civic bodies blame the prevailing political polarisation in the country, the general conflictual relationship between ZANU (PF) and civic bodies, and the frosty relationship between ZANU (PF) and the EU, for undermining the potential of the NDTPF platform to deliver positive EPA outcomes. Anecdotal evidence points to the fact that some national, regional and global civic bodies, including those working on the EPA processes, have over the period under review lost confidence in the ruling governing party to provide leadership in economic policies and programmes, including EPA negotiations with Europe. They cite perennial economic mismanagement, reflected in the decade-long economic meltdown, short-lived macro-economic policies and coordination of the EPA process, especially with respect to formulation of positions and offers. The critical attitude of anti-ZANU (PF) civil society groups has, in some instances, been construed as a strategy for discrediting the former government while mobilising donor funding in support of regime change agenda. It is a fact that the authorities and their allies consider any questioning of state shortcomings in economic management as being anti-indigenisation and against economic empowerment. Further, the ZANU (PF) leadership views any criticism of its shortcomings in economic management as not only a grandstanding political strategy meant to dislodge its hegemony as a champion of indigenisation and economic empowerment, but also a strategy for buttressing EU sanctions.

This atmosphere of tension and mistrust between the state and civil society groups has impacted negatively on the work of the NDTPF. CSO criticism of Robert Mugabe's administration has in many ways served to link the EPA process with prevailing governance malpractices and endemic dubious electoral systems and practices. As a result, all critical civil society voices were deliberately excluded from the EPA process as well as the general socio-economic transformation debate. A significant number of CSOs working in trade issues were excluded from EPA-related meetings and had no access to EPA-related information before and after the RNF and joint ESA-EU meetings held in the region and in Brussels. Of all the EPA-focused CSOs, only the TRADES Centre and SEATINI enjoyed a sound working relationship with the ministry of Trade and Industry. The National Association of NGOs (NANGO), the umbrella body serving most NGOs in the country, participated initially but withdrew as the process progressed, largely due to limited financial resources and the reallocation of available human and financial resources to the governance and human rights agenda.

The antagonistic relationship between the ZANU (PF) government and civil society filters into the work of NDTPF amid claims by a ZIMCODD representative that:

> ... the ZANU (PF) government deliberately excludes some representatives of civic bodies based in the country, who are perceived to be critical to the politically motivated indigenisation and economic empowerment agenda, from attending RNF and Brussels EPA meetings. This is despite the fact that most country-based regional EPA focused organisations' representatives have since the launch of the negotiations been doing sterling EPA work that generated strategic tactics, positions and interventions that were well appreciated by most governments in the ESA configuration and beyond (Mandebvu, interview in Harare, Zimbabwe, 24 June 2011).

EPA-focused CSOs have over this period been active in questioning the EPA's ideology and the rationale of 'fast tracking the process towards predetermined deadlines' (Deve, 2006; Kamidza, 2008) in the face of widespread evidence of the country's unpreparedness to negotiate a beneficial deal. However, limited funding generally renders civic bodies inactive and too weak to mount any serious and critical engagement regarding the NDTPF's activities. This has also resulted in poor mobilisation of citizens and a subsequently low possibility of forming strategic alliances with other key stakeholders, especially the private sector and MPs.

Within their limited industrial and trade capacities, Zimbabwe CSO representatives and their strategic allies mobilised resources for lobbying various EU institutions against fast-tracking the process (Kamidza, 2007), amid growing fears of worsening poverty and social and economic underdevelopment in the short to medium term. Some CSO representatives were very active in the continental "Stop the EPAs" campaign, which influenced the decision to move the deadline set by the EU to conclude a WTO compatible EPAs trade regime by 31 December 2007 to December 2010. Even with the extended deadline, the trade talks could not be brought to a conclusion. Further, the threat of 1 October 2014 when the withdrawal of the MAR 1528 of 2007 takes effect could not lead to the conclusion of negotiating comprehensive EPA in this configuration. Thus, the EPA process lacks serious involvement of potentially critical stakeholders, particularly poor constituencies, and exposes a significant national institutional weakness in collective, inclusive and constructive engagement in the negotiations. It also reflects low citizen mobilisation, particularly of poor constituencies as well as weak strategic networking, synergy building and coalition partnerships between government officials and NSA activists in support of the process. The exclusion of critical CSOs' inputs has, in many instances, contributed to less ambitious EPA outcomes with respect to Zimbabwe and other EPA signatory countries in the same grouping. Many individuals in the civil society movement have questioned the wisdom of signing an iEPA when the Zimbabwean economy was struggling to resuscitate its industrial capacity. Indeed, Zimbabwe's weak articulation of issues, positions and offers vis-à-vis the EC, has resulted in a dangerous and unviable EPA outcome that is likely to fail to support the country's social and economic transition in the short to medium term. Further, the iEPA implementation threatens to become a vicious onslaught on the economy in general, and on new farmers, new entrepreneurs and SMEs' operators in particular, whose market competitiveness may not withstand technology-based EU products.

Critics have linked signs of weak institutional EPA processes to poor management and oversight on the part of the COMESA secretariat's EPA Unit, which is the regional institution driving the process. In particular, civic bodies claim that the COMESA secretariat's EPA Unit has failed to monitor how countries such as Zimbabwe comply with the EPA joint roadmap rules and procedures of engagement in the process. They argue that the regional institution should have insisted that group countries submit reports prior to RNF meetings - a strategy that could have allowed interested stakeholders to review the process and understand the dynamics at each NDTPF platform and subsequently during the RNF negotiation process, thereby encouraging national, regional and international scholars to access country reports and inform Zimbabweans about the dynamics of the process. Without publicity and wider scrutiny, it becomes difficult to assess the NDTPF's accountability, transparency, democratic process and the inclusiveness of the relevant civic bodies in the process.

Due to the deliberate exclusion of civic bodies, publicity about the Zimbabwean EPA process has remained largely low-key, and even absent. Respondents have observed that EPA-related events and activities at the level of the NDTPF, the RNF and Brussels have taken place without media notice. There have been no report back sessions by government officials - either prior to or after participation in the meetings. In particular, the former Industry and Commerce Minister, Welshman Ncube, did not address the nation or consult with other key stakeholders after signing the iEPA. This development renewed state-civil society suspicion about the EPA process, with the latter lamenting a lost opportunity to engage interested constituencies and citizens in monitoring and evaluating the implementation of EPA outcomes.

Regional negotiation forum

The Regional Negotiating Forum (RNF) is a structure that brings together representatives from the NDTPF, the four regional secretariats[1], a regional civic body[2], Brussels-based ambassadors, especially cluster lead spokespersons, and selected observers, to exchange views on issues, interests, strategies and tactics and to ultimately prepare EPA positions and offers for the ESA configuration in their engagement with the EC. The COMESA secretariat coordinates all EPA-related work, including impact assessment studies undertaken in ESA countries, with support from the EAC, the IOC, and IGAD secretariats. The COMESA secretariat also organises and facilitates RNF meetings and monitors the implementation of agreed positions and decisions. The COMESA leadership, including the Secretary General, Deputy Secretary General, Director of Trade, and EPA Unit CTA, have not only been active in the negotiations, but have also directly supervised the process.

Nalunga (2004) observes that since the launch of the EPA roadmap RNF negotiations have become increasingly complex amid organisational deficiencies in terms of technical and financial capacities at the level of the COMESA secretariat and participating countries. Thus, COMESA funding, secured from the EU, has supported three delegates (two government officials and a representative of the private sector) from each ESA country, since the launch of the EPA process. This financial support has ensured the participation of all ESA-EPA countries at both the RNF and joint ESA-EU meetings held in the region and in Brussels. Zimbabwe has received the same level of financial support (the only financial relationship) despite the bilateral standoff with the EU. In addition, some well-resourced and strategic ESA countries have sponsored the participation of additional state officials (from trade and trade-related ministries) and MPs. For instance, some countries (such as Kenya) supported the participation of MPs in both RNF and joint ESA-EU meetings held in the region and in Brussels, while MPs from

---

[1] COMESA, EAC, IOC and IGAD.
[2] SEATINI between February 2004 and 31 December 2005.

Zimbabwe have not been included. Similarly, some ESA member state delegations have supported civil society groups and private sector representatives with resources to join them in all EPA-related meetings.

The COMESA secretariat has often been accused of circulating crucial documents during meetings (Kamidza, 2004). This practice compromises the quality of internal group engagements, as well as the quality of national EPA progress reports on stakeholder preparations and outcomes. This is contrary to the joint EPA roadmap, which emphasises that NDTPF consultative reports should be submitted to the COMESA secretariat well before RNF meetings so that officials may adequately prepare, and which allows translation of documents into the official languages of the ESA group. This is supported by SEATINI's (2005) observation that ESA countries systemically failed to submit reports of their respective consultations to the COMESA secretariat prior to the RNF meetings. This means that most delegations who participated in the meetings were unprepared, while national consultations in some countries, especially Zimbabwe, were severely compromised. For instance, the high level of Zimbabwean state shortcomings, coupled with conflictual state-CSO relationships, greatly undermined the collective articulation of issues and reinforced the adoption of offensive and defensive positions and offers. This not only compromises the depth of engagements within the configuration, but often derails the process entirely.

In the case of Zimbabwe, non-submission of NDTPF reports to the COMESA secretariat poses challenges for the strategic coordination of stakeholder inputs, effective consultations with stakeholders and collective stakeholder decisions with respect to national interests, positions and offers. It not only reflects a lack of preparedness, collective stakeholder participation and strategic contribution to the process, but also shows a high level of politicisation at all stages of the process. Furthermore, continued high levels of political polarisation amid dwindling international support makes it difficult to arrive at a collective articulation of national positions, decisions and offers. This has also undermined the country's effectiveness in RNF meetings. In spite of this, the country concluded an iEPA signed in Mauritius in 2009 by the GNU minister of Industry and Commerce, Welshman Ncube. The lack of technical knowledge, coupled with insufficient consultation was underscored by Angelica Katuruza, the former government chief negotiator, during a combined ESA and SADC configurations' EPA workshop held in Harare in 2009. She pleaded with the Zimbabwe business community to respond to the government's request for additional industrial-sensitive products to be shared with the EU even though it was some time after the country had initialed the iEPA, saying: 'Although Zimbabwe has submitted its offers to the EC, the door is still open for the business sector to submit individual lists of sensitive products for further sharing with the negotiating counterpart' (Katuruza, interview in Johannesburg, South Africa, 28 May 2012).

Other negotiation institutions and structures

Regional preparatory task force

The Regional Preparatory Task Force (RPTF) is an informal body of experts which allows each side (the EU and the ESA) to get a better technical understanding of their counterpart's position, as well as a clearer interpretation of certain relevant issues and developments. The main objective of the RPTF is to prepare for the engagements of the leading ambassadors and EC senior officials by means of scheduling meetings, agenda preparation, and identification of venues. The RPTF also facilitates the exchange of information on negotiations issues, views and positions, and the identification of areas of divergence and convergence between the negotiating parties, thereby enabling each side to adequately prepare for meaningful participation. This structure also prepares ESA ministerial and EU commissioners' meetings. Thus, the RPTF is intended to enable all parties to arrive at their negotiating positions before tabling them.

From the ESA side, representatives of the RPTF comprise Brussels-based ambassadors and their respective officials, COMESA secretariat officials including the EPA Unit CTA, and representatives of the ACP secretariat. The RTPF decisions and process-related agreements are expected to add value to ongoing EPA negotiations outcomes. This structure has a profound impact on the sequencing

119

of negotiating positions within the configuration, and between the configuration and the EC. On the EC side, the representatives of the RPTF are mainly drawn from members of the EU Directorate of Trade.

SEATINI observes that the RPTF has not been engaging regional CSOs, including their representatives who occasionally undertake missions to lobby EU institutions. This suggests that the primary reason for the lack of interaction between the two important relevant stakeholders (RPTF and CSOs) is caused by their different geographical locations - with the RPTF representatives being based in Brussels, and the CSOs in their respective ESA capitals. In cases where RPTF representatives participated in regional meetings in any of the ESA towns, the ESA CSOs failed to interact with them, either formally or informally. This reflects the poor relationship between the COMESA secretariat's EPA Unit, the convener of the RNF meetings, and the CSOs, usually on account of perceptions of unruly behaviour on the part of the latter. The present study confirms this by observing that 'no meeting was organised throughout the EPA process to facilitate interaction between RPTF representatives and regional CSOs' (Machemedze, interview in Harare, Zimbabwe, 25 June 2011 and Makanza, interview in Durban, South Africa, 10 August 2011). The study notes that following the withdrawal of the SEATINI representative in December 2004, all interaction of CSOs with other ESA structures ceased. The study further confirms that all the COMESA organised EPA meetings had congested agendas that did not allow regional CSOs a formal session with RPTF representative(s) for debriefing purposes. This reflects organisational weakness and a poor working relationship between the COMESA secretariat and regional CSOs. It can also be a reflection of the CSOs' weak advocacy strategies. In the final analysis, regional CSOs missed their opportunity to lobby the RPTF.

Kamidza (2004) recalls how the RPTF sequencing of negotiation issues in July 2004 was rejected by the ESA capitals during a meeting held in Antananarivo, Madagascar:

Are we already agreeing to sequence cluster negotiations when national impact assessment studies are yet to be completed? Who prioritises the sequencing of cluster negotiations? Who should provide guidance to this structure in order to synthesise contributions of all relevant stakeholders in this process? Why, in particular, has agriculture, the backbone of many ESA economies, not been prioritized, together with fisheries, development issues and market access for the period July 2004 and March 2005[3]? (Kamidza, 2004: 3).

While RPTF sequencing of negotiations has the potential to confuse the process and to create divisions within the configuration, a development that may result in a bad EPA outcome, regional CSOs could have sharpened their advocacy with a view to influence a more logical sequencing of the negotiations. For instance, the regional CSOs knew where the meeting venues were, and even knew some of the delegates. They could easily have interacted with the representatives of the structure. Indeed, a conventional lobbying tactic would have facilitated interaction.

The regional CSOs could have assigned their European counterparts to lobby the RTPF structure in Brussels. Regional CSOs have a strategic networking and funding relationship with European collaborative CSOs such as Action Aid, Christian Aid, (Holland) Humanistic Institute for Development Cooperation (Hivos), Oxfam Novib, Oxfam America and the Rosa Luxemburg Foundation. These organisations have facilitated sub-regional CSOs' lobbying missions in Europe, as well as the exchange of strategic information and the convening of, or participation in, EPA-related dialogue sessions. This has created space and opportunities for CSOs to lobby EU institutions and citizens on the process and its potential implications for ESA economies. For instance, in May 2005 Christian Aid funded selected CSO representatives from Africa's four configurations on a lobbying mission to Europe, targeting the EU Presidency (United Kingdom), the EU Parliament, various EC Directorates and the ACP secretariat. Unfortunately, the organisers of the lobbying mission (Christian Aid) missed an opportunity to facilitate direct interaction between RPTF representatives and African CSO lobbyists, two of whom were from the ESA region. Indeed, conventional lobbying

---

[3] Para 74 of the adopted 3rd RNF meeting report.

strategy and tactics would have facilitated engagement with the RTPF structure, an outcome that would have facilitated more interaction in subsequent ESA EPA meetings in the region.

ESA EPA unit

At meetings held in Entebbe and Antananarivo, the ESA group agreed to establish a technical office similar to that of the EC, with a mandate to assist in the negotiations at the technical level. Once established, this EPA technical office was headed by a Chief Technical Advisor, whose mandate included preparing ESA meetings, providing technical advice to ESA member states on EPA issues and sequencing negotiations with other EPA structures outside the RNF, such as RPTF and the Council of Ministers. The CTA has also assisted national negotiators and has worked closely with different cluster negotiators based in Brussels. However, some ESA member states were unwilling to contribute financial resources to support this important office, resulting in the EC funding the entire operation itself. This not only exposes the ESA's lack of strategic positioning vis-à-vis the EU, but also the unequal relationship between the parties involved in the negotiations.

Throughout the negotiation period, the EPA unit has remained under-resourced in terms of personnel. It was manned by the CTA, with a secretary to assist in the preparation of meetings with documentation, logistics and office administration. Office operation and staff emoluments are funded by the EU. ESA member states have failed to contribute resources to support the work of this unit, given the frequency of meetings and engagements involved. Contributions from ESA countries would at least have enabled additional staff to be engaged, particularly an assistant to the CTA. It is assumed that the regional CSOs, especially those based in Zimbabwe, would have taken advantage of the unit to enhance their contributions to the process given that the CTA happens to be a Zimbabwean. A close working relationship with the EPA unit would have given the CTA more time to interact with other relevant stakeholders. In particular, a working relationship with Zimbabwe CSOs could have enabled the CTA to harness input from this sector. Since the CTA happens to be a Zimbabwean, it would have provided an excellent opportunity to lobby for national CSOs' direct involvement in the process. Relying on the EU to fund the unit serves to yield effective control of the process to them.

Committee of ambassadors

The Committee of Ambassadors comprises leading cluster spokespersons who are supposed to liaise with the EC on all EPA-related matters, as well as work closely with other ambassadors from the ESA configuration. This Committee has not provided regional CSOs with sufficient space to undertake any advocacy. As noted above, their physical location makes it difficult for regional CSOs to lobby this structure, but the CSOs themselves admit that they failed to explore other means of lobbying.

Council of Ministers

The Council of Ministers comprises all the ministers of Trade, Industry and Commerce in the ESA configuration, and gives political direction to the negotiations, especially with respect to the mandate as informed by unfolding social, economic, and political sensitivities and dynamics. In particular, the Council provides political direction in the event of a declared stalemate. Thus, it only meets when the occasion demands, either in the ESA region or in Brussels. Despite the EU sanctions Samuel Mumbengegwi, the former ZANU (PF) Minister of Trade and Industry, was always allowed to travel in order to participate in EPA-related meetings. In this way ESA unity was maintained during the formative stages of the negotiations, yet subsequently wrecked by isolating him towards the conclusion of the negotiations.

ESA trade ministers also engaged with the EPA negotiation process via other platforms, namely the ACP Council of Ministers, held either in the ACP region or in Brussels, and the AU Ministers of Trade meetings in Ethiopia - the Headquarters of the AU - or the capital city of the current AU Chair. Regional CSOs have not engaged with this structure, which demonstrates their failure to exploit past negotiation strategies and tactics, which included building strong alliances with trade, industry and commerce ministers and their respective permanent secretaries, Brussels-based ambassadors and other technical state institutions.

The EPA process and the 'guerrilla' approach to negotiations

Collins (2009: 17-23) defines guerrilla negotiation tactics as precise and strategic pressures designed to discourage a counterpart's negotiation efforts. Usually this takes the form of strategic silence on certain issues, throwing money at the process, distracting the counterpart and taking advantage of the counterpart's goodwill. Such tactics largely inform the EU-Zimbabwe EPA negotiating process. Benoliel and Hua (2009: 6) describe negotiation as being "challenging, unique, complex and exciting and requiring a mixture of knowledge, skills, experience and intuition." Negotiation entails a combination of moves and countermoves, tactics, strategies, attitudes, mindsets and confidence building, driven by specific commercial interests and social and political considerations. It also entails understanding the fundamental dilemmas and myths which surround the negotiation as well as the counterpart's power, modus operandi and strengths and weaknesses within a context of national interests and defined roles, goals and limits. In managing the negotiation process, parties must avoid common mistakes, which include underestimating the risks associated with poor preparation as:

> The negotiation process involves managing information and communications during the discussions, planning and re-planning, coordinating efforts between negotiators, making moves and counter-moves and making important decisions under conditions of uncertainty and time pressure (Benoliel and Hua 2009: 16)

The EU approach is two-pronged. On the one hand, it makes use of political and economic conditionalities, and on the other, it relentlessly pursues persuasive and offensive commercial interests aimed at securing short to medium term market opportunities for its producers, exporters, investors and consumers. This means sustaining outward expansion of a European capitalist industrial

124

production frontier, thereby summarily increasing the supply of goods on European markets with any excess production having already been assured of a 'secure market' outside the EU (in other words, in EPA economies, especially those with weak productive capacities such as Zimbabwe). This approach not only sustains profit margins and employment levels in the EU, but also extends capitalist tentacles throughout external markets, especially vulnerable economies like Zimbabwe. This scenario is illustrated in Figure 4.2 below: technologically advanced producers, including MCs and TNCs in Europe, increase their respective supplies of goods to EU markets (from S_0 to S_1) but prevent a corresponding fall in price (P_0 to P_1) in the same European market by exporting a corresponding increase in output (surplus Q_0Q_1) to iEPA economies. The fact that the price remains unchanged following the export of excess production means that the profit levels and employment opportunities in Europe have been secured by the EPA trade regime. Indeed, (Q_0Q_1) surplus output is a competitive proxy of a secured market share in iEPA economies. In an economy like Zimbabwe that is still struggling to stimulate industrial capacity utilisation beyond 20% (due to the collapse of most industries, which have been classified as 'infant' or 'distressed'), the EU's Q_0Q_1 surplus output is assured of its market share in the short to medium term. During the SADC EPA ministerial meeting in Gaborone, Botswana, Rob Davies, the South African trade minister, remarked:

EU mercantilist interests and high levels of ambition displayed in the EPA process are certainly poised to displace domestic products with competing and heavily subsidised European products. Sadly, most EPA signatories have not developed countervailing measures to deal with subsidies' induced competitiveness and increased penetration of European products into local markets (Rob Davies, SADC EPA member states ministerial meeting, Gaborone, Botswana, 19 May 2013).

Figure 4.2   Europe's production and export capacity

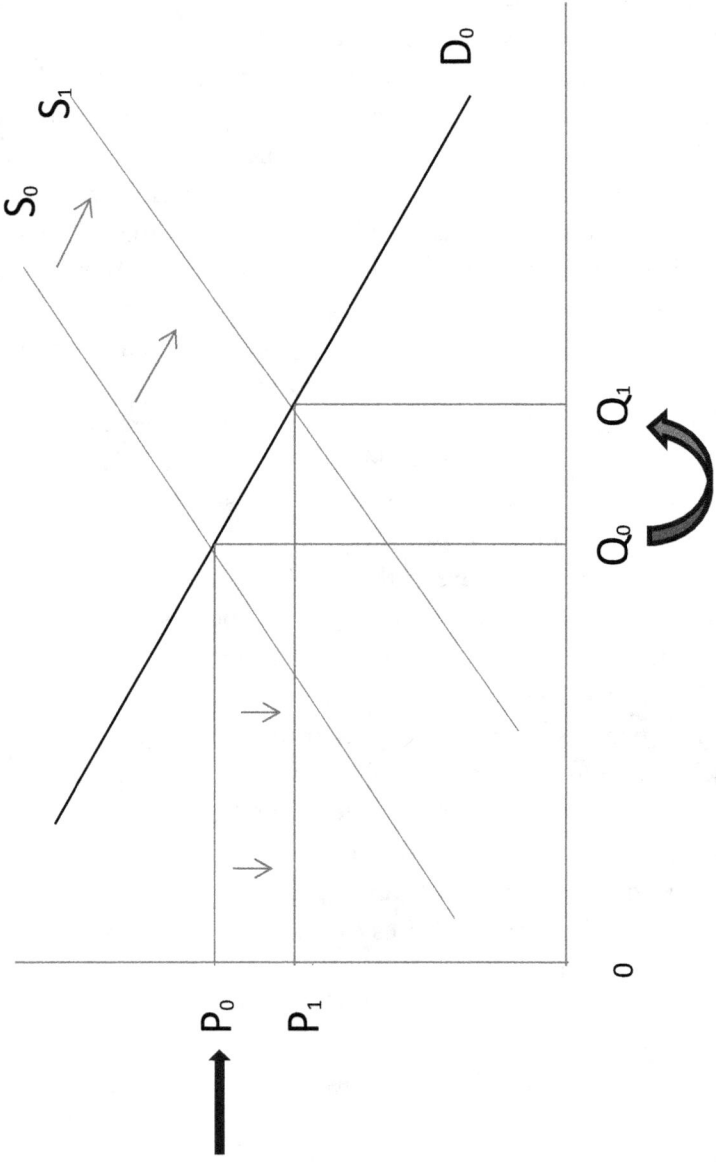

Zimbabwe is about to become open to unfettered access by Europe in terms of production and productivity, largely due to the near collapse of its industrial and export capabilities, estimated at between 4% and 10% of the national industrial capacity utilisation (Nyakazeya, 2009). The collapse occurred at a time of uncertain relations with the EU, in which the latter disputed ZANU-PF's victory in the elections of July 2013, which was overwhelmingly endorsed by African governments. In the short to medium term, Zimbabwean consumers and industrial firms guarantee an open market for European producers and exporters. This onslaught on the economy is benefiting European MCs, TNCs and business lobbies. By signing and ratifying iEPA, Zimbabwe opened 45% of the economy to EU products through tariff line reductions by 2012 (see Table 5.6). This means that Europe's mercantilist and capitalist interests in the Zimbabwean economy will become entrenched in the short to medium term through the - invisible - control of demand and supply forces. It also sends a warning signal to the new 'indigenous economic empowerment entrepreneurs, particularly the new farmers' of future tough competition from European products. The resultant 'made in Europe' market tsunami will assure a corresponding fall in the associated economic profits of local entrepreneurs, as reflected in the Figure below.

Zimbabwe's industrial base has largely consisted in the export of raw commodities, while remaining a net importer of European products and services. This exposes the agricultural sector, now largely indigenised, to corresponding competitive European products. Zimbabwe's new A1 and A2 farmers currently have very low levels of production, compared to their heavily protected and subsidised EU counterparts. For instance, it is calculated that in Europe a single cow receives about US$3 per day compared to over 50% of the ACP human population who live on less than US$1 a day (SEATINI, 2004). Newly settled Zimbabwean farmers are failing to improve the level of production of almost all their commodities compared with the pre-fast track land reform era, and are thereby unlikely to defend the local market from highly competitive EU products. 'Guerrilla' negotiation strategies have ensured that European producers, exporters, and investors are free to unleash an onslaught on 'Zimbabwe's weak, narrow and vulnerable industrial and export capacities' (Machemedze, interview in Harare, Zimbabwe, 25 June 2011). The strategy has the potential to drive the new indigenous entrepreneurs, farmers and SMEs out of business, thereby creating opportunities for displaced former farmers, mining rights owners and other foreign investors (on account of global connections) to reinsert themselves into the economic life of Zimbabwe. Such a development will signal the failure of ZANU (PF)'s attempt to reclaim land rights and make them see that the real economic battles are won at the negotiation table, where agreed tariff liberalisations are implemented through the demand and supply of goods and services.

Diagram 4.1   Potential scenario of trade flows between EU and Zimbabwe under iEPA

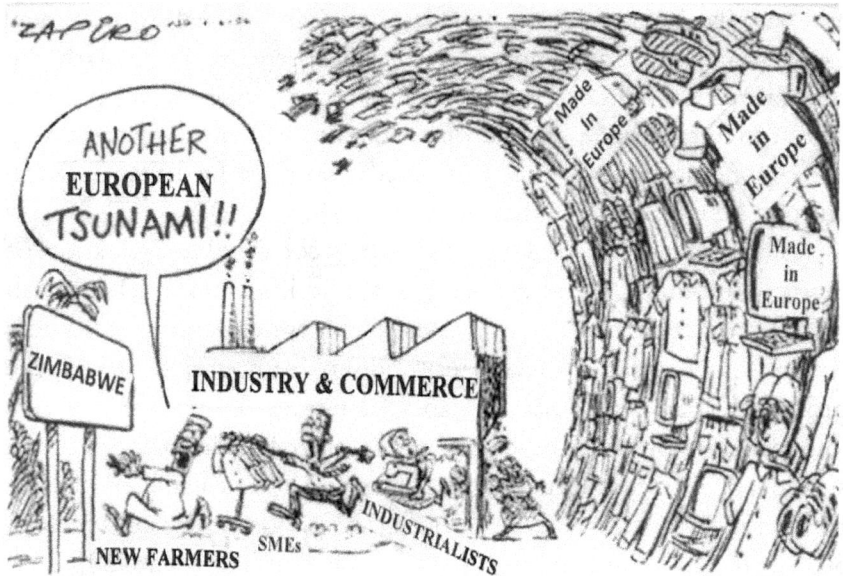

Source: Adapted from Zapiro, 2006

It is almost risible that the EU has always presented itself as being driven by a desire to pursue development-friendly policy objectives, especially sustainable development, building regional markets[94] and implementing poverty alleviation. An ICCO Study[95] (2008: 3) entitled 'Dialogue of the deaf' states:

> In trade negotiations, the EU frequently portrays itself as the ally of developing countries – sensitive to their concerns and looking out for shared interests as a partner in talks; and presents itself as a more benign negotiating partner not ready to leverage concessions or use strong-arm tactics to achieve its political and economic goals (ICCO Study, 2008: 3).

In fact, the strategy of the EU advances its own commercial interests and it is usually supported by a disguised 'developmental aid envelope' designed to entice ACP countries into the negotiating room. While advancing this strategy, Europe argues that it trades very little with ACP countries thereby giving the impression that its industrialists and investors are not very interested in the economic fortunes of their counterpart. In particular, while publicly displaying little interest in Zimbabwe, the mere fact that the bloc agrees:

> … to financially support impact assessment studies and the participation of a three member Zimbabwe delegation (two government officials[96] and one private sector representative) in all RNF and joint ESA-EU meetings held in the region and in Brussels, and to ignore the travel ban on the former Trade and Industry minister, Samuel Mumbengegwi in order to allow his participation in Brussels

---

[94] Building regional markets to support development is a formal objective of the negotiations, laid out in the governing treaty, the Cotonou Partnership Agreement.

[95] A ICCO study that involves a fairly representative sample of thirteen ACP negotiators of whom nine felt EPAs did not support regional integration, eleven confirmed EC pressure to negotiate trade-related issues, eleven confirmed EPAs forced ACP countries to liberate their trade, ten confirmed that aid was made conditional on signing of an EPA, eight confirmed that the EC does not listen to ACP concerns or proposals and only confirmed EPAs as instruments for development.

[96] Initially, EU funding supported two government officials (a trade negotiator and a trade official) and one private sector representative, but later support was given to three government officials.

meetings, points to a well calculated strategy of securing commercial opportunities for European producers, investors and exporters (Mandebvu, interview in Harare, Zimbabwe, 24 June 2011).

While Katuruza attests that the poor bilateral relationship with the EU gave Zimbabwe the space to speak its mind without being manipulated in one-on-one meetings, the fact remains that the country had no opportunity to bilaterally resolve critical and sensitive issues outside the group gathering. Zimbabwe was among the first group of countries in Africa to be congratulated by the EU Trade Commissioner on signing an iEPA (regardless of the prevailing economic situation). This is indicative of 'guerrilla' duplicity, shrewdness and manipulative capacity on the part of the seasoned and experienced EU negotiators.

An ICCO Study (2008) notes that the EU takes pride in its three pillar approach to external relations that consists in flanking trade agreements with a political cooperation and development assistance envelope in order to maximise benefits and complementarities. The ICCO study goes on to accuse the dominant partner of not only ignoring past failures of economic and political conditionalities, but also imposing its views on development policies via trade negotiations, especially on economically stressed economies like Zimbabwe. The study notes:

> The EC Council emphasises the close interdependence between trade policy, development policy, economic development, food security, good governance and democracy, rule of law and legal security and calls on the parties to strengthen coherence between these areas (ICCO Study, 2008: 3).

Meanwhile, EC negotiators have been clever enough not to express their opinions on Zimbabwe's internal political, social and economic deficiencies. They have also avoided adopting any attitude that might have been construed as meddling in bilateral political disputes in trade talks (Chifamba, 2012 and Katuruza, 2012[97]) so as

---

[97] Interview discussions with both chief negotiators – Chifamba and Katuruza based in Harare and Johannesburg, respectively.

not to be accused by ZANU (PF) of pursuing a regime change agenda. As a result, the EU has earned the respect of ESA country officials in general and Zimbabwean officials in particular, thereby enabling it to exploit its superior bilateral bargaining power. As a result, the EU managed to fast-track the EPA process with a view to reaching a conclusion by 31 December 2007, in line with the expiry of the current WTO waiver. However the deadline continues to be pushed forward, resulting in Zimbabwe initialing the iEPA in 2008, signing and ratifying it in 2009 and 2012, respectively.

Using its guerrilla negotiating strategies and tactics, the EU unilaterally violated the principle of partnership in the EPA trade talks by forcing negotiations on controversially trade-related issues as binding commitments on WTO rules and regulations - despite the available option to negotiate in non-binding and cooperative language (Chizema and Masiiwa, 2011) and (Masiiwa, 2012[98]). The EU use of language in the negotiations became increasingly synonymous with binding commitments (Katuruza, 2012[99]), thereby compelling Zimbabwe to opt to forego revenue inflows and the protection of sectors that contribute towards job creation, poverty alleviation or food security and/or food sovereignty.

These guerrilla negotiating strategies and tactics further allow the EC to exploit Zimbabwe's lack of negotiating capacity and the disjuncture in its negotiating structures. The EU exploited the information gap by deliberately presenting strategic and essential EPA issues in different ways to the political leadership and the negotiators (ICCO Study, 2008). The EU was also aware that, without direct bilateral contact, there were no opportunities to clarify group sentiments. Katuruza (2012)[100], the former chief negotiator, confirms that there were no one-on-one meetings between the parties outside the ESA institutional platforms. This allowed the EU to peddle issues in its favour, including controversial proposals.

---

[98] Interview discussion with Medicine Masiiwa, Gaborone, Botswana, 25 August 2012.

[99] Interview discussion with Angelica Katuruza, Johannesburg, South Africa, 28 May 2012.

[100] Interview discussion with Angelica Katuruza, Johannesburg, South Africa, 28 May 2012.

Indeed, following the impasse between Brussels and Harare, the only practical interaction platform between the parties has been the EPA process, that is, engaging the Zimbabwean EPA delegation within the context of ESA group and the political leadership within the context of both the ACP-EU ministerial and AU-EU EPA summit meetings.

While the partnership principle has allowed the widely publicised development aid envelope to be used as an incentive for EPA participating countries, past failure to access EDF resources since the Lomé Conventions[101] clearly indicates a deliberate violation of the partnership principle which states:

> … a partnership would imply that the EPAs truly included the concerns of the ACP parties, rather than the EU framing negotiations primarily and solely in the context of their own needs and constraints. The balance of power in terms of economic clout and resources (including experts) is horribly tilted against the ACP configurations. So it is very hard to see how to have a balanced negotiation in the circumstances (Tandon, 2004: 11).

The guerrilla approach to the EU–Zimbabwe trade talks has resulted in the former becoming increasingly hesitant to consider alternative access to the EU market in the future. The EU seems to believe that an arrangement that forces the ACP countries swallow the bitter pill of trade liberalisation is superior to preference schemes that have not yet delivered. The second reason for EC disregard for alternatives is the political cost; improving or extending preferences to ACP countries has proved to be a harder sell in an EU with 27 member states, most of whom have no historical colonial ties with these countries. The idea of a waiver or other accommodation at the WTO was clearly distasteful to the EC, and they refused a direct request from ACP countries to seek this. The withdrawal of MAR by 1 October 2014 is therefore a development that is seen as exerting pressure on the countries that initialed iEPA, to sign and rectify the agreement while negotiations for the full EPA continue, or risk losing the EU market. It can be inferred that the announcement to withdraw

---

[101] Documentary evidence show that ACP countries have utilised less than 50% of available EDF resources since the Lomé Conventions.

MAR significantly contributed to Zimbabwe's signing and ratifying the iEPA, a development that exposes the country's lack of political will to explore alternatives to the EU market. For instance, in an effort to secure the legality of existing trade preferences to EPA member states, pending the conclusion of the negotiations, the EC should have submitted a formal request to extend the WTO waiver or have issued a formal assurance that, should the deadline be missed, tariffs would not be raised. Instead, the EC was adamant that the deadline would be respected, despite the enormous pressure on ACP relationships that this involved.

ICCO (2004) argues that a country going into any negotiation needs to know a lot about the main interests of its counterpart: know your counterpart's arguments. In this respect, the EU, through its 50-year scenario assessment of each ACP economy (including Zimbabwe), coupled with public information – including that country's challenges in the body politic, the downward spiral of the economy, the conflictual state-CSO relationship, and mistrust in the state-private sector relationship - has significant knowledge about the interests of its counterpart. Through such scenario assessments, the EC might have evaluated the economic strengths (or otherwise) of the new entrepreneur. EU strategies and tactics aimed at maximising its interests include the following:

The EU's unilateral decision to withdraw market access provisions in the middle of negotiations, put pressure on the Zimbabwean parliament to hastily ratify the iEPA in 2012. The EU emphasised the illegality of granting trade preferences after December 2007 when the WTO waiver expired, hence the decision by all 27 member EC Councils, the EC, and the EU Parliament to terminate MAR 1528 of 2007 by October 2014. In this respect, the EC chief negotiator, João Machado, stated:

The EU is the biggest trading partner under WTO, and does not want to be seen to continue breaking the rules. … The EU is the only trading bloc (partner) in the world that willingly continues giving trade preferences and market access even before concluding the on-going EPA negotiations. Thus, the EU must not be viewed as failing the

SADC EPA group by unilaterally and arbitrarily setting the date to withdraw market access provisions. In any case, these market provisions were unilaterally given to ACP countries as a transition support mechanism while negotiating EPA, initially expected to have been concluded by 31 December 2007 (Machado, during the joint EU-SADC EPA countries negotiations, Johannesburg, South Africa, 20-22 March 2013).

The EU often announced that "other configurations have agreed to some provisions, and therefore it would be difficult for the EC Council and EU parliament to accept this group position and offer that is different from other configurations" (Machado, during the joint EU-SADC EPA countries negotiations, Johannesburg, 20-22 March 2013). This strategy is usually linked to market access (rules of origin and tariff offers) or trade-related issues, where EPA counterparts may not have the mandate or the capacity to meaningfully negotiate. The EU chief negotiator would pronounce at the start of negotiations that 'the contentious issue of market access is the make or break of these negotiations.' (Tekere, 2012: 7). This puts pressure on the group or country to make further concessions. For Zimbabwe, which since 2000 has been facing other pressures from the EU, the outcome was not only to concede more, but also to abruptly agree to individually sign and ratify iEPA, regardless of the short to medium term implications for the economy and society.

Singling out a member state or group of countries within a configuration for taking the negotiating process forward in a joint meeting is a strategy aimed at creating division while exerting pressure on those perceived as bent on resisting Europe's strategy. For instance, in a joint meeting with the SADC EPA group, held on 19-22 March 2013 in Johannesburg, South Africa, the EU chief negotiator, João Machado, harshly criticised the Southern African Customs Union (SACU) exclusion lists as being insincere and far below European expectations while heaping praise on Mozambique. This strategy was intended to divide the group and, most importantly, the grouping of SACU itself. It failed because the

SACU countries are bonded together by long-established revenue sharing formulas. SACU member states also wish to correct a 1999 error in which South Africa signed and implemented the Trade Development Cooperation Agreement with the EU leaving out other SACU customs union countries. In the case of the ESA, countries have no common economic and political bonds that compel them to stick together under EU divisive pressures.

Zimbabwean negotiators, despite the prevailing circumstances, devised negotiating strategies and tactics at both the national and regional levels. At the national level, the political leadership heaped praise on the 'look east' policy as an alternative to the traditional trade and development relationship with Europe. Meanwhile, the negotiators insisted on the importance of the historical trade relationship with Europe. This strategy helped reduce mistrust between the state and the business community. It also ensured that at all the EPA engagements, Zimbabwe had allies, and that its disagreements with the negotiating bloc did not filter into the process. This was supported by Elijah Munyuki who claims that:

> There was no visible sign that EU-Zimbabwe bilateral relations were strained as the two sides dealt with political cooperation and economic cooperation separately (at least in public). Both sides also realised that nothing would be gained by either side in linking political and economic aspects of the Cotonou Agreement, as this would expose and isolate Zimbabwe thereby slowing down the ESA EPA processes. Both sides further behaved as if the political impasse did not exist (Munyuki, interview in Gaborone, Botswana, 25 August 2012).

The country's strategies and tactics in the EPA process are summarised in the table below. In this respect, the government through COMESA managed to access EU financial assistance, thereby facilitating the participation of two[102] or three government

---

[102] According to funding criteria, each ESA country receives funding support for two government officials and one for a private sector representative. However, in some instances, the government used all the funding support for its own delegates.

officials in the RNF and joint ESA-EU meetings held in the region and in Brussels, despite the country's suspension from the 10th EDF financial assistance. The table shows that the government, through the COMESA secretariat, successfully mobilised resources to undertake a study on external common tariffs as well as a national consultation between the government and stakeholders interested in the EPA process. Zimbabwe also adopted a strategy of speaking directly with the EU in the context of the ESA group (the only contact between Brussels and Harare at government level), thereby avoiding any reference to conflictual bilateral issues. This removed bilateral politics from the process and allowed for cohesion and unity in the ESA group, as well as ensuring mutual respect between the EU and Zimbabwean negotiators. Zimbabwe also managed to remain part of the group in spite of the many differences, some of which were externally driven. The table also shows that at the regional level, Zimbabwe assisted in maintaining the group's position, including telling the EC that there were 'non-negotiable regional positions' (Katuruza, 2012)[103]. The table further shows the group's strategy of alternating thematic negotiators in order to prevent the EC chief negotiator, João Machado, from focusing on any particular personality(ies)[104].

At the national level, however, there is no indication of any stakeholder consultative engagement in the process. Anecdotal evidence reveals problems in forming reliable and predictable government–NSA strategic alliances on the EPA process, and the involvement of other state institutions such as the MPs in the TDC in particular and other MPs and Senators in general. The former chief negotiator, Angelica Katuruza, acknowledged the challenges facing the government in general and the Industry and Commerce ministry in particular, including confusing EPA issues with the conflictual bilateral relations with the EU, fiscal related constraints, high rate of staff turn-over in trade related portfolios and the EU's economic and

---

[103] Interview discussion with Angelica Katuruza, Johannesburg, 28 May 2012.
[104] Observation during the joint EU-SADC EPA group negotiations, in which João Machado focused his attention on Xavier Carim and Malan Lindeque, the chief negotiators for South Africa and Namibia respectively.

political isolation policy towards the ZANU (PF) government and leadership over this period.

Table 4.1 Zimbabwe's national and regional strategies and tactics for the EPA process

National strategies and tactics	Regional strategies and tactics
Holding preparatory meetings with relevant stakeholders ahead of each round of negotiations (RNF and joint ESA-EU).	Agreeing on strategies and tactics with other group countries ahead of each round of negotiation with the EC.
Pushing for national position reflecting national interests at RNF meetings.	Postponing negotiation on areas where the group feels not ready to engage with the EC.
Requesting the COMESA secretariat to undertake certain studies such as the common external tariff and impact assessment using own resources, as well as funding national level consultations.	Learning to avoid EU 'surprises' by deferring any matter that is introduced without prior notification and/or consultation to a future round of engagement thereby allowing both national and group consultations.
Making use of analytical work done at ministerial level, and the different viewpoints of CSOs[105] with resources and time to participate in the EPA process.	Understanding the merit of what other ESA countries are putting on the table as well as lobbying them with a view to form specific short-term strategic alliances.
Inviting media to EPA meetings held in Zimbabwe for purposes of disseminating information to various constituencies.	Proposing contentious issues to the next round of negotiations in order to allow further consultations at both national and regional levels.
Undertaking mini-studies and analytical work at ministerial level in order to input into the national positions before shared with other ESA countries.	Being wary of EC's tactic and strategy of deliberately leaking information with a view to gauge the group's views in some areas.

---

[105] Particularly TRADES Centre and SEATINI

Holding debriefing sessions after each RNF session or joint ESA-EC negotiating round.	Changing the group's negotiators from time to time in response to EC strategies and tactics.
Keeping the EPA team intact for the sake of continuity (the team has not changed much despite the challenges facing the government).	Ensuring that the chief negotiator for a particular thematic area is not deviating from agreed regional position(s).
	Categorically spelling out 'no go areas' during joint rounds of negotiations.
	Using regional studies to support decision making processes.

Source: Own compilation from interview discussion with Katuruza, 2012

Throughout the process, the EU has constantly reminded the ESA countries that the EPA outcome would produce a 'mutually beneficial developmental and regional integration supportive agreement' (Nalunga, 2004). Many of the EU strategies and tactics have had enormous impact on the economic partnership the EU has been building for decades, and have also had a detrimental effect on trade and development bilateral relations. For instance, the ESA countries claim that the EU wants to hinder the development of regional industries by ensuring that tariff lines remain generally low, while tariff liberalisation commitments have not been harmonised either within the configuration or within existing regional integration initiatives. Already, there is high penetration of EU products into the configuration, including Zimbabwe, as is evident from the growing trade deficit with the EC. However, as shown in the box below, Zimbabwean negotiators claim success in protecting sensitive products and sectors, avoiding agreements that include binding commitments on trade-related issues, back-loading 35% of tariff liberalisation commitments, securing export safeguards that also cover sugar and beef, and securing concessions awarded to other configurations. However, these claims of success have to be judged within the context of the current state of the economy, the dysfunctional GNU administration, and the fractured national body-politic that is struggling to adhere to the agreed GPA provisions.

Box 4.2   Multiple challenges and Zimbabwean negotiators' achievements

In spite of multiple challenges, Zimbabwean negotiators have:

Managed to protect about 20% of the products which are sensitive to Zimbabwe.

Avoided paying customs duties in the EU thereby safeguarding exports including sugar and beef quotas.

Avoided an agreement that includes binding commitments on trade-related issues as requested by the EU on such issues as competition, government procurement and investment, which were rejected by developing countries at Singapore WTO ministerial conference.

Succeeded in demanding concessions given to other configurations from the EU.

Negotiated for longer time frames, and

Managed to back-load tariff liberalised commitments.

Source: Author's compilation from interview discussion with Katuruza, 28 May 2012.

Zimbabwe's formulation of negotiating positions and offers

The EPA process in Zimbabwe presents distinctive features, all of which directly affect state-stakeholders' consultations, subsequent articulation of national issues and interests, and the formulation of national positions and offers. These include tense state-society relations, a contradiction-ridden macro-economic policy environment, politically-induced polarisation with distinct internal and external allies, a conflict-ridden GNU, cold bilateral relations which fuel state-society tensions and limited stakeholder resources. All of these spark mistrust, uncooperativeness and frustration in the key stakeholders, thereby undermining the inclusiveness of the consultation process. This poisons the working relationship between negotiators and relevant stakeholders. As a result, some critical voices have been left out of the process.

The prevailing economic environment in Zimbabwe has over the review period been characterised by partisan economic policies. This has exposed the shortcomings of both the former government and the current GNU in calming the fears of the private sector with respect to interference with sensitive sectors and exclusion of product lists or lines[106] from tariff liberalisation. Equally important is calming the fears of the private sector about the politically motivated indigenisation and economic empowerment programmes[107] in specific sectors of the economy (agriculture, mining, and manufacturing). The grand revolutionary economic empowerment programmes are largely partisan, irrational, unconventional and disregard all economic theory and economic development models. They ignore any scientific analysis of the impacts and implications for the economy's capacity to compete with other economies, including the EU, in both internal and external markets. Critics of the ZANU (PF) driven economic transformation programmes lament the lack of business acumen, competence, commitment, capacity, skills and financial resources. They also decry the government's open tolerance of perennially low levels of productivity. While this has contributed to low levels of ambition in the negotiating round, it equally exposes the vulnerability of the economy in both domestic and external markets. The consultative environment of the EPA process thus continues to be characterised by mistrust among key stakeholders, resulting in a lack of internal engagement between government negotiators and private sector representatives, and officials of other state institutions such as parliament and other relevant stakeholders. This has undermined the articulation and formulation of national issues, offensive and/or defensive interests, positions and offers - an outcome that could only be beneficial to the EU negotiators.

Ideally, consultations involving CSOs and the business sector should have started immediately after the launch of the EPA

---

[106]These product lines are identified by an HS Code at agreed digit levels, usually 6 or 8 digit levels. The parties also have to agree on the data sources with respect to the product tariff lines.

[107] Land reform and economic indigenisation programmes

roadmap. Such consultations would have assisted in aligning national interests with the central objectives of EPA negotiations including enhancing production through an increase in supply and trading capacities, creating new trade, supporting social and economic development and fostering gradual and smooth integration of Zimbabwe into the global economy (Shonhiwa, 2015). Consultations would have also allowed government and stakeholders to build coalitions, along with strategic synergies in all EPA related activities and processes, and so develop coherent national issues, interests, positions and offers. The inclusion of trade related cluster ministries, other state institutions, private sector umbrella bodies and trade and development-focused CSOs and research institutions was a positive measure, but this was counterbalanced by the exclusion of the Consumer Council of Zimbabwe, a body which represents the interests of consumers, CSOs which are critical of the ZANU (PF) government's approach to economic policy, the Zimbabwe Congress of Trade Unions (ZCTU) (despite being an ally of the MDC political party) and academia and research institutions. Given the known strength of the EU's 'guerrilla' strategies and tactics, these omissions reflect major shortcomings on the part of the state. They also reflect the feeble advocacy of the CSOs.

SEATINI (2005) argues that the 'process gives national governments and/or citizens limited space to breathe and think for themselves.' Discussions with some CSOs reveal a deliberate government policy of excluding broad sections of critical CSOs from any level of consultation on economic policy matters. Katuruza (2012),[108] on the other hand, claims success for the government at the various levels of national consultations, sector specific meetings, provincial consultative sessions, and parliamentary portfolio workshops. This assertion was rejected by a significant proportion of CSO representatives who described the EPA process as 'reflecting a significant lack of government's political will to meaningfully and extensively consult them on economic policy including trade

---

[108] Interview discussion with Angelica Katuruza, Johannesburg, 28 May 2012.

negotiations.'[109] Godfrey Kanyenze[110], director of LEDRIZ, the research wing of the ZCTU, laments the dysfunctional nature of the Tripartite Negotiation Forum (TNF) - comprising government, the private sector and labour - with regard to the EPA consultations. Consultations could have replicated the best practices of neighbouring democracies which have high levels of offensive and defensive ambition with regard to not only the EPA process, but also the WTO agenda. For instance, South Africa, a major competitor for the EU's commercial interests in Zimbabwe, uses the National Economic Development and Labour Council, comprising representatives from government, labour, business and community organisations (CSOs) to articulate and develop EPA-related national issues, interests, positions and offers.

Willie Shumba (2012),[111] former Zimbabwean revenue commissioner and a former regular government delegate to EPA meetings, now SADC secretariat senior programme officer, describes government's consultations with CSOs as 'unstructured, selective and a function of a polarised national body politic.' The process excluded CSOs who were perceived as being anti-ZANU (PF)'s economic empowerment and governance practices and therefore (according to ZANU-PF) strong allies of western governments and donors. Yet a number of the excluded CSOs conduct programme activities that interact with people in local communities and rural areas.

While CSOs often decry the difficulties they experience in gaining access to responsible ministers or trade directors, it must be noted that 'EPA preparations and negotiations have all along been done by technical experts in trade related ministries, who generally do not require appointment first before interacting with outside stakeholders.' Focusing on the lower structures would have facilitated the insertion of CSOs' views into the process. CSOs should have

---

[109] Comment by some CSO representatives during interview discussions held between 2011 and 2012.

[110] Interview discussion with Godfrey Kanyenze, Harare, Zimbabwe, 28 June 2011.

[111] Interview discussion with Willie Shumba, Gaborone, Botswana, 14 March 2012.

considered approaching government officials outside the country, or even asked their counterparts in the region and beyond to undertake this on their behalf. Regional networks should have been able to contribute to the process. CSO advocacy seems to have been a failure.

CSOs should have called for human-centered EPA development benchmarks, which would have shown the government that CSOs are not only critical of certain policy frameworks and programmes, but are also supportive of the government's economic development agenda. An approach that took into account variations in the level of development between the EU and Zimbabwe would have allayed state-civil society tensions, regardless of the prevailing economic and political challenges. Munyuki has observed:

> A major weakness of CSOs was their failure to build technical expertise in order to make better informed criticism of the EPA process. Although CSOs were invariably opposed to the process, they did not have strong technical justifications for opposing the process as a lot of their objections were general allegations against the EU's motives. For instance, the Stop-EPAs campaign was launched without any practical idea on what would be the alternative or options for a country like Zimbabwe. Further, Zimbabwean civil society EPA-related slogans, campaign messages and debate should have been framed within the context of economic rights, thereby moving closer to government's wealth redistribution agenda. Most CSOs' arguments were emotional and packaged without proper socio-economic analysis. Further, CSOs perceived that government negotiators were not sympathetic to their concerns thereby worsening the level of mistrust between them and government. As a result, state-CSOs relations in Zimbabwe were very volatile and directly linked to the political polarisation (Munyuki, interview in Gaborone, Botswana, 26 August 2012).

Some MPs in the TDC say that excluding MPs was a major omission, given their three constitutional roles of monitoring the executive (government), representative of the people and legislature of national laws, including trade and associated regulations. The omission ignores the important role played by MPs in domesticating regional and international trade and development agreements and their implementation. It is MPs - by ratifying both bilateral and multilateral trade agreements within the confines of the country's national constitution – who allow trade between parties to take place. Indeed, both the Lower House and the Upper House ratified the iEPA, of which the WTO was notified on 9 February 2012. Commenting on the ratification process, the deputy clerk of the Zimbabwean parliament, Gabriel Chipare said:

> Firstly, the MPs were pressured to debate and ratify iEPA within a short space of time and without due consideration to the fact that they had not been participating consistently in the process as an institution. Secondly, the pressure ignored the fact that some MPs had only been with the legislature for less than 5 years[112]. Lastly, the pressure discounted the fact that this new trade regime, like any other bilateral and multilateral trade agreements, is embedded with socio-economic and political theoretical and technical concepts - all of which would have required more time to unpack before allowing enough time to debate the process, outcome and subsequent implementation. This would have also linked the process to various commercial and political constituencies and the generality of the population (Gapare, interview in Lilongwe, Malawi, 24 November 2012.

Although Angelica Katuruza (2012) claims that parliamentary TDC portfolio workshops were held, due to the political dynamics in the country since 2000, new people have been appointed following every parliamentary election. This situation calls for more capacity building training sessions workshops to be held. Lack of resources denied the MPs any opportunity to participate in the RNF and joint ESA-EU EPA meetings held in the regional capitals and in Brussels.

Throughout the period, the Harare administration presided over a polarised media, both private and public, with the former perceived as being in league with a hostile foreign media and western governments, and pursuing an anti-government agenda based on

---

[112] Zimbabwe's constitutional life-span of Parliament (both Lower and Upper Houses)

exposing every unfolding weakness. Katuruza (2012) further attests that the government could not have interacted with the private media (foreign and domestic), which is heavily critical of the government, not only with respect to political and governance issues, but also the overall management of the economy, including bilateral trade relations with other countries and the EU bloc. However, the private media is significant and its strategic value would have linked the process with broader constituencies, in particular potentially determined and committed agricultural producers, exporters and investors who are not part of any official organisation. Since 2000, national umbrella bodies representing agricultural producers - the key drivers of the economy - have become dysfunctional, largely due to the unfolding economic and political developments in the country. For example, the new farmers[113] (both Model A1 and Model A2) have never been organised within a dedicated umbrella institution that might represent their economic and political interests, including the EPA process. Model A1 and Model A2 farmers belong neither to the Zimbabwe Farmers' Union[114] nor to the Commercial Farmers' Union,[115] both of whose national prominence and significance have dwindled since 2000, hence their absence from the EPA process. These farmer organisations have not lobbied to realign farmers' commercial interests with national strategic policies and external interests, as informed by scenario analysis and projections of both lucrative and depressed markets throughout the world. Neither Model A1 nor Model A2 farmers have been represented in any of the related EPA processes, despite the potential of the new trade regime to have a short to medium term effect on the sector - which is the backbone of the economy. The new farmers are already struggling to

---

[113] Model A1 is for smallholder farming areas (famers) with an average size of six (6) hectares whilst Model 2 is for commercial farmers areas (farmers) with an average size ranging from 30 to 5,000 hectares. By 2005, Zimbabwe had settled 140,866 families under Model 1, drawn mainly from the communal areas and junior workers in government, and 14,500 under Model 2, mainly ruling elites (Kamidza and Mazingi, 2011: 328) or as largely seen by donors and other critics, a sanctuary for the political elites (Matondi, 2011: 96)..[114] Represents smallholder (peasant) farmers, now Model 1.

[114] Represents smallholder (peasant) farmers, now Model 1.

[115] Represents commercial farmers, now Model 2 farmers

satisfy national demand let alone offensively penetrate the EU market or prevent European products from flooding the local market. Farmers struggle to stimulate their production levels to quantities that can sufficiently trigger sustainable forward and backward linkages with the rest of the economy. The EU's agricultural sector is driven to a large extent by MCs and TNCs, some of which have competing operations in the country and the sub-region, and which receive substantial subsidies from EU member states. The EC regards the MCs and TNCs as strategic allies in their bilateral and multilateral trade negotiations. In this process, as reflected in the Figure below, the EU is not only working with its traditional allies (MCs, TNCs and business lobbies), but also with the GFIs (the World Bank and IMF).

The exclusion of the media means that the process has not been brought to the attention of marginalised social groups and the general population, including a significant proportion of civil society and social movements. This means that unorganised entrepreneurs in key politically sensitive sectors, including agriculture and mining, have not been party to the process. Government negotiators should have institutionalised frequent media releases and debriefing sessions both before and after every important EPA-related meeting, platform, or event throughout the process. For instance, the authorities could have instructed the (Zimbabwe Broadcasting Corporation) ZBC daily TV programme entitled 'Murimi waNhasi' (Farmers Today) - which is anchored by academics from the University of Zimbabwe for the purpose of interacting with the new farmers in particular and the nation in general - to include the unfolding developments in the EPA process.

Research institutions provide critical appraisals of economic policy processes, especially indigenisation and economic empowerment programmes, as an integral part of their contribution to the country's socio-economic and political development. In the past, these institutions had a positive relationship with the state despite their often critical attitude towards economic policy, particularly ESAP. The Southern African Political Economic Series Trust and LEDRIZ are two such institutions. However, since 2000, there has been limited interaction between government and the research institutions. On their part, due to various factors including a lack of financial[116] and human[117] resources, the research institutions have not produced any critical reflections on the EPA process. This has greatly undermined rational articulation of national issues and interests, and the subsequent development of national positions, offers, collective strategies and tactics. It has also undermined the formulation of well-focused advocacy activism, the outcome of which would have benefited the country's positions and offers.

Two important policy blueprints, namely the national trade policy (NTP) and the industrial development policy (IDP), both launched in 2012, were unavailable during the EPA process. These would have provided strategic guidance in the articulation of national issues and interests and the development of national positions and offers. They would also have facilitated the engagement and subsequent input of stakeholders.

There has been little collaborative interaction and networking between the Non-State Actors (NSAs) in Zimbabwe. In an environment of political tension, platforms should have been established in order to build coalitions and synergies among NSAs. Multi-stakeholder platforms would have been able to monitor iEPA related issues, especially with respect to protecting tariffs of sensitive products - a condition that is necessary to support infant, distressed and new industries, and intrinsic economic sectors, as defined by both trade and industrial policies.

Government officials and CSO representatives all agree that national level consultative processes have been hampered by budgetary constraints. This has made it extremely difficult for the country to raise fiscal resources to support economic policy directives, including EPA negotiations at a time when, since 2000, grand economic programmes such as the fast-track land reform and indigenous economic empowerment have had priority. Overall, support for government participation was far less than that of other more ambitious economies in the group, including Kenya, Mauritius and Uganda.

---

[116] Lack of donor support
[117] Due to brain drain

147

Zimbabwe's suspension from the 10th EDF financial assistance earmarked for economic and regional integration impacted negatively on the state's ability to deepen and widen the consultation process. The country has not been able to benefit from the EPA financial window, through which other EPA negotiating countries have been able to access resources to build negotiating consultative skills, capacities and synergies. The country was unable to access external resources from other western governments and donors to facilitate discourse, including the EPA process.

The lack of finance also limited the number of consultative meetings that could be held between government officials and other key national and regional stakeholders. In particular, fiscal constraints limited the number of government officials who could attend RNF meetings which over the review period were scheduled to take place almost every month,[118] as determined by the deadlines[119]. These meetings are supposed to involve most of the trade-related government ministries and departments. In addition to the financial limitations, the process has had to contend with a shortage of human resources, since many of the government trade officials are also responsible for other trade and economic integration desks or portfolios. For instance, the same government officials who deal with the EPA process are also responsible for COMESA, SADC, and WTO.

Interim EPA outcome, ratification and implementation process

While the rest of the ACP EPA groups have maintained their original composition, the ESA configuration split into two towards the end of 2007, into the EAC and a reconfigured but still diverse ESA group. Subsequently, the EAC states[120] initialed an iEPA on 23 November 2007 with the EU as a customs union, and negotiations on a full EPA are in progress. The new ESA group comprises the

---

[118] The launch of the roadmap in 2004 envisaged RNF meetings almost every month in light of the 31 December 2007 deadline to conclude the EPA regime.

[119] December 31, 2007, July 2008 and December 2008.

[120] Burundi, Kenya, Rwanda, Tanzania and Uganda

IOC[121], the Horn of Africa[122] and some southern African[123] countries. Meanwhile, Madagascar, Mauritius, Seychelles and Zimbabwe all individually tabled separate market access offers to the EU based on their respective specificities, resulting in the signing of the iEPA on 29 August 2009 in Mauritius.

Following the signing ceremony, the EC Trade directorate heralded the first iEPA in Africa as a major stepping stone towards the wider and more comprehensive EPA deal currently under negotiation between the EU and the whole of the ESA region. These negotiations have been under way since 2008, covering rules and commitments on trade in services, investments, agriculture and rules of origin; trade-related areas such as sustainable development, competition and trade facilitation; and cooperation on sanitary and phytosanitary provisions and technical barriers to trade. On 14 May 2012 Krel De Gucht, the EU Trade Commissioner, remarked:

> Today, our first iEPA with an African region is applied. This is excellent news and I salute the hard work of negotiators and colleagues on all sides. With this trade deal, we hope to accompany the development of our partners in eastern and southern Africa and open up better and lasting business opportunities (www.trade.ec.europa.eu).

In contrast to the above, representatives of some CSOs - including African Network on Debt and Development (AFRODAD), ANSA, LEDRIZ, MWENGO , and ZIMCODD - expressed their astonishment that Zimbabwe, given its economic circumstances within the context of a dysfunctional GNU (Chifamba, 2012) and its hostile economic policy environment, was among the first group of ESA countries to sign and ratify the iEPA with the EU without exhaustive consultation with civil society sector and the private sector[124]. Zimbabwe's ratification process was

---

[121] Madagascar, Mauritius and Seychelles

[122] Comoros, Djibouti, Ethiopia, Eritrea and Sudan

[123] Malawi, Zambia and Zimbabwe

[124] Khumalo, a former Harare EU Delegation official now with the SADC secretariat, argues that the COMESA EPA CTA, Moses Tekere, was instrumental in persuading and advising Zimbabwe to sign the deal.

concluded in both the Lower and Upper House in February 2012. While addressing a seminar workshop on iEPA in August 2012, Aldo Dell'Ariccia, EU Ambassador to Zimbabwe, on the assumption of a full return to normal bilateral relations and a conducive business environment, predicted an improvement in EU exports and a doubling of imports under the new trade regime. The outcome has inspired new confidence in producers and exporters, especially those from Europe. The ratification has inspired the EU bloc to promise funding to support the establishment of a trade and private sector development start-up programme, which, among other things, seeks to improve the business environment, encourage public-private sector dialogue, facilitate SMEs value addition, market competitiveness, export diversification, access market information[125] and upgrade the ZimTrade trade database and the Standards Association of Zimbabwe's laboratories[126]. For instance, public-private sector dialogue sessions will facilitate interactions on the state of the economy including economic policy and trade arrangements and strategies for reviving and sustaining sectoral forward and backward productive and export linkages. The platform will also facilitate engagements on iEPA implementation challenges and opportunities, the implementation of industrial development policy options, including productive value chains, downstream and upstream industrial linkages, mineral beneficiation options and competitiveness and diversification challenges and opportunities.

Table 4.2 below summarises the status of ESA EPA countries that have initialed, signed and ratified the iEPA. The table also reflects existing trade regimes with the EU, the status of notification to the WTO and the ratification process. As illustrated, most countries of the newly configured ESA group countries are not under pressure from the withdrawal of MAR 1528/2007 because they can continue trading with the EU under WTO compatible EBA provisions.

---

[125] EU tools such as a market access database and the export help-desk.
[126] Equipment and software, and staff skills training.

Table 4.2   iEPA status by configuration

EPA Group	Member states	Trade regime	Signature date	Notification to WTO date	Ratification process initiated
ESA	Comoros	iEPA[127]			
	Djibouti	EBA			
	Eritrea	EBA			
	Ethiopia	EBA			
	Sudan	EBA			
	Madagascar	iEPA	29/08/2009	09/02/2012	Yes
	Mauritius	iEPA	29/08/2009	09/02/2012	Yes
	Seychelles	iEPA	29/08/2009	09/02/2012	Yes
	Malawi	EBA			
	Zambia	EBA			
	Zimbabwe	iEPA	29/08/2009	09/02/2012	Yes
ESA / EAC	Burundi	iEPA			
	Kenya	iEPA			
	Rwanda	iEPA			
	Tanzania	iEPA			
	Uganda	iEPA			

Source: Author's compilation from various sources

Zimbabwe signed agreement with the EU includes WTO-compatible market access schedules, and provisions on development cooperation, fisheries and other related issues. The agreement allows the EU to liberalise its market by 100%[128] by value as of 1 January

---

[127] Comoros withdrew at the last minute.
[128] With transition periods for rice and sugar

2008[129] while Zimbabwe is expected to liberalise by 80% by value by 2022, as shown in the graph below. The graph also provides a comparative analysis of the agreed tariff liberalisation schedules and commitments of four ESA countries - that is, the extent to which they are prepared to open up their respective economies to European products across all sectors. The graph also reflects the ability and capacity of the four countries to compete with EU products in the domestic market. Of the four, Zimbabwe shows a slight degree of resistance, though not enough to protect local products from a massive onslaught of competitive European products, while at the same time allowing industrial and sectoral productive capacity utilisation to rebound to its past regional and global competitive status.

Graph 4.3   ESA countries' liberalisation of EU imports, percentages

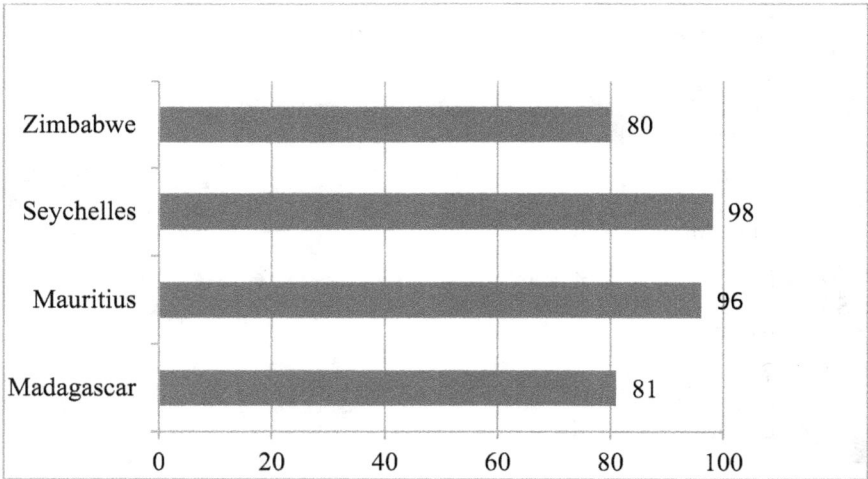

Source: www.acp-eu-trade.org/epa/ESA.php

Of the above liberalisation schedules, 45% would be achieved by 2012 with the remaining 35% to be progressively liberalised until 2022. Though Zimbabwe has already opened close to half of its

---

[129] It is possible that this date may be interpreted to mean "the date the agreement enters into force, that is, when both agree to implement the agreement."

market to EU producers and exporters, the weak industrial productive capacity utilisation, export capacities and market competitiveness are impacting on its commitment to 'domesticate' the iEPA trade regime. Opening up by 45%, at a time when the economy is still struggling to rebound, inevitably favours the commercial interests of European producers, exporters and investors. As Zimbabwe and other iEPA signatories gradually open 80% to 98% of their respective markets to European exports over a period of 15 years, some products that are considered crucial for national industrial development and other political considerations (as reflected in the table below), have been excluded from tariff liberalisation phase-down commitments. This means that the EU, on the basis of differences in economic development between the negotiating parties, has agreed to allow the respective countries to maintain existing tariff levels on certain products.

Table 4.3 List of sensitive products by iEPA signatory

Country	Main exclusions from liberalisation
Comoros	Products of animal origin, fish, beverages, chemicals and vehicles.
Madagascar	Meat, milk and cheese, fish, vegetables, cereals, oils and fats, edible preparations, sugar, cocoa, beverages, tobacco, chemicals, plastic and paper articles, textiles, metal articles, furniture
Mauritius	Live animals and meat, edible products of animal origin, fats, edible preparations and beverages, chemicals, plastics and rubber articles of leather and fur skins, iron and steel, and consumer electronic goods
Seychelles	Meat, fish, beverages, tobacco, leather articles, glass and ceramic products, and vehicles
Zimbabwe	Products of animal origin, cereals, beverages, paper, plastics and rubber, textiles and clothing, footwear, glass and ceramics, consumer electronic and vehicles.

Source: www.acp-eu-trade.org/epa/ESA.php

Zimbabwe, by only identifying 20% of tariff lines for exclusion (ZimTrade, 2012), appears to be less ambitious than the other smaller ESA economies. Zimbabwe's desire to protect sensitive sectors and industries was far below that of Madagascar, a regional country facing similar political tensions and isolation from western governments, including the EU. While some sensitivities can be linked to Zimbabwe's economic and industrial development imperatives, the study raises questions on the moral, economic and political value of wanting to continue to protect, for instance, the Willow-Vale motor industry, given that since 2000 Zimbabwe has experienced an exponential increase in imported second-hand vehicles from Europe, Japan and Korea. However, as can be seen in the table below, the sensitive list excludes some sectors and products including new projects with growth potential currently prioritised in the national industrial development policy of 2012. In this respect, the qualifying criteria for sector prioritisation should include contribution to GDP, employment creation and retention, export earnings and potential for value addition, and forward and backward linkages with other sectors of the economy. In this way, national priorities link policy initiatives with quick turnaround at the industry/sector level, and the potential to increase capacity utilisation levels to a regionally and globally competitive level. These sectors and products have high employment creation potential, and are a significant contributor towards national economic recovery.

It can be inferred that conflictual and uncooperative state-NSA relationships and a politically charged national body politic may have contributed to the compilation of narrow national exclusion lists before they were shared with the EU. Munyuki claims that:

> Although government invited business to pre-negotiations talks on many occasions, the business community's response was very slow. In many instances, the business community and business umbrella organisations and/or lobbies such as industrialists and commercial farmers failed to appear at crucial preparatory meetings (Munyuki, interview in Gaborone, Botswana, 26 August 2013).

Kamidza (2008) supports the above by noting the plea by the former chief negotiator, Angelica Katuruza, to the private sector to submit their sensitivities to government even though the textual iEPA had already been submitted to the EU during a regional workshop held in Harare in 2009. In a subsequent discussion, Katuruza notes:

> Firstly, over the period, the main partner, the business community, was preoccupied with day to day business management and/or survival issues and cared less on the EPA process. Secondly, they cared less about any government economic policy directives, including contributing to or commenting on the process and potential impacts. Lastly, they developed a negative attitude towards economic policies and trade agreements in general and EPA in particular, despite the fact that they are the prime beneficiaries of the outcome and other trade agreements (regional and global) (Katuruza, interview in Johannesburg, South Africa, 28 May 2012).

Table 4.4 Zimbabwe's prioritised agri-business subsectors and products

Sector and products	Importance to the economy
Food and beverages Cane, oil seed, grain, vegetables, meat production and processing	Operations attract small, medium and large-scale producers; High potential for growth; Backbone of the agricultural sector in terms of raw material requirements or provision; and Significant stimulus of agro-based raw material supply industries (seed, chemicals and fertilisers), printing and packaging, milling and energy.

Clothing and textiles Cotton, polyester, acrylic, yarn, sanitary pads, clothing, under-garments, cotton wool, blankets and carpets	Vehicle for manufacturing development due to its quick turnaround from investment to production. High adaptability in operations of SMEs to bigger corporate entities. Huge scope for value addition and for backward and forward integration
Leather and footwear Quality leather and footwear products	High potential to enhance value addition thereby benefiting producers, collectors and merchants of hides. High potential to encourage associated manufacturers
Wood and timber Quality timber products	High potential to stimulate furniture related industries, exploiting both exotic and indigenous hardwoods and softwoods High potential to establish a niche in the EU and global markets

Source: Industrial Development Policy, 2012: 17-24

From the exclusion list of sensitive products it can be inferred that Zimbabwean negotiators either failed to present compelling arguments for the merits of the country's infant industries, industries under distress or sensitive sectors such as agriculture. This means that the negotiators failed to clearly articulate potential impacts of iEPA implementation on human and social development while negotiating the new trade regime with Europe. On the other hand, a relatively small or weak exclusion list and lack of concessions can be attributed to insufficient state-private sector consultation (see Katuruza above) and the deliberate exclusion of civil society from the process. It could also be a product of the former ruling ZANU (PF) party's macro-economic mismanagement and partisan indigenous economic empowerment programmes, which hardened the EU negotiators' attitude toward them. Finally, this could be a product of limited bilateral contact or interaction between the negotiating parties. As confirmed by Katuruza, the EU's only contact with Zimbabwe was within the context of the ESA EPA processes. The absence of any broader interaction reduced the options for lobbying and articulating national interests within the Cotonou Trade, Development, and Political Agreement Framework that considers agriculture as the main area of focus (Commonwealth Secretariat, 2010). In any other situation, most sectors and industries would have qualified for distress protection in the form of an exclusion list. Possibly, as Chifamba argues, the level of ambition reflects the mandate given to the negotiators to merely aim at securing future markets for the economy, a development that was exploited by the EU.

Zimbabwe's failure to protect its sensitive and infant industries has to be assessed in the light of EU-Zimbabwe trade relations which, since the Lomé Conventions, have been characterised by the application of import and export duties and taxes, sharing of lists of sensitive products, and other safeguard mechanisms that have been considered important instruments for sustainable agricultural growth and development and food security. In the context of the ongoing EPA processes, potential increments in economic production and export competitiveness are a source of compensation for the loss of fiscal revenues as a result of tariff cuts. The economic meltdown, lasting more than a decade, coupled with massive withdrawals of donor funding and investment, have undermined the country's ability to service and finance the huge challenges of social and economic underdevelopment, social inequality and humanitarian assistance, because tariffs constitute a significant proportion of government revenue.

Now that the trade agreement has been ratified, implementation is underway. Regardless of the lack of proper consultation during the negotiations and ratification[130], the state needs the cooperation of all the stakeholders in the implementation of iEPA. The current focus of the iEPA implementation commitments are reflected in the box below. Broadly, it entails establishing an EPA implementation unit under the Ministry of Industry and Commerce to spearhead all work related to the domestication of the iEPA - including research analysis, awareness raising and the buy-in of all stakeholders and the general population.

---

[130] CSOs were generally unaware. The process was also rushed through according to the Deputy Clerk of Parliament.

Box 4.3   Zimbabwe iEPA implementation support requirements
Undertaking needs assessment of the legal framework and administrative and human resource requirements.
Domesticating iEPA in terms of Zimbabwean laws, including the customs book.
Establishing a Zimbabwean EPA implementation unit, preferably under the Ministry of Industry and Commerce.
Pursuing accompanying measures to finance EPA-related adjustment costs including capacity building, modernisation and re-structuring of industries affected by trade liberalisation.
Launching an awareness programme to inform all stakeholders (civil society, MPs and the business community) of the rights, obligations and opportunities contained in the iEPA.

Source: Compiled from various sources

In addition, the parties agreed to facilitate the implementation of the iEPA and to support regional integration and development strategies. The level of cooperation is based on the ESA development cooperation strategy and a jointly agreed-on development matrix. This entails mobilising resources from EU member states and other donors through the Aid for Trade commitments in support of iEPA implementation requirements and related adjustment costs. The country can also access funding from the 10th EDF financial framework. While this sounds promising, caution has to be exercised because of the prevailing hostile attitudes of the bilateral partners and confrontational state-civil society relations. The EU has already instructed that the allocated 10th EDF resources be channeled into humanitarian assistance, governance and human rights projects.

In addition, there are issues of capacity with respect to accessing EDF and the entrenched complex bureaucratic machinery in Brussels. ACP countries have in the past absorbed less than 45% of the first 9th EDF financial windows (see Table 3.6). This means that the degree to which the country is able to access the promised 'developmental assistance envelope' through cooperation, determines the appropriate iEPA implementation scenario described in the table below. These scenarios are a function of the country's ability to rejuvenate industrial production and productivities, export capabilities and competiveness, leading to improved capacity to generate fiscal revenue. In addition, implementation will be determined by the nature of the relationship between the negotiating parties, and between the national stakeholders in the prevailing political environment.

Table 4.5 iEPA implementation - Zimbabwean approach

Scenario 1	Scenario 2
A cautious approach, determined by the desire to minimise threats from: o revenue loss; o investor confidence; o infant and strategic sectors or industries; and o social cohesion (inequality and uneven development).	A fast approach, determined by the desire to: o generate more revenue; and o facilitate; ▪ technology transfers; ▪ value addition; ▪ economies of scale and specialisation; ▪ job creation (poverty alleviation); ▪ FDI flows; and ▪ human resources development.

Source: Compiled from various sources

Ongoing comprehensive negotiations would be concluded at a regional level to foster regional integration within the group. Critics have, however, warned the ESA negotiators to prepare to individually square up with the EU at the negotiating table, as was the case during the conclusion of the iEPA. Already a precedent has been set in which individual ESA countries have signed an iEPA based on individual market access offers, leading to a new trade in goods agreement being ratified by parliament, despite having negotiated as a bloc. This suggests that it is possible for individual ESA group countries to sign the comprehensive EPA with the EU. This calls for careful consideration on the part of the Zimbabwean negotiating team in order to avoid errors that will harm the country's commercial and political interests in the short to medium term. Such an eventuality (which is highly probable) would mean that the EU has been fronting the ESA group in order to intensify interaction with the lower echelons of the Zimbabwean government as a proxy to quickly seal a medium to long term future trade regime with the current antagonist. This example of EU guerrilla negotiating tactics opens the Zimbabwean economy to the former's operators, investors and exporters, including MCs and TNCs. Given that Zimbabwean entrepreneurs in the short to medium term would be able to compete with products originating from Europe, the study predicts the future exodus of some of the local entrepreneurs, thereby creating opportunities for expropriated commercial farmers and mining owners to invest in the country once more.

Conclusion

A review of the trade regime with Europe has been undertaken by institutions and structures that were established during the launch of the ESA-EU EPA negotiations roadmap in February 2004. These institutions and structures have been guiding the process at different levels (national, RNF, and joint EU-ESA). At the national level, the negotiating structure that was/is supposedly involved in all the preparatory EPA work and reviews, has been the NDPTF, comprising government officials from all trade related ministries and other state institutions and representatives of NSAs. However, as discussed above, the structure confronted numerous challenges. These challenges caused it to be subsumed within the normal trade coordination process in the Ministry of Industry and Commerce. Thus, the NDTPF has existed in name only as it could not be publicly identified with the process up to the iEPA signing - yet it could have been easily incorporated into the proposed 'EPA Implementing Unit'.

The ESA-EU EPA roadmap established a structure that was supposed to interact with the EC for the purposes of advancing the negotiations. This is the RNF, comprising ESA delegations, ESA REC representatives, the Brussels based ESA group, representatives of the Committee of Ambassadors and a Seatini official representing the CSOs[131]. The COMESA secretariat has coordinated the process with support from other ESA REC secretariats, namely EAC, IGAD, and IOC. In order to streamline the coordination process, the ESA group, with financial support from the EU, agreed to establish the EPA unit under the COMESA Directorate of Trade, headed by the CTA with a secretary to facilitate coordination of the process by managing meetings, communication flows, arrangements and logistics. The CTA has provided technical and intellectual leadership at all levels, in addition to attending to specific requirements of the ESA countries. The unit has also been liaising with the EU in the process, especially with respect to joint ESA-EU meetings. On paper the unit is accessible to all relevant stakeholders, but this has not been the case in practice.

The CSOs' coordination, strategic networking, and synergy building with government negotiators, MPs and the private sector in the EPA process has not been as robust and intense as it had been in the EU-ACP and the WTO trade talks. Coordination seems to have been undermined by the domestic stakeholder relationship coupled with the government's decision to exclude those perceived to have critical views. This indicates that the process suffered from a lack of clear strategy. Such a strategy would have helped coordinate the CSOs' advocacy and strategic engagements with government negotiators and the private sector. All the above weaknesses demonstrate that the process is indeed an 'onslaught on the national economy' in the short to medium term.

---

[131] The SEATINI representative was dismissed in 2005.

Chapter Five

Zimbabwe's State Shortcomings and Civil Society Advocacy

Introduction

This chapter discusses state shortcomings and civil society advocacy in the EPA process. This is premised on the notion that international trade negotiations are becoming an important arena in which Zimbabwe in particular and African countries in general have opportunities (consultative policy spaces and platforms) that can only be exploited if their governments collaborate with all the relevant stakeholders. This requires cooperation, collective consultation and participation of both the government and the NSAs if the challenges are to be overcome. The Zimbabwean authorities and the NSAs would have to create sustainable consultative EPA networks and partnerships alongside their counterparts in other African countries.

Vast fault lines exist within the ZANU (PF)/GNU administration. At the same time, CSOs' resources, both financial and human, are too limited to enable them to engage the Zimbabwean authorities, RECs' EPA units and EU institutions. These problems have undermined collective identification of both offensive and defensive political and commercial issues, interests, positions and offers; collective analysis of unfolding issues, interests and positions; and strategic stakeholders' networking and synergy building. They have fueled state-civil society mistrust and intransigence, leading to the deliberate exclusion of critical CSOs input on economic policies, including the EPA process.

The chapter is divided into three sections. The first section describes the practical functions of the RECs (COMESA and SADC) secretariats to locate opportunities and challenges for CSOs activism in the process in Zimbabwe, Africa and beyond. The second section focuses on the extent and implications of the fault lines within the state-civil society relationship. The section further interrogates the nexus between donor funding and CSOs' advocacy activities. The third section highlights emerging real and potential fears, implications, and policy options as the process unfolds and concludes by highlighting the persistence of state shortcomings and the conflictual state-civil society relationships that have characterised the GNU administration throughout this process.

COMESA and SADC secretariats[132] and civil society activism

Despite the directive of the ESA roadmap for countries to deposit their respective impact assessment studies (IAS), and NDTPF consultative reports with the regional secretariat (COMESA), Kamidza (2004) reports that only five countries had done so at the beginning of 2005. It is not clear which countries submitted and if the remaining countries eventually complied with the directive. Most CSOs' representatives interviewed by Kamidza concurred that the IAS and NDTPF reports in some ESA countries, including Zimbabwe, were not a collective exercise. Had they been inclusive, this could have enhanced the EPA-related advocacy work of CSOs at various levels (country, configuration, region and EU). It could have also facilitated robust and rigorous engagements on the findings, with a view to translating difficult proposals or positions into stakeholder expectations or inclusive developments and pro-poor outcomes.

Throughout the process, the participation of civic bodies has been constrained by limited democratic space, poor state-civic relationships and outright exclusion by the coordinating institutions and structures in Lusaka and Gaborone - the capital cities of COMESA and the SADC respectively. For instance, SEATINI, the roadmap's designated representative of civil society, was booted out of the internal processes in December 2004, largely due to their strong views on the way the process was unfolding (Kamidza, 2004). This effectively ended the inside-outside strategy in which controversial process issues, crucial information or emerging positions had to be shared with other national and sub-regional civil

---

[132] ESA and SADC Secretariats have established EPA Units to provide technical and intellectual leadership to this process. In this section, the author has opted to use 'intellectual leadership' instead of 'Secretariat' in some cases.

society activists. Failure to share process information between government negotiators, ambassadors and officials on the one hand and civil society activists working on trade and development issues on the other not only undermined engagement, but also generated mistrust of the process at national, configuration and regional levels.

While it was evident that the inclusion of CSOs in formal discussions outside their respective government delegation was not applicable, the sector failed to articulate constructive and systematic forms of engagement in the process. Throughout the process, the CSOs have not explained why their representatives failed to develop or commission analytical work on the process with a view to share with government negotiators and thereby adding value to the process and outcome.

These shortcomings, which were replicated in all other continental EPA configurations, compelled African CSOs, in collaboration with their northern counterparts to develop and implement a lobbying and advocacy strategy targeting EPA negotiating institutions, structures and personalities, both in Brussels and the various EU member states. However, the lobbying efforts undertaken in the EU institutions, although they highlighted the likely negative impact of the proposed EPA in southern Africa, they suffered from lack of up to date information (Masiiwa, 2012).

CSO advocacy and campaign missions were undertaken at various levels and intervals, aimed at directly lobbying and engaging the EU's political institutions such as the EU Council, the EU Parliament and the EU presidency and the EU's technical institutions and structures, including the EU Commissioner, Directorate-General Trade, Directorate-General Development and Directorate-General Agriculture and Rural Development. They targeted development research institutions to lobby for pro-poor and pro-development comparative synthesis and analysis of the unfolding EPA process in the six configurations and Europe. This helped to counter the EU's strategy of exerting pressure on 'configuration X' during their introductory remarks at the joint meetings, usually by saying that 'configuration Y' has already accepted the EU's proposal or position or made 'tremendous progress' on the proposal or issue. The advocacy also targeted stakeholders with access to the corridors of

EPA power, with a view to ensuring a pro-poor and pro-developmental trade regime between Europe and Africa. This activity contributed significantly to the EU's decision to extend the deadline for concluding ACP-EU EPA negotiations beyond 31 December 2007.

The CSO advocacy campaign focused mainly on Africa and culminated in the launch of the 'Stop EPAs Campaign' in March 2004 in Nairobi, by CSOs affiliated to the ATN based in Accra. The nature of the activity varied by targeted audience, but usually took the form of direct persuasive exchanges supported by evidence of potential EPA outcomes and implications. They identified sympathetic African governments and produced detailed explanations of why the 31 December 2007 deadline would disappoint African producers, exporters, investors and consumers. The CSOs complemented this by holding meetings, including at the margins of the annual AU organised African Trade Ministers meeting. They also mobilised other constituencies interested in Africa's trade and development to resist fast-tracking the process without the participation of all key stakeholders. Indeed, the work resulted in several extensions of the set deadlines, thereby allowing negotiators to navigate slowly towards pro-poor and pro-development EPA outcomes. In spite of the above, a number of challenges and fault lines impacted negatively on the CSOs' advocacy work in the ESA configuration in general and Zimbabwe in particular. While the sector narrated the challenges and fault lines, especially in the Zimbabwean context, there was no corresponding articulation of solutions and alternative ways of engagements in a manner that would unify all relevant stakeholders.

CSO advocacy targeted RECs and authorities in their respective governments at different levels. These included those driving the EPA process, such as the COMESA and SADC secretariats, and those who had been providing support, including the EAC, IGAD and IOC (for ESA) and SACU (for SADC EPA). Their activities were largely premised on the fact that the ESA configuration through COMESA had not organised a single dedicated meeting with NSAs, particularly civil society, to share the implications of the unfolding negotiations, or the effects on the citizen's livelihoods. This failure to organise dedicated EPA meetings with NSAs prompted CSOs to successfully mobilise resources for the purpose of organising meetings with the COMESA and SADC EPA units' Chief Technical Advisors (CTAs). Subsequently, the regional CSOs organised a number of EPA dialogue sessions aimed at facilitating interaction and sharing information, strategies and tactics under the intellectual leadership of two EPA configurations[133]. The CSO organised EPA dialogue sessions included:

a regional conference, whose theme was "ESA and SADC experiences in negotiating EPAs with the EU" organised by the TRADES Centre based in Harare, in February 2009;

a regional workshop, whose theme was "EPAs and Economic Development in ESA Countries" organised by the Consumer Unity and Trust Society – Africa Resource Centre (CUTS-ARC) based in Lusaka, in October 2006; and

a regional roundtable discussion, whose theme was "EPAs negotiations: Challenges and Opportunities for Poverty Eradication in Southern Africa" organised by the Southern Africa Regional Poverty Network (SAPRN) based in Pretoria, in October 2006.

With respect to all these events, the sector did not indicate whether the main dialogue session negotiating points or arguments were shared with their national and configuration authorities, with a view to adding value to the process.

The COMESA and SADC secretariats' EPA units' CTAs failed to avail themselves of these funded policy dialogue sessions[134]. This has since been described as a violation of the principle of consultation with all national and regional stakeholders. It shows a lack of openness and desire to interact with both moderate and radical CSOs in the process. Indeed, the Zimbabwean authorities have continually and deliberately excluded all CSOs that they consider too radical and adversarial. SADC officials attended none of the funded dialogue sessions, while ESA officials only attended the Trades Centre conference in Harare. ESA and COMESA officials

---

[133] ESA and SADC configurations
[134] Regional conference, roundtable discussion and workshop

disdained the 21st plenary assembly of the SADC Parliamentary Forum meeting held in Johannesburg on 10-17 November 2006, which had the theme "Enhancing the role of Parliaments in Governance and Development at Regional Level: Trade and Development Issues relating to the ACP-EU Trade negotiations".

Besides mistrust between the RECs' EPA unit officials and member state authorities and representatives of civil society, the above reveals the challenges of coordinating regional parliamentary work in the EPA process through sub-regional EPA units. Ironically, while sub-regional member states had unlimited access to sub-regional EPA units, other organs (parliamentarians) had difficulty interacting with the sub-regional EPA units' CTAs and their respective governments' negotiators and officials. These platforms could have facilitated direct interaction and engagement between MPs and regional member state officials, especially since most MPs did not participate in the RNF meetings.

At the TRADES Centre conference[135] (see above), COMESA technical officials circulated the ESA-EPA draft negotiating document that was officially submitted to the EU with a deadline for response of 30 September 2006. Kamidza (2008: 6) observes that Moses Tekere, ESA-EPA CTA, when asked about the rationale of sharing negotiations positions and offers with the EC before exhausting internal (ESA) consultations, said: 'It is a wise strategy meant to outwit our counterparts in the EU. The ball is now in the EU's court, and a timed response is likely to work in favour of the happy ESA family.' This was the first time that the regional CSOs had seen the draft. However, they could still have opted to undertake further work with a view to producing a critique of Tekere's assertion as well as supporting those countries eager to conclude the deal as individuals.

The failure to consult widely and deeply with other interested stakeholders at various stages of the process reflects COMESA's, and by extension Zimbabwe's, shortcomings throughout the process. It also reflects the extent of the difficulties faced by CSOs in lobbying

---

[135] The only dialogue session in which regional civil society groups made an effort to bring together COMESA and SADC technical and intellectual leadership to share their respective experiences in negotiating EPA with them.

and engaging political and technical personalities at the sub-regional RECs compared to the EU. Lack of dialogue fuels fears of negative implications and outcomes that are likely to tie ESA economies to European producers, exporters and investors in an unbalanced framework that will perpetuate an unjust trade regime with the potential to undermine economic growth and development and regional integration efforts. Deve (2009), reporting on the outcome of the Harare Conference, remarked:

> … this mirrors the competitive race of African configurations all wanting to be the first to reach out to the EU's negotiating machinery in spite of limited capacity, tight timeframe and space to assess outcomes in light of emerging national and regional economic units and consumers' aspirations. Being the first to knock at the EU negotiating machinery's doors not only fuels pessimism on the process, but also points to a bleak future for ESA economies under a legally binding trade regime (Deve, 10 September 2009).

The ESA-EPA intellectual leadership[136] opted for text-based negotiations, that is, a compiled comprehensive wish list document which highlights:

the scope of the agreement coverage: trade cooperation, trade related issues, trade in services, fisheries, economic and development cooperation, development finance cooperation, institutional framework and dispute settlements;

a schedule for eliminating customs duties a day after the agreement's entry into force, that is, 10 years for capital goods and raw materials, 20 years for intermediate goods and 25 years for finished goods; and

the exclusion lists of sensitive products from liberalisation commitment.

The above forms the basis for actual negotiations with the EU, and ESA-EPA CTA expected these provisions to improve the respective economies' industrial productive capabilities, export

---

[136] Its role is to guide the EPA process, provides technical direction and is responsible and/or accountable for the outcomes.

competitiveness and trading capacities, as well as their ability to attract FDI and an assortment of technologies. However, the ESA-EPA draft text fuels the CSOs' fear that the EPA outcomes may fail to assist the developmental objectives of the respective economies, saying:

> .... every five years the ESA-EU EPA Council shall undertake a formal and comprehensive review to ascertain if the development benchmarks have been attained by individual ESA countries as well as to determine whether EU's trade and development policies and assistance have contributed to individual ESA countries achieving the development benchmarks (ESA-EU Draft Text, 2006: 8).

Further, CSOs' advocacy work focuses on associated EPA adjustment costs that were estimated by the European Research Office in 2006 (see the table below). As can be seen, revenue losses include falling fiscal revenues necessary to support government expenditures, including agricultural research and development, infrastructural development, social development and poverty alleviation programmes; dwindling resources to support trade facilitation and export diversification initiatives; production and employment initiatives; and skills and production improvement. Madagascar and Zimbabwe's adjustment cost levels are both high, signifying huge future challenges in satisfying fiscal expenditures and any initiatives meant to support respective industrial production capacities, export competitiveness and production and export diversification. This is instructive since the two countries have political challenges that impact negatively on any form of economic recovery.

Table 5.1 Estimated EPA-related adjustment costs by country, € million

Country	Fiscal adjustment	Trade facilitation & export diversification	Production & employment adjustment	Skills/ production enhancement	Total adjustment costs
Angola	40	45	40	45	170
Botswana	30	12	25	15	82
Lesotho	40	25	25	35	125
Mozambique	60	90	50	65	265
Namibia	40	12	12	15	79
Swaziland	60	12	25	15	112
Tanzania	70	65	40	65	240
Madagascar	90	65	40	65	260
Malawi	40	45	20	30	135
Mauritius	40	12	12	15	79
Seychelles	30	30	6	15	81
Zambia	50	45	25	45	165
Zimbabwe	40	20	25	30	115

Source: European Research Office, December 2006

Throughout the EPA process, CSOs have been concerned with poverty (currently estimated at 60% of the population in many ESA member states) as well as high levels of unemployment, socio-economic under-development and growing inequalities. They have also been concerned about the potential negative impact of the EPA outcomes, especially on economic units, and in particular small and medium sized entrepreneurs and new farmers (in the case of Zimbabwe), who are now exposed to an EPA-driven bilateral and global market environment and conditions. Yet both the COMESA and SADC intellectual leadership (EPA units' CTAs) seem unwilling to consult other stakeholders, such as civil society groups. There is also no evidence that the EPA unit CTAs engage the business community in dedicated sessions other than meetings where they form part of government delegations, in which they express their feelings on the process through the government negotiators.

The regional CSOs' representatives noted and agreed that the EPA process contains a number of contentious and complex issues that demand thorough and strategic preparation, coordination and synergy building between the various stakeholders. This requires an inclusive, constructive, and sound state-NSAs working relationship. They further observed limited political will to widely consult or involve other stakeholders at national, configuration and EU levels. Of the three levels, they absolved the EU, at least for entertaining African CSO representatives, which would have been difficult to do at both the configuration and national levels. With respect to Zimbabwe, there was absolutely no interaction between the state's political and technical personalities and regional and/or national activists. Such developments have future short to medium term implications, especially on vulnerable infant and sensitive sectors of the economy such as agriculture and manufacturing as well as social welfare.

Anecdotal evidence acknowledges that agriculture supports about 70% of the population for household consumption, and plays a minor role in both commercial agricultural markets and agro-processing activities. This fuels CSOs' fear that EPAs are likely to flood ESA markets with subsidised agricultural products, a development that has future negative implications for the sector and the entire economy, especially in Zimbabwe, where new farmers are still establishing themselves. Regional CSOs complain that the EPA process has failed to provide platforms for farmer organisations to contribute to the process, given the fact that most ESA countries are largely dominated by agriculture, agriculture-related activities and agriculturally linked sectoral industrial processes. They also expressed concern because the unfolding dynamics and importance of the sector should have qualified them for a dedicated session. Furthermore, the CSOs observe that COMESA's insensitivity in this regard has future implications, especially for smallholder farmers, other producers of agriculture-related products, industrial development and competitiveness - given the sector's strong forward and backward linkages with the rest of the economy - as well as consumers, with respect to balancing food security and food sovereignty objectives. The CSOs have thus been arguing that 'consultation is not about making assumptions about other social and economic units', (Makanza, interview in Durban, South Africa, 10 August 2011) but rather about direct or indirect soliciting of their views. They, therefore, called upon regional political and technical leadership to also incorporate the radical views of broader constituencies, including the 'Stop the EPAs' campaign.

In Harare, the ESA-EPA CTA appealed to CSOs and other participants to popularise the ESA-EPA document in their various constituencies. This raises the following questions: Should CSOs focus on the weakness of the document with a view to improving the final output, or on lobbying for its acceptance in the EU negotiating machinery? Should CSOs focus on inherent COMESA intellectual leadership weaknesses and failure to widely consult broader constituencies before serving the 'menu' on the EU table? Should CSOs focus on COMESA's intellectual leadership's lack of organic team spirit to call for a review of the process to date with the view to improve negotiating tactics, strategies and mandate? This prompts Deve (2009) to argue that requesting constructive engagement on a document that has already been shared with the counterpart for consideration highlights a high degree of contempt of other stakeholders' intellects, energies and activism; a display of mistrust between COMESA and CSOs, and a lack of team spirit, strategic networking, and synergy building - all of which are a necessary condition for positive socio-economic developmental EPA outcomes.

The regional CSOs agree that the ESA region can improve its negotiating capacities by involving all the available actors and critical voices. They also agree that a broad array of critical voices requires efficient coordination as well as analysis, dissemination and sharing of critical information on the process. For this to happen, an 'open door policy', has to be adopted, coupled with the expressed intent to accommodate different views. The CSOs further agree that coordination is about accountability of outcomes, reaching out to broader constituencies, and building strategic alliances, synergies and networks aimed at ensuring policy driven strategies and the positive outcomes necessary to promote pro-poor development and improve livelihoods. Given the success of the "Stop EPAs Campaign", the CSOs should have foreseen the implications and dangers of the EU political structures' decision to withdraw MAR.

The CSOs' concerns were echoed by the former South African President, Thabo Mbeki, in his opening remarks to the 21st Plenary Assembly of the SADC Parliamentary Forum, held in Johannesburg on 10-17 November 2006[137]: "How do we ensure that EPAs currently being negotiated with the EU by all SADC member-states do not serve as an obstacle to the envisaged SADC customs union?" Subsequent to the meeting, regional MPs claimed that "the EPAs issues, positions and offers have not been shared adequately with other organs of the state in respective member-states". Negotiators have not interacted with MPs on the EPA processes in the context of their three roles: oversight of the executive, representing the people, and legislating national laws and regulations. Since then, annual regional parliamentary forum meetings have included a dedicated session on EPA processes in southern Africa in order to clarify issues and concerns in the MPs' three constitutional mandates: oversight, legislation and representation. This also means that consultation and coordination between government negotiators and other state organs has remained very poor. By now, the ESA-EPA

---

[137] COMESA and SADC Secretariats

intellectual leadership should have developed a database of national and regional activists and MPs in order to facilitate easier coordination of their input.

State-stakeholder relationship and civil society advocacy

Stakeholder participation and consultation on the EPA process in Zimbabwe has been the responsibility of the ministry of Trade and Industry (now Industry and Commerce). This entails identifying stakeholders from other trade-related ministries, parastatals, private sector bodies, CSOs and labour. The ministry's failure to adequately implement the above reflects state shortcomings and suggests a general lack of political will to involve and consult with all the relevant civic bodies in the EPA process. This has undermined the potential for harnessing all the available financial and human resources for a national common course. The government's narrow and partisan approach to engaging the EU in EPA process has marginalised the voice of vulnerable groups in society, including that of unorganised entrepreneurs. There was also no political will to encourage all stakeholders to mobilise resources in support of the EPA process, especially knowing that there were no possibilities of donor funding as well as fiscal limitations. Engagement of all stakeholders would have allowed collective identification of priorities, issues of national concern and interests and strategic approaches and tactics during the negotiation.

SEATINI, MWENGO and the TRADES Centre admit that the former Trade and Industry ministry (now Industry and Commerce) had throughout the process consistently invited them to every national preparatory engagement prior to the RNF and joint ESA-EU EPA related meetings. They have also participated in these meetings as part of the government delegation. For instance, SEATINI, a Harare-based regional trade organisation specialising in trade negotiations, officially represented ESA civil society groups in all the EPA related RNF and joint ESA-EU meetings held in the region and in Brussels between January and December 2004 as per the EPA roadmap. The organisation developed a good relationship with the Trade and Industry ministry, resulting in the signing of a memorandum of understanding (MoU) with the ministry of Foreign Affairs' Department of International Relations, aimed at facilitating dialogue sessions on topical thematic areas[138] of trade and development. As an insider in both the Trade and Industry ministry and RNF trade sessions, SEATINI succeeded in passing crucial lobbying information to other national and sub-regional CSOs. However, following the organisation's removal from the RNF framework[139], and faced with the exodus of key technical staff[140] and diminishing funding[141], the influence of SEATINI in shaping advocacy and activism in the EPA process dwindled. The TRADES Centre, considered by the civil society sector to be pro-government, produced the country's EPA-IAS and facilitated stakeholders' engagement in the findings and recommendations that eventually shaped the country's positions, interests and offers. The TRADES Centre also facilitated an EPA-related conference in Harare and Bulawayo to review and engage with the EPA-IAS findings and recommendations, national imperatives and the economic transformation agenda. Notwithstanding the above, the EPA-IAS suffered from minimal engagement between government and critical key stakeholders, namely, the civil society fraternity and the business community, which limited the potential for building national synergies, coalitions and partnerships in support of a better deal for Zimbabwe. It also reduced the potential for a pro-development and pro-poor EPA outcome based on collective articulation of the country's developmental aspirations. MWENGO, though considered pro-government and which had a cordial working

---

[138] Topics presented included 'Assessing political risk in the SADC with specific reference to Zimbabwe and the New Partnership for Africa's Development.

[139] Participating support was withdrawn in July 2004 and February 2005 for the two representatives on account of insisting on editorial freedom in its monthly "Electronic Bulletin," in line with the insider-outsider strategy.

[140] Two key officials (an economist and policy expert, and a trade lawyer) resigned to join diaspora jobs in South Africa and Botswana, respectively, in July 2005, mainly on account of the country's deteriorating economic situation, while another media expert went for further education (Masters) in the same year.

[141] On account of the staff exodus and donor funding models in Zimbabwe that prioritise governance, democracy and human rights activities while excluding economic programme activities including trade negotiations.

relationship with the former Trade and Industry ministry, also suffered from staff shortages and remained inactive.

While SEATINI, TRADES Centre and MWENGO had good working relationship with government, they would have invested effort and time to ensure that the contributions of other civil society groups added value to the formal process. Other Harare based CSOs were excluded from directly engaging with the ministry on account of the official perception that they are allies of the MDC formations and the EU. This worsened the level of mistrust and hostility between the Mugabe government and civil society in a context where donor funding of programmes and projects linked to the citizens' constituency has often been regarded by the state as an extension of the opposition parties' antagonism towards its authority in almost all sectors of governance, social development and the economy. Indeed, CSOs have for more than a decade been dependent on donor funding due to lack of alternative sources of funding or own resources. As a result, many of them have oriented their strategies and activities in line with donor priorities, losing independence and fueling the authorities' perception of them as "agents of the governments and donors of the West". It is undisputed that most of the excluded CSOs at some stage publicly sympathised with the MDC formations, in addition to publicly expressing strong views against the ZANU (PF) government's economic mismanagement and partisan approach to economic transformation and empowerment. That alone precipitated their exclusion while fueling state-CSO mistrust and lack of cooperation on economic policies including trade talks. This also fueled state shortcomings and paranoia about CSOs from the region and beyond, thereby denying them access to the country's EPA-IAS (a national strategic document).

The CSOs argued that engagement in the process would be based solely on national economic interests rather than political alignment. Firstly, the CSOs cited their undisputed and impressive record of engaging with the IMF and World Bank sponsored ESAP. They further questioned the state's approach to policy implementation as well as its reluctance to consider alternative policy options. Secondly, they pointed out their undisputed record of mobilising various constituencies in support of government policy space, then under threat from the World Bank and the IMF. Thirdly, they cited the leadership abilities of LEDRIZ, the research arm of the ZCTU, which successfully mobilised resources and regional activists, academic and research institutions and labour, culminating in an ANSA policy dialogue platform and a publication with a set of alternatives to the neo-liberal policies in the region. By excluding such CSOs, the government dismissed potential sources of strategic analysis, and views that could have contributed positively to the articulation of national issues, interests, positions and offers. Indeed, the hardline stance whereby organisations were labelled anti-ZANU (PF) not only made it extremely difficult for the Trade and Industry ministry to even consider their views in the process, but also firmly closed any window of opportunity for lobbying and advocacy work in the process.

Some of these organisations are highly respected in the region, and were allowed to contribute to other regional EPA processes. Unfortunately the EPA process, because of embedded sensitivities about future commercial interests with respect to the EU, makes it difficult for other sub-regional member states to act as conduits of civil society advocacy work in Zimbabwe. Leaders of sub-regional member states regard Zimbabwe's civil society-EU nexus, which Harare often describes as an instrument of regime change, as too sensitive to interact or engage with publicly on matters of national importance. So the only route for CSO advocacy and lobbying was through the Zimbabwean state. While a sound state-civil society relationship on trade related issues is a necessary condition for constructive and effective engagement and participation, it is not a sufficient condition for the country to secure a better deal in this round of negotiations. Indeed, in the absence of a state-stakeholder relationship, it is idle for the EPA to attempt to address the multi-dimensional nature of the country's current social and economic developmental challenges - including growing poverty, societal inequalities, and underdevelopment; under-equipped, under-funded and static industrial production; and value addition processes and export diversification. It is difficult at this stage to qualitatively ascertain the impact of excluding critical CSOs from the process in terms of securing a pro-poor and pro-development outcome[142].

The Commonwealth Secretariat Hub and Spokes Project (2012) observes that most ACP countries, including Zimbabwe, have 'multi-stakeholder trade consultative networks' to inform trade policy making and input into bilateral and multilateral trade negotiations. More often than not, any 'trade consultative network' that may exist, is over-represented by government officials at the expense of the private sector and CSOs. This means that countries may struggle to build sustainable and lasting pro-trade development outcomes, including input into trade policies and trade negotiations. Willie Shumba, 2013, the SADC secretariat's senior customs officer, in his presentation to regional trade and integration stakeholders during the SADC Trade Negotiating Forum held in Gaborone, Botswana, observed that while other regional countries with troubled political environments such as the DRC, Lesotho, Madagascar, Malawi and Swaziland have succeeded in establishing active customs-business forums in support of their respective trade and economic development goals, Zimbabwe is yet to do so.

Communication between stakeholders is necessary to sustain investments made in the trade and development dialogue in the context of the country's industrialisation strategy. It is imperative for government, business, and civil society formations to work together to share unbiased and rigorous analyses of achievements, best practices and challenges in the current EPA process. Mutual tolerance and understanding sustains collective responsibilities on matters of trade and industrial policy formulations, trade negotiations and the implementation of regional and international trade agreements. Zimbabwe needs to come up with a sustainable mechanism that will rally all the relevant stakeholders behind the government in future bilateral, regional and multilateral trade and development cooperation negotiations. This suggests rejuvenating the public-NSAs consultative trade and industrial policy dialogue platforms. It also suggests supporting and encouraging national institutions and structures to be active, not only in national trade and

---

[142] The EPA objectives have all the nuances that the EPA Framework seeks inter alia to secure pro-poor and pro-development outcomes.

development discussions and practices, but also in regional and global networking. This has huge potential for galvanising current and future collective political will in support of the country's commercial interests and concerns.

Government officials argue that the main driver of negotiations was the country's future needs in the global economy. Though this assertion is linked to short to medium term national commercial interests, it suffers from poor strategic consultations with stakeholders and rational and collective analysis of the short to medium term strategic goals in the proposed reciprocal trade regime with the EU. The process also suffers from a lack of collective and inclusive articulation of national commercial interests in the context of the country's ambitions. The process further suffers from negative perceptions about the relationship between government and the NSAs. In the light of this, CSO advocacy has failed to link the country's present situation of unimpressive socio-economic development with the potential EPA outcome. Secondly, the CSOs have failed to demonstrate the dangers of an economy that is open to European operators, producers, exporters and investors, some of which have strong lobbies that include MCs and TNCs. Thirdly, the CSOs have failed to advocate for the participation of new economic entrepreneurs from all sectors of the economy, most of whom are yet to be organised under effective umbrella bodies, with the objective of protecting their interests in regional, bilateral, and multilateral trade negotiations. As opposed to the ESAP era, most CSO advocacy messages - although predicting the general and specific future social, economic and political ramifications of the new trade regime - were not based on rigorous and scientific scholarly analyses, and had no empirical basis. Most of the published materials on EPA advocacy were produced by activists, and are emotional, one-sided and offer no alternative suggestions for an ideal process and outcome. While the advocacy messages targeted officials of the Trade and Industry ministry they forgot that the negotiators had been given a mandate by political principals - who were not targeted for lobbying purposes. Lastly, their advocacy showed that the CSOs were not working closely with national, regional, continental and global research institutions, which would have allowed rational, scientific, conceptual and contextual analyses to filter into some of the lobbying messages.

The eagerness of both parties to fast-track the EPA process that culminated in the signing of the latter by the Minister of Industry and Commerce, Welshman Ncube in 2009 in Mauritius was at odds with all the prevailing and projected social, economic and political indicators. The economy - that had contracted for eight consecutive years to about 50% of GDP, and was struggling to recover under the GNU administration. Expectations of in-flows of FDIs, regional and national investment as well as unlocking financial resources from the international community failed to materialise because the provisions of the GPA had been disregarded. The social and humanitarian crisis continued to absorb significant fiscal resources. The parties in the inclusive government continued to publicly contradict each other, especially with regard to economic policies and programmes. All this generated an inconclusive debate about whether the economy could be downgraded from 'developing' to 'LDC' - which would have allowed trade with the EU to continue under EBA and DFQF initiatives. However, the CSOs, having failed to dissuade the government negotiators from succumbing to EU pressure in Mauritius, were left in limbo. The prevailing social, economic and political indicators should have enabled the CSOs in their advocacy activities to point out the consequences of splitting the ESA configuration, and the perils of individual small, weak, and vulnerable economies signing the iEPA. They should have highlighted the violations of the joint ESA-EU roadmap in 2004 and the EU's potential to extract huge concessions for the European TNCs, MCs and other operators and investors at the expense of Zimbabwe's sustainable socio-economic development and political stability. Indeed, Zimbabwean CSOs, under the leadership of the ZIMCODD advocacy programme, made a spirited effort to downgrade the economy to LDC status on the basis of its huge and growing external debts and obligations, coupled with negative social and economic indicators. Zimbabwe would then, like the rest of the LDCs, be under no pressure to initial and sign the iEPA. The CSOs, under the leadership of AFRODAD, also argued that the economy should be classified as a highly indebted poor country on account of its huge and growing external debt. The CSOs observed that the country's debt and associated obligations was denying the government the necessary resources to improve social development and the conditions of the people. The debt also denied the country the resources to rejuvenate and revitalise industrial productive capacity utilisation which, at the birth of the GNU in February 2009, was estimated at less than 15%. The debt further, denied the country the necessary resources to revitalise downstream economic activities, value addition in export production, export competitiveness and supply-side development.

The signing and ratification of the iEPA served merely to ensure that trade in goods between Europe and Zimbabwe was legal before the WTO members, lest the EU face legal battles from other non-ACP WTO countries. According to João Aguiar Machado, the EU commission deputy director general of Trade and the chief negotiator:

> ... big member countries of the WTO such as the USA and Canada, which have commercial interests in ACP economies, are already questioning the legality status of the trade regime between the EU and non-ratified iEPA countries, despite the fact that negotiations for the full EPAs are underway (Machado, during the joint EU-SADC EPA group negotiations, Johannesburg, South Africa, 20-22 March 2013).

Machado further cited conformity with the WTO regulations as the main reason why the three political structures[143] of the EU have unanimously voted in favour of the withdrawal of MAR 1528 of 2007 by 1 October 2014. This will result in non-LDC EPA countries that are without an alternative preferential trade regime but are trading under the Most Favoured Nation status, enjoying the same treatment as all the WTO members. On this basis, it is possible that the Zimbabwean negotiators might have opted for an early signing in order to avoid the sudden withdrawal of MAR, thereby swiftly cutting trade flows between the negotiating parties, which has remained

---

[143] The EU Council, the European Parliament and the EU Commission.

impressive throughout the period under review. By remaining silent on the potential negative impact of MRA withdrawal, the CSOs lost an opportunity to come together with the government negotiators and officials on this process in particular and economic policy in general. The CSOs should have opted to discredit MAR decisions as well as alerting different constituencies on the implications and dangers of such a move. Either way, the CSOs would have proved that they are also fierce critics of the three political EU institutions that are accused of being not only anti-ZANU (PF), but also pro-MDC[144] and its allies.

Proposed advocacy and lobbying for CSOs in Zimbabwe should therefore have entailed forming strategic networks with other key stakeholders - including the business community and broad sections of the sector (social movements) - working on trade and development with a view to exerting pressure on the negotiators to summarise national interests, positions and offers in the iEPA framework for wider consumption. Concerted pressure should have been brought to bear on government through the ministries of Industry and Commerce, Regional Integration and other trade-related portfolios with a view to popularising these summaries in the main vernacular languages: Ndebele and Shona, in order for the citizens to understand and engage in the new trade regime with Europe. Furthermore, CSOs working with other NSA components should have exerted pressure on government negotiators to debrief the nation before and after each major EPA meeting or process.

It is known that the negotiators have not been sharing any EPA information with respect to potential opportunities and challenges with diverse strategic stakeholders, including industrial bodies such as the CZI and ZNCC as well as with research institutions and labour. While in the case of labour[145] this is understandable, the situation is

---

[144] The three EU institutions have since 2002 directed that 10th EDF resources be allocated towards humanitarian assistance and governance and human rights activities, areas that favour the MDC. Following the formation of the GNU, the three EU structures ensured that more 10th EDF resources are diverted towards soft sectors, namely health and education portfolios under MDC formations.

[145] Due to the deep connection with the MDC, that is, labour being the foundation of the MDC party.

different with the CZI and ZNCC, whose members would either benefit or suffer as a result of the new trade regime, and are entitled to know how this will affect them. The CSOs should have developed friendships and partnerships with the business umbrella bodies, while creating opportunities for using these bodies as conduits for interfacing with government negotiators at all levels. Success in the above would have enabled the CSOs to focus on forming strategic stakeholder alliances with government negotiators. It would also have supported collective harmonisation of iEPA trade liberalisation schedules commitments, with the current and future regional trade and integration commitments already agreed upon - or likely to be agreed upon - under COMESA FTA, SADC FTA and the Tripartite FTA (comprising COMESA, EAC and SADC).

CSOs should have stepped up lobbying and campaigns for the allocation of resources (donor funding and fiscal) with a view to ensuring that views of the unfolding process were balanced. In particular, CSO advocacy should have aimed to support the development and establishment of technical institutions, and the introduction of trade negotiations courses at different levels. This would help to build a broad base of qualified officers and activists with sound knowledge, skills, and capacities to simultaneously deal with bilateral and multilateral trade negotiations as well as regional integration agendas. While this level of critical mass would come too late to help in the current negotiations round, it would be an asset in subsequent engagements and future trade negotiations (bilateral, regional or multilateral) in order to ensure fair publicity and scrutiny of the process and outcomes. This level of consultation is essential for mainstreaming trade and industrial policy objectives within the broad trade and regional integration agenda, socio-economic development, pluralistic governance and the body politic.

Negotiations in all configurations are done in thematic Technical Working Groups (TWGs), structures comprised of junior government officials who not only prepare background materials for senior government officials, but also form the main body of all respective government delegations to EPA related meetings. The TWG officers, who are experts in certain areas, are approachable and flexible in their interactions with stakeholders. The structures not only report to senior officials (chief negotiators), but also produce thematic texts or records that are used by senior officials during their internal group negotiations or joint negotiations with the EU. Furthermore, TWG officials not only advise their respective chief negotiators, but also develop textual proposals of group positions and offers on all the areas that are under negotiation with the EU. Unfortunately, the CSOs have disregarded this structure. It also appears that the CSOs have been targeting higher level senior officials and ministers while the real negotiations take place at a lower level.

These challenges have undermined CSO offensive lobbying of government and other key stakeholders working on trade and development issues in Zimbabwe as well as the constituencies of producers, consumers and vulnerable groups in society. State-civil society relations are symbolic and virtually non-existent since, in most cases, CSO efforts with respect to the country's economic affairs are conducted according to donor funding patterns and intervention objectives, often with scant regard for relevance or even rationality. Since 2002 the 10th EDF has concentrated on democratisation, electoral reforms, human rights and governance activities, while no funding was made available for the EPA process. The EU cites the poor bilateral relations between it and the Zimbabwean leadership as the main reason why 10th EDF resources (channeled through the national authorising officer, located in the ministry of Finance) were not accessible to NSAs, particularly civil society groups.

Thus, discourse among the CSOs on economic matters (including trade negotiations) turned into a political mine-field, becoming increasingly irrational, uncooperative and irresponsible. At the negotiating table poor state-NSA relations lead to poor stakeholder wisdom, effort, and resources vis-à-vis politically and economically focused EU institutions which have the full support of MC and TNC lobbies. The Zimbabwean negotiators' ineffectiveness paves the way for short-term gains and a trade regime that is favourable for the EU. It is sad to observe that most national stakeholders working on trade and development remain at the periphery of the process amid limited government outreach programmes on account of the non-availability of resources — from the EU and other donors on the one hand, and from government fiscal sources on the other. It is common knowledge that there has been no donor funding for the Zimbabwean government's policy space, including activities related to trade negotiations, and the government has been unable to fund these activities from its own resources.

Donor funding and civil society advocacy

The EU's institutions and structures are well endowed with all the necessary financial, human and technical[146] resources to advance EPA negotiations with all six configurations. For their part, the ESA countries have few resources of any kind, and have had to rely on the financial benevolence of the negotiating counterpart - the EU - to support the process. As a result, interest groups have become frustrated or have opted out of the process. Of all the ESA countries, Zimbabwe is in worst condition: there has been a massive exodus of foreign funding coupled with high fiscal prioritisation of economic empowerment at the expense of trade negotiations. In addition, the country's industrial capacity utilisation, productivity and export competitiveness have declined significantly. Lack of donor funding has denied CSOs the opportunity to develop advocacy activities which would have influenced increased fiscal allocation in support of the EPA process.

Throughout the process, ESA member states have been guaranteed financial support from the EU (air tickets, accommodation and daily subsistence allowances) for three participants at both RNF and joint ESA-EU meetings held in the region and in Brussels. The EU has been categorical in stating that the funding support would cover two government negotiators and one private sector representative. This decision was announced during the launch of the EPA roadmap, and so, is not a product of CSO advocacy work. Zimbabwe in particular, despite its frosty bilateral relations with the EU, has benefited from this support. However, as foreign currency in-flows dwindled, especially from

---

[146] Includes technical experts, specialised skills, short to long term consultancy and equipment.

mid-2005, the government made use of the funds earmarked for the private sector representative.

It is interesting that the EU decided to bankroll the EPA processes and activities of the ESA group, since it is considered a 'hybrid configuration,' with no legal status as a recipient of donor money. The ESA was not formed by a legally binding instrument such as a treaty or MoU. The ESA group's activities have been coordinated by COMESA with moral support from three RECs (EAC, IGAD and IOC). As coordinator, COMESA was then identified by the EU as the appropriate secretariat for coordinating disbursements coming from the EU in support of this process. This is in spite of the fact that not all the countries of the original ESA group (before the split into EAC and the reconfigured ESA) are members of COMESA. Tanzania, for example, which the CSOs successfully lobbied to join with other EAC countries, is not a member of COMESA. By using COMESA as a conduit to fund all EPA-related activities of ESA the EU, as a donor, has opted to ignore the basic rules and principles of funding institutional activities. Kamidza, in his assessment of donor funding for CSOs working on EPA issues, remarked:

> …. because the donor is an interested party, who expects to gain from the conclusion of EPA round of negotiations, they simply overlook the ESA's legal and structural deficiencies. ….. because the EU is a domineering party, which expects to secure markets through rushed EPA process, simply overlooks basic donor principles of funding organisations, institutions and structures. …Basic funding principles dictate that under normal circumstances, no donor could have bankrolled the activities of a recipient through another entity's structure the way the EU is supporting ESA-EPA activities through COMESA secretariat (Kamidza, 2008: 9).

Throughout the entire EPA process, no EU funding was made available to support the participation of national and sub-regional CSOs in RNF and joint ESA-EU meetings held in the region and Brussels. It is also regrettable that the ESA group officially withdrew SEATINI's representatives from all EPA-related meetings, which weakened the state-civil society consultative process at all levels. A few donor agents and philanthropists working with economic justice network programmes supported CSO participation in the process, though not in any sustained or structured way. The donors/donor agents and philanthropists who have supported the process are listed in the table below. Inadequate donor funding has, to a large extent, restricted CSOs' advocacy to unstructured and inconsistent activities, often without any clear outcome in view. State shortcomings and fault lines increasingly worsened, to the extent that the GNU's economic policy-making process became paralysed. The EU's support of the participation of three trade officials at the same time as employing divide and conquer tactics with respect to the ESA group and its guerrilla negotiating strategy and tactics has survived public scrutiny.

Table 5.2   Donor agents and philanthropists who funded government and CSOs in the EPA process

Donor	What was supported?
EU	Government officials/negotiators' participation in EPA meetings, and impact assessment study.
African Capacity Building Foundation	CSO representatives' participation in AU organised meeting.
Action Aid	CSO representatives' participation in RNF meetings, consultation sessions with government and other civic bodies, and advocacy at national level, and CSO organising an EPA conference.
Afrika Groups of Sweden	CSO hosting national EPA workshop.
Christian Aid	CSO representatives lobbying mission to the EU, and CSOs hosting national EPA workshop.
Friedrich-Ebert-Stiftung	CSO representatives' participation in Brussels meetings, consultation sessions with government and other civic bodies, advocacy at national levels and CSO organising an EPA workshop.

Foreign Trade Union Organisations (FNV and FOS Belgium)	CSO representatives' participation at the NDTPF and RNF, and advocacy at national level, CSO consultation sessions with government and other civic bodies, and organising an EPA conference.
Hivos	CSO representatives' participation at RNF.
Oxfam America	CSO representatives' participation at RNF, consultation sessions with government and advocacy at national level, organising EPA workshops.
Oxfam Novib	CSO representatives' participation at RNF, consultation sessions with government and other civic bodies, and advocacy at national level, and CSO organising an EPA workshop.
Rosa Luxemburg Foundation	CSO representatives' participation at the NDTPF and in Brussels meetings, organising an EPA conference, workshops.

Source: Compiled from study questionnaire responses for this book.

Few civil society representatives have been able to participate in RNF meetings. Only two CSOs[147] from all those working on EPA issues have participated in joint ESA-EU proceedings as part of the Zimbabwean delegation. The country has thus been an opportunity to build synergies and coalitions between government negotiators and the broader section of CSO representatives, who over the decade have been able to build strategic trade-related networks across the continent as well as in Europe. This has also prevented the Trade and Industry (now Industry and Commerce) ministry from receiving any moral or technical support from the civil society sector. This is important, given the politically charged environment and the ruling party's view of civil society as 'swimming in EU money.'

Indeed, limited funding for the EPA has greatly compromised CSO activities that might have contributed significantly to the articulation of issues and interests and the development of positions

---

[147] TRADES Centre and SEATINI

and offers. Civic bodies, whose work typically involves interacting with both policy-makers and grassroots communities, would have been the natural advocates of pro-poor developmental policies during the process of developing Zimbabwe's positions. They would also have given voice to unorganised constituencies in the process.

While most ESA countries have the opportunity to access promised developmental assistance through the 10th EDF, Zimbabwe does not qualify for this. This means that the country cannot prioritise improving existing supply-side constraints to facilitate trade in goods. This also means that the country has to normalize the bilateral relations with the EU through the ongoing re-engagement. But the country can continue to trade with the EU, regardless of the supply-side bottlenecks, a development that blocks the flow of trade, giving EU products an advantage in the market. However, a combination of limited resources and the hardline position of the government vis-à-vis critical CSOs, frustrated civil society advocacy prowess in engaging with emerging EPA national challenges in particular, and those relating to both the ESA group and the EU in general as highlighted in the table below.

Table 5.3 Emerging EPA challenges by level

National level
Limited financial resources to undertake wide and deep consultations, and own supervised industrial or sectoral studies.
Politically charged environment undermines effective national consultations.
Lack of skills and capacity to adequately prepare for the negotiations.
Deploying chief negotiators to regional missions[148] undermines continuity in the pursuit of national interests, positions and offers.
Numerous areas of negotiation areas requiring a very large team of experts and specialists - including economists, trade policy analysts, political and social analysts, lawyers and statisticians - who were not easy to find, given the brain drain across all sectors of the economy.

---

[148] The chief negotiator between 2004 and 2006 was posted to the Embassy in Zambia, and the chief negotiator between 2007 and 2008 posted to the Embassy in Pretoria.

The business community – the main stakeholder – has throughout the negotiation process been preoccupied with day to day business management issues, and has shown little interest in the EPA process.

Configuration level

Co-ordination at the regional level, resulting in negotiating parties playing their cards close to their chests.

Maintaining the group's cohesion given the continuous dangling of the 'development aid envelope' by the EU.

Different tariff liberalisation commitments among ESA countries (see Table 6.6), which also conflict with existing regional integration commitments.

Divergent interests among ESA member states.

EU level

Getting the EU to the negotiating table has not been easy given that the same (EU) negotiators have also been negotiating with other ACP configurations.

Thorough knowledge on the part of the EU of ESA countries vis-à-vis its commercial interests.

Dealing with the EC's specific mandate backed by a large pool of experts and specialists in all the areas under negotiation.

Engaging EU with huge resources, all the necessary data and access to impact assessment studies' findings and recommendations of all ESA countries and extensive experiences in trade negotiations.

Source: Compiled from study questionnaire responses for this book.

Emerging concerns and implications for the future: trade and industrial policies

There is increasing consensus in African policy circles that trade is a powerful engine for economic growth and development (Kalenga, 2011) and that promoting the participation of ACP countries in international trade requires effective, trusted and accountable trade consultative networks that are mainstreamed as part of the national trade policy framework (Commonwealth Secretariat Hub and Spokes Project, 2012). This ensures that the trade policy framework balances a country's capacity to generate

191

foreign currency and to produce competitive products destined for external markets. It entails balancing the flow of imports and exports with the government's prevailing social and economic objective(s). For instance, in pursuit of the goal of maximising consumer welfare, the government may opt for growth in imports which invariably introduces competition in the domestic market, leading to a reduction in the price of goods.

Ugarteche (2000: 73) observes that foreign competition forces an accelerated rate of domestic economic change and produces new opportunities to learn new technologies and new management practices that can be used to improve domestic productivity. Ugarteche (Ibid: 1) further notes that in economies with small domestic markets, primary production spearheads economic modernisation, while raw materials become a growing source of generating foreign currency to meet national import demands. In such economies, employment is not a concern as small to medium sized industries and emerging informal sector entrepreneurs increasingly become a vital source of job creation, income, poverty alleviation and livelihoods.

The above is characteristic of the Zimbabwean economy over this period which, as a result of the economic meltdown, informal cross border trading activities became the main source of jobs, livelihoods and also a reliable source of fiscal revenue - a trend that continued under the GNU administration. This reflects deficiencies in the macro-economic policy framework and weak implementation thereof. Between 2000 and 2008, the country launched a series of macro-economic policy blueprints. However, these remained on paper. These macro-economic blueprints are summarised in the table below. The list shows the short life-span of all these policies, the country's deficiency in implementing macro-economic policy, perennial macro-economic policy failures, and a lack of any collective approach to the macro-economic policy making process and implementation. The table also reflects the growing frustrations among stakeholders, fueling state-NSA tensions. Lastly, the table provides evidence of why it has been difficult to harness stakeholder resources in support of collective, inclusive and effective participation in the EPA trade negotiations.

Table 5.4 Zimbabwe's macro-economic policy frameworks visions, objectives, and targets, 2000 – 2007

Millennium Economic Recovery Programme (2000 – 2001)
The vision was to mobilise all stakeholders (government, business, labour and civil society) to implement a set of measures that would restore macro-economic stability in the country.
National Economic Revival Programme (2003)
The objective was to achieve macro-economic stability including a reduction in inflation and stimulating national output, productivity and foreign currency earning capacity.
Macro-Economic Policy Framework (2005-2006)
Outlined policy interventions and programmes targeted every economic sector, covering agricultural development, industrialisation, infrastructural development, investment promotion, social service delivery, poverty reduction, economic empowerment, youth development and gender equality, macro-economic stabilisation and strengthening institutional capacity.
National Economic Development Priority Programme (2006)
The aim was to mobilise foreign currency in three to six months and to restore industrial production, which was on the verge of collapsing.
Zimbabwe's Economic Development Strategy (2007)
The aim was to consolidate the country's economic development strategies aimed at achieving sustainable, balanced, and robust economic growth and development. However, issues contain therein are summarily repackaged from previous policies and/or policy pronouncements.

Sources: Kamidza and Mazingi, 2011, p. 320-323

The short life-span of all of these macro-economic policy frameworks reflects a high degree of uncertainty, government-NSA mistrust, and low confidence in the country's economic affairs. So far, every one of the macro-economic policy directives and interventions have failed to restore macro-economic stability in the country. The ZANU (PF) administration has failed dismally to embrace macro-economic policy frameworks as 'national policy tools' capable of stimulating economic activity and production across the sectors, regardless of the country's political and bilateral fault lines. The GNU at its inception raised national expectations (across the political divide) that it would create the necessary confidence-building measures to involve not only domestic and foreign economic entrepreneurs and investors, but also national constituencies and the general population in the design of macro-economic policies and their subsequent implementation in support of economic recovery, and thus to improve national product competitiveness vis-à-vis European products in both EU and local markets. For instance, the Short-Term Emergency Recovery Programme, launched on 18 March 2009, adopted the use of multiple currencies as legal tender and the Rand as a reference currency; dismantled foreign exchange controls; and promised to revive the productive sectors and create a conducive investment climate.

In line with the GNU's objective of inspiring industrialists to prioritise their allocation of resources to favour industrial production, industrial productivity, export competitiveness and industrial research and development, a trade policy was developed and launched in September 2012. The policy has the potential to support the national economy by providing strategic guidance in linking industrial production processes with external markets and investors. It also has the potential to significantly turn the economy around as it contains both sectoral and national industrial policy options, linking national productive capacities and consumers with external consumers and exporters of goods and services, for example, by using import tariffs as instruments capable of enhancing the country's economic growth and competitiveness. Unfortunately the policy was introduced long after the signature and ratification of the iEPA. This means that Zimbabwean stakeholders have to navigate a tricky and complex process without the guidance of this important document. It also means the country has formulated levels of trade liberalisation schedules and commitments and identified the sensitive sectoral products to be exempted from liberalisation commitments without the strategic input and guidance of the trade policy. Furthermore, the Zimbabwean negotiators, by failing to demand the development of the trade policy prior to the trade talks, implicitly succumbed to the domination of Europe's MCs, TNCs and other producers, investors, and operators.

The Zimbabwean GNU also launched its industrial policy well after the iEPA was signed and ratified. This means that the EPA negotiations continue without an industrial policy to inform, guide and advise stakeholders, and the business community in particular, on future industrial and sectoral development potential. The industrial policy should have assisted in the identification of sensitive and strategic sectors and associated products, and in the development and articulation of sensitive sectoral issues, interests and positions prior to exchanging textual proposals and offers with the EU. Neither the proposals nor the offers that culminated in the ratified iEPA were developed and articulated from an informed point of view. This goes against the revolutionised economic empowerment and transformation crusade, but also suggests that the new indigenous economic entrepreneurs, while celebrating economic freedom, will soon lose ground in both local and EU markets largely due to the fact that they had no input into the process that led to the agreed trade regime. The development and articulation of the country's national and sectoral positions and offers were informed by the findings of an impact assessment study that was done in 2005, which was not thoroughly interrogated by most stakeholders - owing to the prevailing political environment, limited fiscal resources and absence of donor funding support. Collective articulation of issues and interests across all sectors could have assisted negotiators to push for a viable and sustainable trade regime with Europe capable of supporting sectoral development in the form of present and future forward and backward sectoral linkages in the economy.

The trade and industrial policy frameworks should together have provided sound and strategic analyses based on the stakeholders' collective contributions. The policy blue-prints should have formed the basis for linking Zimbabwean economic sectors and consumers with EU consumers and investors. The policy documents should have highlighted the country's present and future industrial development capabilities at a regional level, the EU and global markets as well as the potential and viability of export diversification and product competitiveness. The two policies should have supported and created new public-NSA[149] platforms that would continuously engage and interact on economic policies, trade policy, trade negotiations (including the EPA process), and the implementation of regional and international trade agreements. The two policies should have also assisted in building synergies and coalitions between government and NSAs, and within the NSA fraternity (business, labour, and civil society) leading to collective wisdom in the development and articulation of strategies and tactics in pursuit of national issues, interests, positions and offers. Lastly, both trade and industrial policies could have assisted in the development of appropriate new export and import taxes or increases thereof, leading to more government revenue to support social and economic development, including industrial sector improvement and production capacities and productivity, especially in agriculture and manufacturing.

Emerging concerns and implications for the future: industrial production and export competitiveness

Zimbabwean industrial productive structures over the period under review have been extremely weak. This can be seen in the general economic meltdown and hyper-inflationary environment, and an industrial operating capacity estimated in 2008 at between 4% and 10% (Nyakazeya, 2009). This level of industrial capacity could not compete with regional, EU, and global levels. The low industrial capacity is a function of the decade-long MDC – ZANU (PF) political contestation, which compelled ZANU PF to adopt the political survival strategy of grand-standing economic empowerment and transformation programmes, particularly the fast-track land reform and indigenisation agendas. The political contestation is also responsible for the massive exodus of foreign and domestic investors from the economy. Even when the two belligerent parties agreed to govern the country jointly as the GNU, they struggled to mobilise the necessary external and domestic financial resources in support of

---

[149] Representatives of the private sector (Confederations of Industries and Chambers of Commerce) and civil society formations working on trade and development and regional economic integration initiatives.

industrialisation, downstream industrial activities and export capabilities, which remain extremely weak in a country that has huge potential in natural (agriculture and mining) resources and human capital formation[150], and a population that is known for being educated, skilled, disciplined and hard-working. Weak, uncompetitive industrialisation and low capacity utilisation translate into low levels of export diversification and competitiveness. The industrial and export bases have remained weak, narrow and almost entirely oriented towards primary and unprocessed commodities, particularly mineral products (diamonds, articles of base metals and precious or semi-precious stones) and agricultural products (unprocessed foodstuffs, beverages and tobacco). Most of these commodities, particularly minerals, are currently fetching low prices on the international market.

The country's need for foreign currency remains huge and smart sanctions have been applied against leading ZANU (PF) members and associated companies. Since 2000, the country has not qualified to access the 10th EDF development aid window that is designed to assist ACP countries in redressing industrial production challenges and supply-side bottlenecks that could undermine trade flows with Europe. The country does not qualify to borrow money from the GFIs (the World Band and the IMF), not only due to the sanctions, but also because of the huge and growing external debt overhang. All this means that the government is unable, especially prior to the introduction of the multi-currency regime, to satisfy national

---

[150] The South African government regards Zimbabwe as a strategic source of human resources on the basis of its highly educated, skilled, disciplined and hard-working citizens. Thus, the decision to relax the visa requirements for Zimbabweans entering the Republic of South Africa in October 2008 following the signing of the GPA from 'less than a month one-entry' to 'three months multiple entry' that can be extended by a further month at any Home Affairs Office while inside the country. Following the formation of the GNU on 9 February 2009, South Africa further relaxed the visa requirements of Zimbabweans already in the country by regularising their stay. This entailed appealing (through extensive multi-media campaign advertisements on radio and television channels and newspapers) to every Zimbabwean to apply to the nearest Department of Home Affairs for a stay of four years regardless of specific skills and work experience, type of work, and with or without relevant documents such as certificates, passports and national identification cards.

requirements, particularly external debt service obligations, and the importation of industrial and consumer goods. On-going debt service continues to divert scarce resources away from supporting industrialisation, export diversification, research and skills development, and technological advancement. This also means that the country's industrial and export capabilities are likely to take longer than expected to revive and transform. Although progress in the macro-economic policy environment in general and industrial and trade policies in particular are necessary ingredients for industrial development, export capacity development, and/or diversification possibilities, the reality of the Zimbabwean economy points to a huge opening for EU commercial interests.

Thus the fear of an unbalanced EPA outcome that will not be able to support Zimbabwe's industrial and export development. The stage is set for EU products to flood the local market, thereby entrenching the European capitalist (investors and operators) foothold in Zimbabwe. Such an outcome negates the anti-colonial agenda as well as the much-touted revolutionary claims of the land rights programme. The EPA outcome is set to tie the Zimbabwean economy to Europe in a skewed fashion that undermines national producers of goods in the short to medium term. The EPA is also likely to intensify a further opening up of the national economy to EU competition in particular and other international economies in general thereby firmly entrenching the neo-liberal policy project of the 1980s and 1990s that was characterised by trade 'liberalisation.' The 'one-size-fits-all' economic reform blueprint did not benefit Zimbabwe, especially in terms of industrial downsizing and closure, and job and income losses. 'ESAP' could be said to signal the beginning of the current political tension, with its accompanying social development challenges such as widespread poverty, and economic challenges that included industrial stagnation due to aging equipment that could not be replaced. The EPA is unlikely to provide any positive options for the country's industrial strategy and development objectives. In fact, the EPA may result in a loss of industrial competitiveness and employment opportunities, as well as cuts in tariff levels leading to revenue losses. Such a development compromises government efforts to improve the economic empowerment programmes, policies and initiatives that currently underpin the country's industrialisation and agriculturalisation processes. The economy may continue to fail to attract international capital in the form of foreign investors and funding from GFIs and foreign governments due largely to the political fault lines and contradictory economic policies.

Furthermore, by negotiating trade-related issues such as protecting infant industries, government procurement, intellectual property rights and competition policy, Zimbabwe is likely to lose its options in this regard. According to the ESA-EU Report (2011), Zimbabwe requires urgent technical assistance and capacity-building support in the area of competition policy and sanitary and phytosanitary issues with respect to live animals, beef products, cut flowers and vegetables (mange tout peas, peas and beans), tobacco, sugar and cotton. This not only inhibits efforts towards building sectoral and industrial capacity, but also limits the market competitiveness of local products and efforts to enter fast-growing markets such as those of the emerging economies of China, India, and Brazil. Had the bilateral relationship between the negotiating parties been good, specific components of trade-related assistance, especially strengthening tax collection and the tax administration system, particularly where revenue shortfalls due to a reduction in tariffs are expected to be high, might have come well before the implementation of iEPA's trade liberalisation.

The EPA outcomes are unlikely to create viable economic activities given limited market information coupled with challenges related to industrial diversification and competitive initiatives, which Zimbabwe does not have the technological capacity to control. The risk is therefore high that the country will rely too heavily on the EU market, even though opportunities in other thriving regions such as the BRICS[151] become available. The Eurozone crisis has dampened the spirit of entrepreneurs who fear that a new trade regime is set to undermine short to medium term economic recovery. The crisis has also dampened the spirit of negotiators, who fear that the proposed trade regime with Europe has the potential to lock the Zimbabwean

---

[151] Brazil, Russia, India, China and South Africa

economy into an unhealthy trade imbalance for decades to come and may not necessarily lead to economic and social development benefits for the country. Even government officials view the EPA process and its expected outcome as an 'economic onslaught' on the local economy. Some civil society activists view EPA as an 'ideological economic onslaught' on the Zimbabwean economy, whose external debt is growing fast while the country's ability to generate foreign currency is dwindling at the same rate.

The economic meltdown translated into a narrow, undiversified and low value industrial and export base. This leads to a situation of vulnerability with respect to regional, Eurozone and global market competitors. It also translates into serious constraints on the capacity to generate foreign currency, as predicted by a UNECA (2005) study which concluded that the impacts of an EPA on Zimbabwe would be an estimated revenue shortfall of US$18.4 million. This is confirmed by the fact that, since 2000, Zimbabwe has failed to diversify from traditional to non-traditional exports, and also from the traditional, and now shrinking, dominant Eurozone market to fast-growing new markets in the emerging economies. Tadeus Chifamba (interview in Harare, Zimbabwe, 14 September 2012) remarks: "the Eurozone crisis has vindicated the voice that argued against joining the EPA process, preferring to vigorously promote the 'look east' policy." Following a massive fall in the country's industrial capacity utilisation to less than 10% in 2008 (Nyakazeya, 2009), the divided 'inclusive' government - often referred to as dysfunctional - failed to unlock the necessary external resources from western foreign governments and GFIs. It also failed to mobilise domestic and foreign investors to revitalise and recapitalise industrial production processes. This means that the economy is highly unlikely to build or improve industrial capacity to diversify production and exports in the short to medium term, or to promote labour-intensive industries in the manufacturing sector and in other related downstream industrial activities. Further, trade barriers and other cross-border transaction costs (on account of the failure to access the blocked 10th EDF resources promised during the start of the negotiations specifically for this purpose) continue to rise, thereby undermining any feasible potential to manufacture exportable goods.

The above does not augur well for an economy that still has extremely high levels of unemployment, which is currently estimated at over 90% of the total labour force.

Since the launch of the joint ESA-EU EPA roadmap in February 2004, both parties to the EPA negotiations have been aware of Zimbabwe's economic and political challenges. Since then, the country has been experiencing shrinking industrial production and productivity as well as falling export competitiveness. Following massive withdrawals of investors (both domestic and foreign), an unorthodox nationalistic and populist economic reorganisation policy agenda epitomised by 'radicalised land reform' (Moyo and Yeros, 2007), domestic political contestation and polarisation and isolation from the international community, including the EU, the economy has recorded massive de-industrialisation and de-agriculturalisation that by 2008 culminated in less than 10% industrial capacity utilisation and the worst hyper-inflationary environment in the world. All the sectors of the economy are struggling to improve levels of production and capacity utilisation after the ratification of the iEPA in 2012.

Emerging concerns and implications for the future: supply-side constraints

The United Nations Economic and Social Council (2004) argues that countries derive greater benefit from increases in market access if they build competitive enterprises that are able to produce products and services at reasonable cost structures. This entails combining measures that enhance productive capacity with measures that facilitate cross-border trade, thereby further reducing the cost of conducting trade. It also entails reducing supply-side constraints that prevent an economy from exploiting its comparative advantage under any trade liberalisation arrangement. In this respect, prevailing supply-side bottlenecks mean that the production processes in an economy are unable to keep pace with rising domestic or external demands, and this makes both products and services uncompetitive. Subbarao (2012) attributes the supply-side constraints to a variety of factors, including inadequate air, rail and road infrastructure, lack of credit and low-cost access to reliable market information, and non-availability of a skilled labour force and technology.

Many African countries continue to experience poor trade performance on account of high supply-side constraints (Hodge, 2002). Locally produced commodities cannot compete favourably in domestic, EU, and other global markets. They continue to suffer from a high presence of supply-side bottlenecks, which some scholars and civil society activists blame for limiting the capacity of most ACP countries to maximise trade flows under the EBA dispensation of (DFQF) non-reciprocal market access in the EU. Furthermore, these supply-side constraints were largely neglected by the development instruments of the Lomé Conventions, and so the countries failed to exploit the potential and promised benefits from the EU trade preferences. This is further supported by the Cotonou Monitoring Group of European Development NGOs' networks (2002) seminar discussions, which observed that 'the experience under the Lomé Convention has demonstrated that ACP countries face major problems in producing and supplying goods competitively within an increasingly liberalised trading environment'. Kohnert (2008) blames the EU for failing to deliver the promised development programmes and packages meant to redress supply-side constraints in order to even the trading playing field. Kamidza (2007; 2008) identifies the following as key supply-bottlenecks, which are present in most ACP countries, including Zimbabwe:

> ... unreliable public utilities (electricity and water); poor public infrastructure (run down roads, bridges and railways); weak institutional policy frameworks (fluctuating exchange rates, high inflation rates and poor fiscal measures); low labour productivity (arising from poor education, health and housing provisions); and an unfavourable investment climate, coupled with inadequate resources to foster socio-economic transformation (Kamidza, 2007: 8; Kamidza, 2008: 17).

Meyn (2005) observes that redressing the above supply-side bottlenecks is a crucial step towards improving the country's export capacity. This is supported by constituencies, including some radical

CSOs who have persistently been calling for pro-development EPA outcomes within the broader anti-EPAs campaign under the leadership of the ATN, based in Accra. At numerous meetings of the ESA processes and CSO lobbying missions to the EU institutions and structures have continuously raised the need for the EU to honour its promise of delivering the 'development aid envelope' through which supply-side improvements could be financed. However, there is currently no tangible evidence that any country has been able to access the EU resources meant to redress supply-side constraints. Most ACP economies are under stress due to these widespread supply-side bottlenecks.

Zimbabwe has struggled to maximise trade related benefits under the Lomé Conventions trade arrangement dispensation. The Cotonou Monitoring Group of European Development NGOs' networks (Ibid) argues that Zimbabwe's shortage of skilled labour has obliged the clothing and textile industry to apply technologies that are about four generations behind those used in developed economies, including the East Asian 'tiger' economies.

Over this period, the EU's Trade Development and Political Cooperation policy has worsened Zimbabwe's fragility and vulnerability. The decision made by all three political structures of the EU in 2002 to deny the government access to the 10th EDF development aid resources and the imposition of smart sanctions on ZANU (PF) ruling elites and associated companies that was supported by other western governments and GFIs negatively impacted the economy in general, and the ability to improve supply-side constraints in particular. Thus, the call to improve the supply-side bottlenecks that has featured in several joint ESA-EU trade negotiations, under the 'standing agenda of developmental aid envelope' is meaningless, with no evidence of EU remorse for 'political misjudgment' on the EPA win-win outcome objective. For Zimbabwe, the EPA process embodies the 'EU's predatory onslaught on the economy in the short to medium term'.

Supply-side constraints (see table below) could not and are unlikely to be prioritised, largely due to limited fiscal resources and continued evidence of contradictions within the GNU with regard to policy directives, especially concerning farm invasions and indigenisation. This is aggravated by non-committal to GPA provisions, thereby fueling political tensions between belligerent political parties and mistrust between the government and NSAs. Furthermore, the post-31 July Mugabe administration continue to experience fiscal resources limitation and access to eternal funding support that is necessary to improve supply-side bottlenecks in the economy. Meanwhile, since 2000, the country has experienced frequent power shortages that not only hold back manufacturing productivity and exports, but also discourage start-up industries, especially those SMEs which might have been able to compete with EU products. The CZI (2012) complained about the poor service provided by the Zimbabwe Electricity Supply Authority and the frequent power outages due to many years of under-investment, underpricing of electricity, poor management and an absence of workable legal and regulatory frameworks for private sector investment.

Furthermore, Zimbabwe continues to suffer from a weak regulatory environment, particularly for utilities, resulting in high production costs for firms, thereby eroding the competitiveness of export products. The physical infrastructure is poor, with a lack of efficient and reliable transport networks and facilities which limits the flow of goods between Zimbabwe and the EU, and other regional economies and countries. Supply-side constraints, especially the high cost of transport and infrastructure (roads, ports, border facilities and railways) which currently constitute the greatest portion of marketing costs not only in the SADC region but also in European markets, if not addressed soon, will undermine the competitiveness of Zimbabwean products in the local as well as other markets, particularly the EU. The country also continues to suffer from trade-related transport costs associated with border controls and procedures, storage and market facilities, the telecommunication system and facilities and utilities (power and water). In particular, the country's fixed-line telephone services are limited and unreliable, with notoriously high call charges while the establishment and/or operation of modern communication systems is constrained by lack of skills and capital investment. This has further been compromised by a failure to meet international quality standards, lack of information on available market openings, limited competitiveness of local industries and the lack of an entrepreneurial culture. All these factors are critical for the Zimbabwean economy, particularly with regard to agricultural growth and development, agro-processing and manufacturing. As a result of these supply-side bottlenecks, Zimbabwe has lost any competitiveness that it might have once had, both in the region and internationally (Mushowe, 2012).

Table 5.5 Zimbabwe's main supply-side constraints

Antiquated equipment, machinery and technology which hampers efficiency in production as well as demands frequent maintenance.
High input cost, resulting in: o   overall high cost of production for most goods relative to the EU and regional countries. o   cost production structures with variables that ordinarily would be excluded in a normal sound economy.
Low agricultural and mining output resulting in high importation of raw materials which are no longer available locally thereby choking the supply to the agro-mining based supply chain.
Low industrial capacity utilisation.
Physical infrastructure (roads and railways) in need of urgent repair and upgrade, especially the unreliable national railway of Zimbabwe, a bulk carrier of industrial goods, and increasingly expensive road transport.
Skills flight due to massive brain-drain, especially from 2000 to 2008, which contributed to shortages of skilled labour, and/or poor workmanship.
Tight liquidity conditions, characterised by lack of long term funding and supplier credit, hence a huge bearing on competitiveness.
Uncompetitive, expensive and often limited options procurement system.
Unfavourable investment climate fueled by political tension and policy contradictions.
Unreliable and costly utilities (water and electricity), in need of urgent revamp and upgrade.
Wage pressures unrelated to productivity.
Weak institutional policy frameworks (fluctuating exchange rates, high inflation rates and poor fiscal measures).

Source: Adapted from Mushowe (2012) and other sources

While ZANU (PF) received significant sympathy from emerging countries such as Russia and China - a development that gave rise to the 'look east policy', it is yet to translate into significant improvements in supply-side constraints. Zimbabwe's more than decade-long relationship with China, whose commodity-exchange financing model with respect to physical infrastructural development, should have resulted in much improved existing supply-side constraints. This would have enabled the country to supply products to both local and EU markets. Yet little of any concrete value has emerged.

Because of the political polarisation in Zimbabwe, the previous ZANU (PF) government lacked the capacity to mobilise investment resources. This was worsened by the imposition of smart sanctions against the ZANU (PF) leadership and associated firms, which fueled the political divide in the country. The GNU administration also failed to unlock external resources from the international community, including western governments and GFIs, or to lure MCs, TNCs and other foreign investors to support the country's economic transformation, especially industrial recapitalisation across all sectors of the economy. Access to external resources would not only have rejuvenated the economy, but also provided options for financing supply-side constraints, especially the provision of electricity and water. Further, the current ZANU (PF) is struggling to attract domestic, regional and foreign investors as well as GFIs' resources to rejuvenate the country's industrial and export capabilities.

Emerging concerns and implications for the future: disruptions of national and regional markets

Unlike the Lomé Conventions and the Cotonou Agreement in which the EU treated the ACP countries as a single region, the EPA negotiations split them into six configurations[152]. Europe engineered this disintegration by dangling a 'developmental aid purse', available (in theory) to those countries that were ready to enter into non-

---

[152] The six configurations are (Pacific) PACP, (Caribbean) CARIFORUM, (West Africa) ECOWAS, (eastern and southern Africa) ESA, (Central Africa) CEMAC and (southern Africa) SADC EPA.

reciprocal EPA negotiations. While the Pacific and Caribbean each have a configuration, the African countries were bundled into four small, weak, vulnerable and fragmented configurations. The four African groups often had no historical cultural, social, economic and political links between them, as is the case with the ESA, whereas the EU is substantially enlarged from 15 by 30 April 2004[153] to current powerful, united, 27 member region. The dangling of a 'developmental aid envelope' ensures EC control not only of its negotiating counterparts, but also the agenda and process, leading to an outcome that is likely to promote and entrench Europe's commercial interests in the sub-region. Yash Tandon explains the EU's 'divide-and-rule tactics,' aimed at controlling the agenda, process and outcome:

> We are aware of well-documented threats the EU has made in the past, including withdrawing development aid, existing trade, aid and investments, contracts and budgetary support; interfering with national and regional security policies; re-imposing trade barriers; and removing ambassadorial representations from WTO and ACP-EU headquarters where key events take place (Tandon, 2004: 3).

The sub-regions of eastern and southern Africa highlight the divisive character of the EPA process, as reflected in the figure below, which shows the multiple memberships of countries in the region. It also confirms that the EPA process has created another layer of regional integration with its own programme of action (structured and systematic negotiation rounds), and time-lines for tariff liberalisation scheduling and commitments. Only Angola and Mozambique belong to one regional integration scheme (SADC) in addition to belonging to the SADC EPA configuration.

---

[153] The EU prior to 1 May 2004 accession of ten countries comprised of Austria, Belgium, Denmark, Finland, France, Germany, Greece, Ireland, Italy, Luxembourg, Netherlands, Portugal, Spain, Sweden and United Kingdom.

Figure 5.1 RECs and EPA groups in eastern and southern Africa[154]

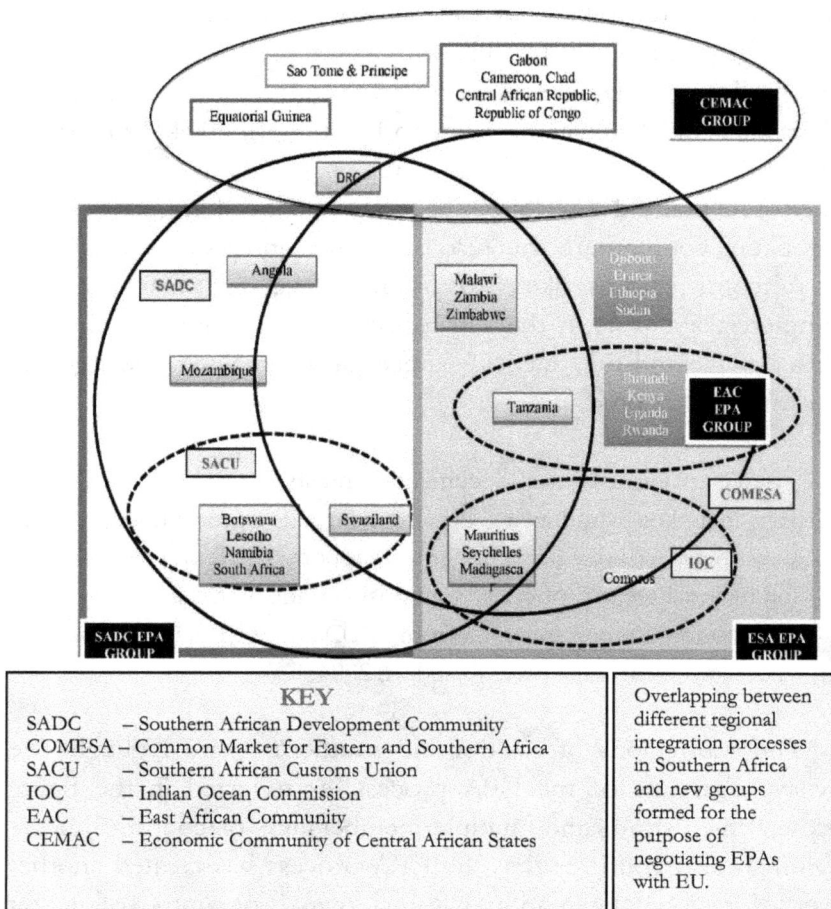

KEY	
SADC	– Southern African Development Community
COMESA	– Common Market for Eastern and Southern Africa
SACU	– Southern African Customs Union
IOC	– Indian Ocean Commission
EAC	– East African Community
CEMAC	– Economic Community of Central African States

Overlapping between different regional integration processes in Southern Africa and new groups formed for the purpose of negotiating EPAs with EU.

Source: Author compilation from various sources

The diagram above demonstrates that EU negotiators, by supporting various EPA configurations in full knowledge of the overlapping memberships in the sub-region, have been controlling the process in order to indirectly force countries to comply with

---

[154] The EU and EU member states have been the main funders of RECs in eastern and southern Africa since their respective formations. The EU is the sole funder of the EPA negotiation process in ACP countries.

Europe's commercial interests[155]. It also demonstrates that the process ignores the fact that Zimbabwe is a party to bilateral and regional trade agreements (SADC and COMESA), which overlap in terms of trading partners but may differ in product coverage and regulatory stringency including with respect to rules of origin. EU-Republic of Zimbabwe Report (2015) notes that not only does Zimbabwe have bilateral trade agreements with Botswana, DRC, Malawi, Mozambique, Namibia and South Africa, but also that the simple average tariff rates for Zimbabwe's preferential partners range from 0.2% (SADC excluding South Africa) to 11.4% (South Africa). This demonstrates that the process supports the capitalist agenda of carving up the markets for European investors, producers and exporters, especially in vulnerable countries like Zimbabwe. As a result, the EPA process and outcome has compromised the impetus, direction and time-frames for deeper regional integration, the basis through which these countries are to increasingly become integrated into the EU market and the global economy in line with EPA objectives. Furthermore, the EPA process and outcome has compromised sub-regional political leadership support for existing regional integration initiatives established by treaties and supported by various protocols, Memorandum of Understandings, and the Heads of State and Governments' Summit Communiqué. This is illustrated in the EU and SADC secretariat's commissioned study of 2012 that developed a 'Trade Facility' with two separate financial support windows for the SADC EPA countries and those in other configurations (EAC[156], ESA[157] and CEMAC[158]). While the goal is to fast track the implementation of the EPA agreement provisions, such a development will directly or indirectly disrupt both regional and national markets. Indeed, new developments point to the fact that the process and outcomes also cause disruptions in national and regional markets, mainly on account of tariff liberalisation scheduling

---

[155] The disintegration of the ACP regional bloc into four configurations, and of ESA configurations into two groups (EAC and reconfigured ESA) was engineered by Europe's dangling of a 'developmental aid purse' – the EDF resources, as argued elsewhere in the thesis.

[156] Tanzania.

[157] Madagascar, Mauritius, Malawi, Seychelles, Zambia and Zimbabwe.

[158] DRC.

and commitments that are different from those currently obtaining in sub-regional RECs (See Table 5.6 below). For Zimbabwe, this poses challenges with respect to prioritising iEPA implementation and the goals of on-going regional integration, and the ability to generate fiscal revenues without any derogation, as was the case under the SADC FTA.

The EPA processes, as reflected by the iEPA outcomes, totally disregarded the provisions of existing regional economic integration initiatives in terms of tariff liberalisation (tariff phase-down), agreed integrative milestones and resource mobilisation strategies. Bilal and Rampa (2006) argue that the EPA process may derail regional integration by imposing too fast a pace and overstretching the capacity of some regions and creating tensions because of the overlapping memberships. In this respect, the process produces two outcomes that have a direct bearing on existing regional integration goals in the sub-region. Firstly, it compounds the multiplicity of overlapping regional memberships by creating yet another bloc that has not only been meeting more often but is also committed to different tariff schedules. The EPA bloc already has a financing window aimed at ensuring quick implementation of agreed EPA provisions. Secondly, the process has undermined the allegiance of member states to existing regional schemes, since the choice to participate in a configuration has largely been a sovereign decision based on future trade ambitions with the EU. In this case, some member states of the SADC region - such as Madagascar, Mauritius, Malawi, Seychelles, Tanzania, Zambia, and Zimbabwe - preferred the ESA group, while the DRC opted for CEMAC. Some of these countries, including Malawi, Tanzania, Zambia, and Zimbabwe, are original members of the SADC. The table below reveals individual ESA countries' tariff liberalisation scheduling and commitments, alongside those of the EAC and SACU[159] region

---

[159] In this respect, the SACU refers only to those member states (BLS) that had signed iEPA before the configuration with the EU agreed to set aside the ratification process while negotiations for a comprehensive EPA continue.

Table 5.6 iEPA tariff liberalisation schedule and commitment[160], percentages

Country	2008	2010	2012	2013	2017	2018	2022	2023	2033	Total
EAC[161]		64.0						80.0	82.0	82.0
Madagascar				37.0			80.7			80.7
Mauritius	24.5				53.6		95.6			95.6
Seychelles				62.0	77.0		97.5			97.5
Zimbabwe			45.0				80.0			80.0
BLS[162]		86.0								86.0
Mozambique	78.5									80.5

Source: Author's compilation from various sources

While some SADC member states opt for mid- or back-loading tariff liberalisation under the SADC FTA, the negotiators under the iEPA appeared to have succumbed to the EU guerrilla negotiating strategies, tactics, and divisive agendas by front-loading their respective commitments. For instance, both Mozambique and Zimbabwe, which back-loaded their respective tariff phases under the SADC FTA, agreed under the iEPA to open their respective economies to EU products by 78.5% and 45% respectively. These outcomes are an affront to the objective of deepening existing regional integration schemes in the sub-region. In particular, sub-regional RECs have, through the financial support of the EU and other development partners, developed regional integration milestones with a strict roadmap to follow. However, the implementation of the EPA outcomes is set to disrupt these milestones, resulting in disruptions of regional and national markets due to potential flooding of EU products into the sub-region. The porous borders in the region mean that imported EU products end up in non-EPA implementing countries, thus negating economic

---

[160] Cumulative value of imports from the EU to be liberalised by specified year.

[161] EAC countries sign as a bloc, so this is a proxy of Tanzania.

[162] Botswana, Lesotho and Swaziland.

integration among ACP economies, and between ACP countries and the global economy.

The EU's 'divide-and-conquer strategies and tactics' cited by Tandon (2004), aimed at controlling the EPA agenda, processes and outcomes, are reflected in the division of the ESA group into two parts by the end of December 2007. Bundling the ESA countries into two configurations in this way means that these countries have to comply with tariff reduction schedule commitments, rules of origin[163], and other liberalisation requirements that are different from each other when previously they were working together to secure a beneficial trade regime with Europe. The reconfigured ESA group shown in the map below clearly illustrates that the countries' economic units and citizens have no historical cultural, social, economic or political ties, giving the impression of three distinct groups agreeing to continue the negotiations as a unit vis-à-vis the united and enlarged EU bloc. The three distinct groups are IGAD, IOC and the former Federation of Rhodesia and Nyasaland[164] countries. As a result, the EU guerrilla onslaught focused on securing individual deals with island economies[165] and Zimbabwe, while the rest continue to trade under the EBA regime since they are LDCs. The map further flags potential challenges since the EPA's goal is to support regional integration within the configuration. The map confirms that the EPA process has the potential to disrupt regional and national markets and dispels any notion of 'regional integration within the configuration' on the basis that the trade and development trajectories of the 'newly configured economies' suffer from a lack of well-developed social, economic, and political ties or relationships. There are currently insignificant trade flows between southern African countries and those in the Horn of Africa. There are also no common borders between the southern African group of countries and those in the Horn of Africa and the IOC. The above rejects the

---

[163] Rules of origin are legal procedures that track the origin of products in order to prevent third countries from taking advantage of any new trade agreement. In this respect, EPA offers Zimbabwe flexible rules of origin or regulatory rate that measure preferences on the basis of tariffs only, and the associated cumulation with other configuration economies as well as with other EPA signatory states.

[164] Malawi, Zambia and Zimbabwe.

[165] Madagascar, Mauritius and Seychelles.

notion that the implementation of an EPA regime promote regional economic integration within the configuration.

Map 5.1   Configuration mapping of eastern and southern African counties

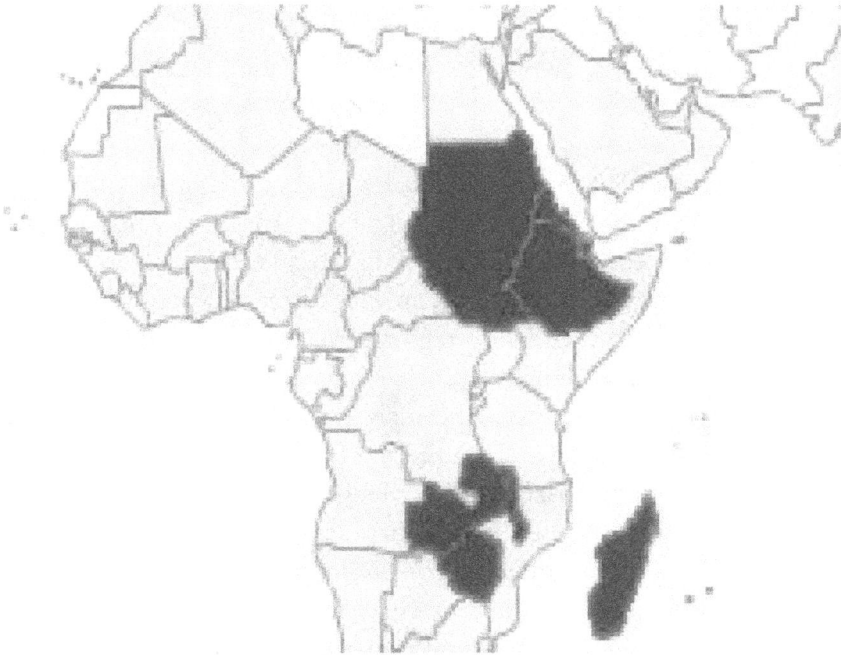

Source: http://ec.europa.eu/trade/policy/countries-and-regions/regions/esa/

However, Zimbabwe under the SADC FTA successfully negotiated trade concessions that are explicit with regard to industrial development, export capacity building and fiscal revenue flows for the limping economy. They include the following:

Securing a derogation, allowing the country to push compliance on agreed FTA tariff phase-downs towards the end of the cycle by substantially mid- and back-loading tariff reductions; that is, postponing tariff reductions towards the final years of FTA implementation. This contradicts the iEPA tariff liberalisation phase-down in which the country significantly front-loaded tariff reductions by 45%.

Securing the space to generate about 70% of the country's revenue from customs taxes as well as having space to resist any significant scaling down of tariff walls under the FTA on account of wanting to sustain fiscal revenue flows to support growing national needs without censoring from other regional countries.

Having the space to resist pressure under the SADC TNF to remove the new surtax imposed by the GNU on some regional products that should be at zero tariffs without censoring from other regional member states.

Under the EPA process, Zimbabwe risks losing most of the gains secured under the SADC FTA, while the iEPA risks becoming an affront to the leadership objective of the regional countries, which is to assist the economic transition process through derogation on tariff phase-down in line with the regional mandate of mediating in the political conflict in Zimbabwe.

The fact that the EU - the main donor of regional integration projects in the eastern and southern African sub-regions - agreed to different trade liberalisation scheduling and commitments, illustrates the superiority of its guerrilla negotiating tactics and its control of the process. Most importantly, by concluding and signing an iEPA with Zimbabwe - a staunch critic at every international public platform including the UN Assembly and the ACP-EU meetings - vindicates the predatory nature of the capitalist bloc in scoring victories in this process.

Firstly, the EU succeeded in isolating Zimbabwe's EPA negotiating machinery (team of negotiators, officials and other stakeholders) from the rest of the ESA countries' representatives, who were/are more concerned about the group's cohesion in the process than entertaining any EU-Zimbabwe bilateral fights.

Secondly, the EU succeeded in securing a trade regime with a sworn adversary whose economic productive and export capacity is too weak to withstand the wholesale entry of European products into the local market. Zimbabwe's economic export capacity is too weak to penetrate the European market. The Zimbabwean manufacturing sector is very small, narrow, and weak, and certainly not in any position to compete with EU products in the short to medium term, a situation that favours the EU's MCs, TNCs and other operators, producers and exporters.

Thirdly, the developments that resulted in the ratification of the iEPA signified the defeat of ZANU (PF)'s anti-colonial agenda, since the new economic entrepreneurs, especially in the agriculture sector, will be competing with the EU in the market according to the forces of demand and supply.

Fourthly, the forces of demand and supply are set to provide the EU with an opportunity to punish ZANU (PF) leadership for its unorthodox method of reclaiming land rights[166] from white commercial farmers and insisting on a 51% shareholding in companies and other equities. In particular, Zimbabwe's chief negotiators and officials seem to have underestimated the strength of the EU's cohesive and defensive economic interests in its relations with Zimbabwe. They also underestimated the influence of former coloniser, the United Kingdom's, commercial presence in the country across all sectors of the economy, particularly in agriculture, manufacturing, mining, and finance. They also underestimated the grievances of some EU member states, such as the Netherlands, Germany and Switzerland, whose bilateral investment promotion and protection treaties[167] were violated by the ZANU (PF) government in its crusade against foreign control and ownership of the means of production, particularly in the agricultural sector.

Fifthly, the developments and outcomes clearly show that the revolutionary credentials of ZANU (PF), while succeeding in defeating imperialist control and ownership of the means of production, were found wanting in the negotiating room, where strategies and tactics became increasingly subtle with short to medium term impacts. In

---

[166] ZANU (PF) leadership, from the onset of the fast-track land reform, advanced the thesis that the land occupied by white commercial farmers was taken by force during the colonial era, and therefore they were simply reclaiming it back, hence only improvements made on it should be compensated.

[167] Dutch, German and Swiss nationals' ex-commercial farmers successfully sued Mugabe government at the International Centre for the Settlement of Investment Disputes in respect to land which was violently and forcibly acquired during the land revolution notwithstanding the existence of Bilateral Investment Promotion and Protection Agreements (Magaisa, June 2016).

particular, the EPA negotiation outcome exposes state shortcomings in mobilising all the relevant stakeholders regardless of their known views about partisan economic programmes, and being fully aware of the resourcefulness of the negotiating partner.

The economy, in the short to medium term, will be swamped with EU products resulting in uncompetitive entrepreneurs fleeing the domestic market. There is no significant immediate prospect of trade creation with respect to the Zimbabwean economy. This development sustains current levels of de-industrialisation, as was the case in the mid-1990s when South African products wiped out much of Zimbabwe's industry. Local products will not be competitive in the EU market. Assuming full return to political normalcy with good governance, democratic values and respect of property rights, former commercial farm owners and EU nationals and investors including MCs and TNCs will be among the first buyers.

A TRADES Centre (2002) study, based on the assumption that all tariffs on imports from the EU will be eliminated by 2020, reveals that most countries in the SADC region are set to incur substantial revenue losses as shown in the table below. The implications for the regional and national economies cannot be ignored. Significant cumulative revenue losses of about 49.5%, 37.7%, 33.2%, 28.0% and 24.1% are expected in Mauritius, Tanzania, Zimbabwe, Mozambique and Namibia respectively which will have a ripple effect on their national markets (Kamidza, 2007; Bilal and Szepesi, 2003). For Zimbabwe, a loss of 33% will lead to significant limitations in terms of redressing short to long term industrial and export capacities and market competitiveness. It also translates into limited social services delivery (health care, education, housing, and water), limited infrastructural development, agricultural research and development, human resource development, poverty alleviation and the living conditions of citizens. Unfortunately, such a development not only guarantees European products and services easy access to the Zimbabwean market for a longer period, but also disrupts market forces of demand and supply.

Table 5.7 Tariff revenue losses as percentages of total import revenues

Country	T<50 per cent in 2012	T<50 per cent in 2016	T<50 per cent in 2020	Total Loss
Botswana	1.9	2.7	3.1	7.7
Malawi	4.2	5.9	6.8	16.9
Mauritius	9.9	13.8	15.8	39.5
Mozambique	7.0	9.8	11.2	28.0
Namibia	6.0	8.4	9.6	24.1
South Africa	2.6	3.6	4.1	10.3
Swaziland	2.5	3.5	4.0	10.0
Tanzania	9.4	13.2	15.1	37.7
Zimbabwe	8.3	11.6	13.3	33.2

Source: Kamidza, 2007 (also adapted from Bilal and Szepesi, 2003)

Conclusion

This chapter explored the relationship between COMESA and the SADC EPA units, the drivers of the EPA process and regional CSOs, showing the opportunities exploited and the challenges that persisted throughout the process to the extent of compromising civil society's input. It showed how the CSOs lobbied the three EU political structures and related institutions but omitted to do the same with respect to the COMESA and SADC secretariats, as seen in the snubbing of civil society-organised dedicated dialogue sessions by the respective EPA units' CTAs. The CSOs' failure to systematically lobby and engage with Zimbabwean authorities in terms of mobilising all the available opinions while raising awareness of the counterpart's capacity and manipulative abilities in the process, was also discussed.

The chapter further explored the state-CSOs relationship in the context of the historical fault lines that continue to fuel mistrust and lack of cooperation between the two parties, leading to the government excluding civil society organisations or representatives considered too radical and opposed to its views on the economy, including the EPA process. The chapter further explored the political dynamics and landscape over this period which made it impossible for the state to consult and involve civil society groups considered critical of the former ZANU (PF) government or the ZANU (PF) party's economic empowerment programmes and policies, including the EPA negotiations. The exclusion of some CSOs reflects a lack of transparency and inclusive involvement in the EPA process. This also raises questions about the partisan selection or identification criteria of the trade and development-focused CSOs who participated in the process, which undermines the possibility of formulating and developing negotiating issues, interests, positions and offers in the cultural context of co-existence and diversity of opinion. As a result, the EU was able to exploit the Zimbabwean state shortcomings in its dealings with the prevailing economic environment and the political discourse in the country.

Donors have not systematically or consistently funded the CSOs' activities, including advocacy in the process, and this has hampered their expected impact. Conversely, the same donors - including the EU through its 10th EDF resource window - have been supporting democracy, governance and human rights programmes, thereby fueling the friction between the former ZANU (PF) government and some sections of civil society. In this respect, CSOs such as LEDRIZ and ZIMCODD, although working on EPAs, are known to be ideologically close to the MDC party, which is perceived by ZANU (PF) as a strong ally of the EU that imposed 'smart sanctions and travel bans' on the leadership, as well as refusing any interaction outside ESA meetings – the point of direct contact between the EU and Zimbabwean authorities. This also prevented interested citizens, especially research analysts and students, from occasionally interacting with government officials about the process.

The discussion explored emerging real and potential fears, implications and policy options from the unfolding process, demonstrating the challenges likely to undermine the sale of Zimbabwean products in both local and EU markets. The iEPA (or full EPA) is likely to impact negatively on the implementation of trade and industrial policies, the ability of the country to improve industrial production and export competitiveness, the capacity of the economy to redress supply-side constraints and the capacity of the economy to minimise the impact of disruptions in national markets.

Chapter Six

Bilateral Re-Engagement and Interim EPA Implementation

Introduction and context of re-engagement

ZANU (PF)'s landslide victory in the harmonised (parliamentary and presidential) election of 31 July 2013 was endorsed by the AU, COMESA, SADC, and the United Nations. This not only resulted in the party's comprehensive recapture of the state, but also confirmed its grip on power (Chatham House Report, 2014). But western donors and governments (Australia, Canada, the EU and the United States of America) in particular expressed deep concerns about the credibility of the polls and the general lack of pluralistic democratic values, partisan application of the rule of law, and bad record of human rights. Thus, they resolved to maintain the isolation of ZANU (PF)'s leadership and associated companies. The above contentious issues forestalled any chance of Zimbabwe re-engaging with the international community at a time when the economy not only needed external resources in the form of FDIs, GFIs concessionary loans and donor grants, but was also desperately in need of regional and domestic investment.

Though the GNU Administration stabilised the economy, there was no real economic growth because the impressive figures did not translate into any substantial increase in human development indicators or employment (Chatham House Report, 2014). The macroeconomic policy environment was lacking certainty and predictability on account of public contradictions among government officials. There was no consensus within government, and between government and other key stakeholders on macroeconomic policy, and on how to unlock donor and GFIs resources and attract domestic, regional and foreign investors. In particular, lack of consensus within the GNU had frustrated every effort towards re-engaging the EU and other western governments which would have ended more than seventeen years of political crisis

(Chatham House Report, 2014). Furthermore, the political parties in the GNU failed to resume dialogue with the western governments with a view to eventually normalise economic ties, particularly with the EU – the world's largest importer and exporter of goods and services. As a result, the economy continued to struggle to unlock much-needed external financial and technical resources. Mutsaka (2010) presents undisputed reasons why the inclusive government failed to re-engage the EU. Firstly, ZANU (PF's) insistent demand that targeted sanctions, imposed in 2002, be lifted, despite its failure to commit to furthering the implementation of GPA reform measures. This hardened the attitude of the EU and its member states, displeased with the lack of pluralistic democratic and governance reforms, legal, media and electoral reforms, and respect for human and property rights. This was publicly expressed on several occasions. In particular, they accused ZANU (PF) anti-reformists of slowing down the reform process, including those agreed by the GPA. Secondly, Robert Mugabe's deep mistrust of the European bloc and its allies. Thirdly, ZANU (PF) leadership's suspicions about the EU's perceived preference of the MDC formations and their decade-long demands, while not fully engaging them on the issue of sanctions. Fourthly, discord within the all-party delegation during meetings with European representatives. Lastly, the attitude of the EU hardened the stance of former ruling party officials who insisted on 'no further GPA reforms' without the removal of imposed sanctions.

In order to resolve the daunting and insurmountable economic challenges confronting the post-GNU government there is urgent need for cooperation with other key local and foreign stakeholders, and equally urgent re-engagement with the western governments and donors, notwithstanding their disapproval of the government's macroeconomic programmes, lack of democratic, governance and electoral malpractices, and its bad record on human and property rights. The Chatham House Report (2014) argues that the government's macroeconomic policy options are increasingly restricted by a liquidity crisis in an externally determined monetary policy[168] environment. An EU-Republic of Zimbabwe Report (2015) concurs that the economy still struggles to improve productive output, largely due to relatively high production costs; use of old plants and equipment; unreliable supplies of raw materials and other related inputs into the production process; and exorbitant tariffs for key utilities (electricity, water, fuel and coal). Zimbabwean firms have high production costs which erode the competitiveness of export products as well as the high cost of transport and logistical infrastructures (roads, ports, border facilities and railways) which currently constitute the greatest portion of marketing costs not only in the COMESA and SADC regions, but also in the European markets. The economy suffers from limited access to and high costs of industrial related financing capital, as summarised in the box below. This undermines the role of trade as the engine for sustainable economic growth and development. Increased trade volumes would stimulate the productive sectors of the economy towards higher productivity, efficiency, and international competitiveness. The high cost of finance capital and its limited circulation in the economy not only undermines the development of high-tech, innovative industries, value chains and anti-competitive domestic markets, but also iEPA's potential competitiveness against Zimbabwean products in both the local and the EU markets.

Since its election victory the ZANU (PF) government has stopped blaming the EU and other western nations for the country's continued economic underperformance, signaling a softening of approach on its part. This also indicates government's intention to upgrade its portfolio of international economic relations, not only by accelerating collaboration with the World Bank, the IMF, the AfDB, the Paris Club and other international financial institutions, but also by re-engaging western governments, especially the EU, which is the second largest trading partner after South Africa. Pilling and England (2016) posit that successful talks between ZANU (PF) and multilateral institutions (AfDB, IMF and the World Bank) would not only enable Zimbabwe to clear nearly US$1.9 billion of debt in arrears, but also access international funding, which is a prerequisite

---

[168] Since the adoption of the multi-currency system in 2009, the country ceded monetary policy to international actors.

for the revival of the economy, thereby ending fifteen years of exclusion from global lending financial windows.

Box 6.1	Inadequate and costly capital for the financing of exports, investment or other links with foreign firms

Lack of access to sufficient capital to initiate and sustain international business activities

Problems in obtaining credit due to banking inefficiencies and reluctance (especially in the case of credit applications by small businesses)

High cost of credit

Problems in understanding the different international payments procedures and general problems in obtaining payment for goods and services

Complexity of financial requirements

Higher cost of doing international business because of the additional expenses incurred by foreign tariffs, transportation and shipping, promotion and marketing, insurance etc. which are combined with normal operating expenses

Source: EU-Republic of Zimbabwe Report (2015)

The government is under pressure to adopt policies that will build international business confidence, support technocratic and entrepreneurial expertise at home, and encourage domestic governance, economic reforms and pro-poor policies. The government is also under pressure to improve its record on pluralistic democratic values, political and economic governance, human and property tights, rule of law and electoral legitimacy. Furthermore, there has been pressure from the continent and the EU bloc for sustained re-engagement with the ZANU (PF) government with a view to restoring economic and political relations between Brussels and Harare. European analysis described re-engagement policy as the 'best possible way forward,' notwithstanding widespread criticism of continued human rights abuse, partial application of the rule of law and concerns about investment security issues (Mananavire, 2015). This is further supported by Bell (2014), who argues that the Brussels-based Antwerp World Diamond Council relentlessly lobbied the EU for the removal of targeted measures in order to secure its economic interests in Zimbabwe. Mukori (2014) argues that increasing mutual cooperation between the Zimbabwean government and the Chinese, Israelis and Indians in the diamond sector, caused Belgium - owner of an old diamond industry - to threaten to disrupt the unity of the EU by unilaterally re-engaging with the ZANU (PF) regime.

The apparently peaceful environment and the new political reality has compelled the EU and its member states to soften its perception of the ZANU (PF) leadership with a view to resuming and intensifying re-engagement with the government of Zimbabwe, despite its failure to implement GPA-related reforms, and the constitutional and democratic reforms that had been agreed by the inclusive government. A ZEN Conference Report (2014) credits moderate or reform-minded elements within ZANU (PF), some of whom were actually the main victims of the Cabinet reshuffle, with working towards normalising bilateral relations. This re-engagement has the full backing of EU member states. This is supported by Bell (ibid), who argues that the EU has been steadily re-engaging with the ZANU PF regime despite the flawed and highly disputed elections of 31 July 2013, and lack of commitment to the reforms previously stipulated by Brussels.

Empirical evidence shows that since 2014, the EU bloc has made overtures in support of normalising bilateral relations with the ZANU (PF) government. Firstly, on 20 February 2014 the EU agreed to suspend the remaining measures under Art. 96 of the Cotonou Agreement on the ZANU (PF) leadership and related companies, except for those on President Robert Mugabe, his wife, Grace Mugabe, five[169] members of Zimbabwe's security apparatus and the Zimbabwe Defence Industries and Arms Embargo[170]. The EU upheld these measures in two subsequent annual reviews (February 2015 and February 2016). On the one hand, maintaining sanctions

---

[169] Happyton Mabhuya Bonyongwe, Augustine Chihuri, Constantine Chiwenga, Perence Shiri (a.k.a. Bigboy Samson Chikerema) and Phillip Valerio (a.k.a. Valentine) Sibanda

[170] An embargo on arms and related materiel, and ban on exports of equipment for internal repression.

satisfies its traditional allies[171] and on the other hand, resuming bilateral relations with the Zimbabwean government is in the interests of some within Europe and Zimbabwe and beyond, who believe that more than a decade of political sequestration has been ineffective. President Robert Mugabe was invited to attend the fourth EU–Africa summit in Brussels in April 2014, in response to African pressure as well as the EU's desire to normalise bilateral relations. However, President Robert Mugabe boycotted the Summit when his wife, Grace Mugabe, was denied a visa. The EU avoided specific benchmarking for fear of being accused of wanting to effect 'regime change' in the country. The EU steered the re-engagement process via two contradictory principles. It treated Zimbabwe as a "normal" country in line with the Cotonou Agreement's proclamation that ACP member states should be treated as equals as much as possible, and by acknowledging the country's exceptional political and economic historical situation and circumstances. The EU approach on re-engagement has avoided mention of Zimbabwe's democratic, governance, electoral, legal and human rights deficiencies in regional and international platforms. The EU is offering a development assistance envelope of financial and technical resources through the 11th EDF in support of sustainable economic growth and transformation as well as supporting the establishment of institutional systems of democracy, good governance and human rights. In the interests of economic growth and trade development, the 11th EDF was conceptualised on the basis of identified challenges including greater integration into Europe and the global economy and the consequential need to restructure the economy and companies to become more competitive at both the local and international level.

Following the suspension of the application of Cotonou Agreement's Article 96, by the European Council Decision of 24 July 2012, in October 2012, the Zimbabwe government and the EU launched and completed the 11th EDF programming exercise. This identified three focal sectors for funding: health, agriculture based

---

[171] These are local (opposition parties - MDC formations - and civil society groups) and external (western governments and donors, and some governments in Africa and beyond)

economic development, and governance and institution building. In addition, the EU has already pledged on different occasions various sectoral rescue financial packages worth 'multimillion Euros' (See table 5.1) demonstrating its commitment to the ongoing re-engagement exercise with the ZANU (PF) government. In November 2014, the Danish Trade and Development Minister, Mogens Jensen, visited Zimbabwe to assess DANIDA funded programmes and projects in the field of agriculture and the judiciary. He announced his country's willingness to normalise more than a decade of frosty bilateral relations with the ZANU (PF) government. Furthermore, Denmark, which re-established a diplomatic presence in 2009, having closed her Embassy in 2002, became the latest European nation to deliver the message of re-engagement with Harare. The Danish Minister was also the first EU member state leader to visit the country since the start of political and economic isolation measures and ZANU PF's disputed electoral victory of 31 July 2013. Denmark is one of Zimbabwe's largest bilateral development partners, with an investment portfolio of US$95 million, a Denmark-Zimbabwe Development Partnership Programme (2013-15) that seeks to enhance democratic institutions while promoting universal human rights. In June 2015, Denmark announced that it was giving a US$20 million grant in support of water, energy and infrastructure rehabilitation. Denmark is a member of the Zimbabwe Multi Donor Trust Fund, established in 2010, that supports economic recovery efforts. Other individual European countries with a strong bilateral development presence in the country[172] include the United Kingdom, Germany, Sweden, the Netherlands and the Czech Republic (EU Report, 2014).

To demonstrate concrete positive re-engagement, the EU and Zimbabwe signed an agreement in July 2015 to normalise bilateral relations and start cooperation. This is confirmed by the current Zimbabwean Minister of Finance, Economic Planning and Development (MoFEDP), Patrick Chinamasa, who states, ".... we have faith that the lapse of sanctions would, as promised by the EU, pave way for the normalisation of economic and political relations

---

[172] These nations together with Denmark have been continually supporting civil societies' substantial activities in the country.

between Brussels and Harare. …..." (Bell, 2014: 1). All this raises the following questions: has the re-engagement been sufficient to attract potential investors into the economy? Has the re-engagement been sufficient to improve the prevailing macroeconomic environment for medium and long term investors? Can the re-engagement guarantee the security of foreign investments and bilateral investment treaties? Has the re-engagement taken account of partisan programmes such as the indigenisation law, in terms of predictability and transparency? Has the re-engagement been in accordance with the rule of law and can it build mechanisms in support of bilateral treaties?

The re-engagement supports efforts towards, *inter alia*, normalising economic and political bilateral relations, redressing the decade-long social and economic development challenges, and reviving the economy through prudent macroeconomic policies including the implementation of an iEPA trade regime that entered into force on 14 May 2012. This raises two questions. Is the re-engagement process supporting the implementation of an iEPA whose main goal is to maximise benefits to local producers, exporters and consumers? Is it representing the interests of the private sector with respect to building the requisite productive and export capacities and related advocacy skills and expertise, as well as business information packaging and distribution in support of implementing the new trade regime? With respect to the above questions, the re-engagement in support of iEPA has been contextualised within the framework of the country's trade and economic policies, namely, the NTP (2012), IDP (2012) and the Zim-Asset (2013-2018). Of the three, Zim-Asset which was developed through a consultative process involving government officials and representatives of civil society, the private sector and the donor community, seeks to rejuvenate key sectors of the economy (EU-Republic of Zimbabwe Report, 2015). In this respect, the commitment of the donor community, particularly the EU, is reflected in the funding of some sectoral areas identified in the economic blueprint (see subsequent tables in this chapter). In May 2014 the Zimbabwe government and EU Delegation officials organised a joint consultative workshop that was attended by representatives from business and CSOs in order to validate the National Indicative Programme (NIP) worth €234 million[173], which was eventually signed on 16 February 2015. The EU Ambassador, Aldo Dell'Ariccia, described Zim-Asset as a work-in-progress rather than a substantive document of policy intent (Bell, 2014). Notwithstanding the identification of business opportunities through re-engagement in the tourism, energy, mining industry and transport sectors which could be exploited in the context of iEPA framework, European businesses have expressed concerns about the dubious tender procedures, fear of the return of the Zimbabwe dollar[174] (which would trigger hyperinflation in a foreign currency scarce economy) and the indigenisation and empowerment policy.

Changes in the post-July 2013 political landscape have a direct bearing on the re-engagement between ZANU (PF) and the EU and its member states. Ngwenya (2014) argues that for more than a decade the EU has commanded high levels of respect from Zimbabwe's civil society and opposition political sectors for two main reasons. First, the EU remains one of the few international blocs that maintained the stance that the legitimacy of the Zimbabwe government and Robert Mugabe's presidency are dubious. The EU has, until recently, adhered to a strict regime of restrictions on the ZANU (PF) leadership and associated companies as a way of protesting their illegitimacy. Second, civil society has benefited immensely from EU programmatic and institutional support, especially in the areas of democratisation, constitutionalism and election monitoring. Matsaka (2014) maintains that as late as April 2014, the EU was still concerned about the manner in which the July 2013 elections were held, insisting that the process did not conform to best democratic and electoral practices. This reassured the CSOs that re-engagement with ZANU (PF) government would not take place any time soon. The news that the EU was re-engaging with Robert Mugabe's government without any significant demonstration

---

[173] This was announced by the Head of the EU Delegation in Harare during the iEPA validation workshop held on 22 July 2015, the development assistance envelope supports health, agriculture-based economic development, and governance and institution building.

[174] RBZ proposal to introduce bond notes in circulation by end of October 2016 has generated wide-spread stiff resistance from the business community and ordinary citizens.

that the issues in dispute would be resolved[175], hurriedly announced by Dell'Ariccia, the EU Ambassador, took civil society, opposition parties and social media by surprise. Pilling and England (2016) report that opposition parties questioned the wisdom of the international community in wanting to re-engage with the Mugabe administration when the conditions that gave rise to Zimbabwe's isolation still stand. The ongoing efforts by European nations to re-engage with ZANU PF have been described as a "travesty of justice", because they don't take into account either the past or current destructive policies of Robert Mugabe's party (SW Radio Africa, 2014).

Changes in the post-July 2013 political landscape are open to various interpretations by the country's opposition parties and civil society groups. However, this should be summarized as a period of retrospect, reform and renewal. With respect to the EU-Zimbabwe government funding relationship, the parties have already established a National Authorising Office within MoFEDP with the responsibility of managing EDF resources. Opposition parties and civil society groups should work with the ZANU (PF) government towards consensual or bipartisan politics, particularly in the context and interests of re-engagement, in order to redress the social and economic challenges facing the country. Civil society groups in particular should prepare to participate in the national process, being invited by the relevant government ministries. This is a departure from the previous strategy of 'bulldozing participation' as observed in the NANGO/EU Report (2014: 10), stating:

> There is room for all stakeholders to participate in the national social and economic policy framework. In particular, civil society's participation will be considered given the acknowledgement that the sector has the potential to manoeuvre the policy cycle. Thus, its participation in the policy dialogue will be by invitation. NANGO/EU Report (2014: 10)

---

[175] Deficiencies in democracy, good governance, rule of law, human rights and electoral legitimacy as well as social and economic reforms

The funding relationship between the EU and CSOs should be better defined, targeted at achieving strategic objectives. Cases of donors "setting the agenda" could be avoided by the CSOs inviting proposals for funding. The EU appreciates the willingness shown by Zimbabwe government to re-engage and the Zimbabwean authorities commend the ongoing re-engagement which does not insist on commitment to democratic reforms and free and fair elections. In this regard, in the interests of building confidence, the Zimbabwe Electoral Commission should reconsider re-instating the EU's observer status in future elections.

Trade flows and brief outline of iEPA features

Zimbabwe's current tariff structure and other trade taxes shape prices in ways that create incentives to market goods at home compared to selling them abroad. Table 6.1 below shows that between 2002 and 2014 the country imported more goods and services than it exported. The table also reflects how the bilateral economic relationship between the parties withstood political pressure, in particular, the imposition of smart economic sanctions on the ZANU (PF) government; absence of direct contact between the Zimbabwe government and the EU and/or EU member states; rhetorical posturing and grand-standing at global meetings and summits; and accusations and counteraccusations of a regime change agenda. At the member state level, the table shows a significant economic relationship between Belgium, France, Germany, Italy, Netherlands, Portugal, Spain, UK and Scandinavian economies (Denmark, Finland and Sweden) and Zimbabwe. The table further reveal that the remaining European countries maintain an economic presence in the Zimbabwean economy. Their respective trade flows over the period, though consistent, were not all that significant.

Table 6.1 Zimbabwe's trade with European countries, 2002 – 2014, € Million

Countries		2002	2003	2004	2005	2006	2007	2008	2009	2010	2011	2012	2013	2014
Austria	M	11.3	12.5	4.3	1.3	1.0	0.4	0.5	0.3	0.8	0.6	0.3	0.2	0.2
	X	4.6	2.6	2.1	1.8	1.3	0.7	0.8	0.7	2.3	0.9	0.9	1.5	3.8
Belgium	M	18.9	12.5	17.1	14.3	13.7	11.8	5.2	13.1	9.0	6.6	30.1	52.1	97.6
	X	9.6	8.6	8.3	5.3	6.1	9.4	7.1	8.5	18.0	7.0	6.3	13.9	27.0
Bulgaria	M	9.8	6.8	6.8	4.5	4.9	2.8	4.1	5.4	0.5	8.7	4.7	9.9	8.8
	X	0.0	0.2	-	0.1	0.0	0.1	0.1	0.2	0.2	0.9	1.6	0.6	0.4
Croatia	M	4.3	2.4	2.0	0.7	0.2	0.4	0.2	0.1	0.1	0.1	0.1	0.0	0.0
	X	0.0	0.0	0.0	-	-	-	-	-	-	0.0	0.0	0.0	-
Cyprus	M	0.0	0.0	0.0	0.0	0.0	0.0	0.0	0.0	-	0.0	0.0	0.0	0.0
	X	0.4	0.2	0.0	0.1	0.1	0.1	0.6	0.2	0.2	0.7	0.8	0.3	0.6
Czech Rep.	M	-	2.2	1.0	0.0	0.0	0.0	0.0	0.0	0.0	0.1	0.1	0.0	0.0
	X	-	0.5	0.4	0.3	0.3	0.2	0.0	0.3	0.6	3.0	1.0	1.2	0.9
Denmark	M	11.5	10.5	11.3	4.0	3.2	3.4	3.7	2.1	0.4	0.1	0.2	0.3	0.3
	X	3.7	3.9	2.9	2.7	2.3	1.7	2.1	1.2	4.4	3.4	7.0	4.5	5.4
Finland	M	1.7	1.3	0.9	1.0	2.8	0.2	0.6	0.3	0.2	0.0	0.3	0.2	0.4
	X	7.0	6.6	3.7	2.9	3.0	6.2	6.7	5.1	5.9	9.0	8.3	6.2	11.9
France	M	18.1	16.7	14.2	8.3	8.3	10.8	10.7	7.8	11.8	16.8	17.3	16.3	42.0
	X	15.7	18.8	10.0	8.9	9.1	11.6	7.9	7.7	10.9	15.2	21.0	20.7	14.7
Germany	M	145.5	119.8	85.1	50.8	71.9	52.1	47.5	20.6	19.5	40.6	45.2	51.4	44.8
	X	44.9	45.6	44.3	29.3	53.6	37.5	42.0	18.6	36.2	49.3	57.3	37.7	31.3
Greece	M	9.7	7.6	6.1	4.0	2.0	2.9	1.0	0.7	1.8	0.0	0.2	2.2	0.1

Country														
(cont.)	X	0.3	0.2	0.1	0.6	0.6	0.5	0.4	0.5	0.1	0.5	0.5	0.2	0.8
Hungary	M	2.1	1.9	1.2	1.1	0.9	4.1	0.8	0.9	1.4	0.6	1.6	1.6	1.2
	X	0.0	0.3	0.4	0.1	0.1	0.6	0.3	0.7	0.7	0.8	2.4	0.5	1.3
Ireland	M	1.7	0.7	0.2	0.1	0.2	0.1	0.0	0.2	0.0	0.2	0.3	2.4	0.2
	X	3.4	2.8	1.9	2.0	1.5	0.7	0.6	1.7	1.2	1.0	2.2	0.3	2.5
Italy	M	57.5	53.1	88.2	72.1	76.4	82.3	82.3	28.8	67.0	119.3	98.6	85.7	86.3
	X	12.6	9.4	11.6	8.3	7.1	7.4	13.3	5.6	16.9	18.5	24.3	40.2	18.3
Netherlands	M	125.4	105.0	81.4	86.2	82.2	104.8	55.4	58.9	88.3	73.8	63.5	72.1	84.1
	X	14.9	19.1	18.4	16.2	11.2	26.8	13.6	15.9	24.6	23.1	22.9	25.2	17.8
Poland	M	26.7	7.8	3.3	3.7	2.7	3.5	3.5	4.4	5.8	10.2	10.8	15.3	21.2
	X	0.1	0.1	0.1	0.2	0.1	0.2	0.3	0.2	1.5	0.4	0.9	3.9	14.2
Portugal	M	23.6	18.4	11.6	18.1	18.0	6.0	21.2	26.7	22.2	45.6	46.6	19.0	34.0
	X	2.9	2.4	3.1	0.1	0.3	0.5	0.1	0.6	0.2	2.2	1.6	2.0	4.5
Romania	M	4.0	1.6	2.2	1.5	1.2	0.4	0.7	2.3	15.0	9.6	55.4	6.5	23.1
	X	0.0	0.0	0.0	0.0	-	0.0	0.0	0.0	0.0	1.8	1.7	1.0	0.1
Slovakia	M	0.6	1.4	0.1	0.1	0.0	0.0	0.0	0.0	-	0.0	0.0	0.0	0.0
	X	0.3	0.0	0.1	0.7	0.2	0.2	0.1	2.2	0.0	0.3	0.0	0.0	0.1
Slovenia	M	3.5	3.2	0.6	0.9	0.8	1.1	0.8	0.6	0.8	0.8	1.1	1.4	1.2
	X	-	0.0	0.1	0.0	0.0	-	0.0	0.0	0.0	0.0	0.0	-	0.0
Spain	M	36.6	31.8	32.8	34.6	30.7	24.8	33.3	7.3	20.7	45.0	18.0	11.3	28.6
	X	5.8	3.0	3.2	2.1	2.1	4.0	2.0	0.9	2.2	3.5	3.4	3.3	5.5
Sweden	M	6.8	3.2	3.8	12.6	18.9	7.3	2.7	16.9	27.9	25.6	43.1	12.8	1.0
	X	3.9	0.7	0.8	0.9	1.8	1.8	6.8	2.0	0.4	0.5	1.0	1.0	8.6
UK	M	145.4	99.5	91.5	93.0	70.7	44.3	39.4	54.0	33.7	66.8	23.6	40.5	34.5
	X	53.9	42.1	38.0	32.1	28.3	31.9	24.6	21.0	34.4	64.0	74.2	60.3	50.1

| Total Imports | 6656 | 5182 | 4630 | 4013 | 3939 | 3585 | 3137 | 2364 | 299.4 | 446.0 | 417.5 | 387.6 | 5103 |
| Total Exports | 184.1 | 169.7 | 1526 | 1268 | 1463 | 147.8 | 129.7 | 1084 | 189.1 | 2320 | 2823 | 240.7 | 220.6 |

Source: ZimTrade, 2015; NB. Croatia, Estonia, Luxembourg, Malta, Latvia and Lithuania have been omitted due to insignificant trade flows with Zimbabwe over this period.

Note: X stands for Export; M stands for Import; and - means data not available

Zimbabwe's exported non-mineral products attract a tariff structure that provides higher returns for exporters selling in the region than the EU and global markets. The above illustrates how tariffs and trade taxes form a wall of protection that makes it more profitable to sell at home, which discourages exports. This further means that the local producers find it more profitable to sell at home than in the region, the EU and beyond. But incentives to produce for the domestic market undermine overall expansion of the value-added goods industries while tariffs and trade taxes on intermediate inputs weaken competitiveness. Therefore, the SMEs policy calls for a systematic and periodic review of the customs duty and tariff regime with a view to enhancing their ability to import cheap raw materials while manufacturing entrepreneurs enhance product competitiveness locally and internationally (EU-Republic of Zimbabwe Report, 2015). Further, the SMEs lobbies for a constant review of the tariff regime in order to respond to changing domestic and international circumstances and simplification of procedures and processes at border posts.

The iEPA agreement[176] covers free movement of goods, non-tariff measures, trade defence measures, rules of origin, fisheries, economic and development cooperation, dispute avoidance and settlement (mechanisms for settling disputes), institutional and general provisions and areas for future negotiations (EU-Republic of Zimbabwe Report, 2015). Further, the agreement eliminates tariffs (elimination of duties and quotas for imports from Zimbabwe to the EU as well as gradual liberalisation of EU exports to Zimbabwe) and redresses behind-the-border barriers that impede the flow of goods and services between parties. It also encourages investment, enhances cooperation, and addresses other issues including intellectual property, e-commerce and government procurement. Thus, in the spirit of cooperation commitment, the EU agrees to fund Zimbabwe's envisaged short, medium and long-term sectoral needs expressed via a 'Development Matrix[177]' in order not only to

---

[176] iEPA is made up of 6 Chapters, 4 annexes and 2 protocols

[177] This covers infrastructure development; productive sectors; regional integration; trade policy and regulations; trade development; adjustment cost; and institutions.

facilitate iEPA implementation, but also to build the economy's productive capacities, industrial capacity utilisation, and export capabilities with a view to reaping positive tangible benefits from the new trade regime. The main features of the agreement in terms of defensive and offensive measures are thus summarised in diagram 6.1 below.

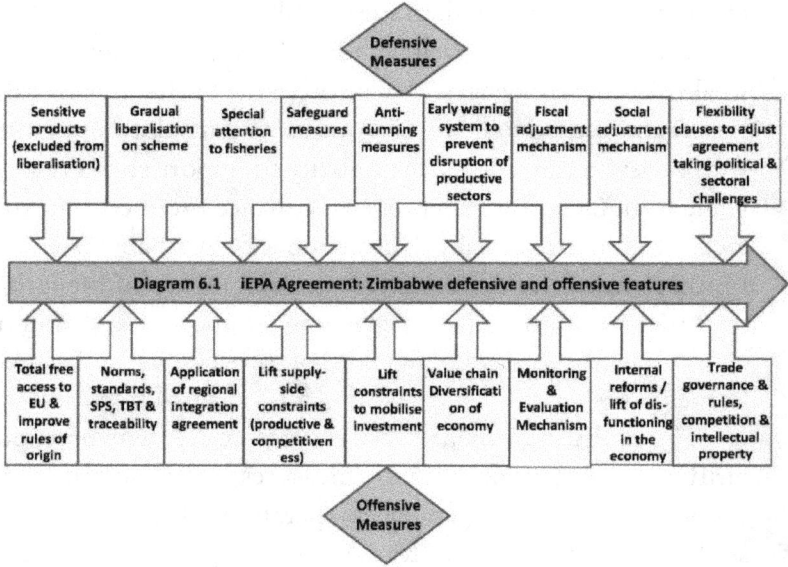

Defensive Measures								
Sensitive products (excluded from liberalisation)	Gradual liberalisation on scheme	Special attention to fisheries	Safeguard measures	Anti-dumping measures	Early warning system to prevent disruption of productive sectors	Fiscal adjustment mechanism	Social adjustment mechanism	Flexibility clauses to adjust agreement taking political & sectoral challenges

Diagram 6.1   iEPA Agreement: Zimbabwe defensive and offensive features

Total free access to EU & improve rules of origin	Norms, standards, SPS, TBT & traceability	Application of regional integration agreement	Lift supply-side constraints (productive & competitiveness)	Lift constraints to mobilise investment	Value chain Diversification of economy	Monitoring & Evaluation Mechanism	Internal reforms / lift of dis-functioning in the economy	Trade governance & rules, competition & intellectual property
								Offensive Measures

Source: Adapted from EU-Republic of Zimbabwe Report (2015)

As shown in the diagram, Harare negotiators protected the local 'limping economy'[178] by not only excluding some sensitive products from liberalization, but also by adding a comparable tariff advantage vis-à-vis products from Europe. In particular, this protects domestically produced, usually agricultural commodities or products from competing EU imports. The fiscal and social adjustments are built-in mechanisms aimed at committing the EU to make available funding support through the 11th EDF for appropriate government programmes. The country can also invoke anti-dumping measures and safeguard measures that are incorporated in the agreement in order to protect the economy in case European imports threaten to

---

[178] According to the ruling governing party, the economy require about US$27 billion to turn it around (Ndlovu, 2016).

cause injury to domestic industries or disturbances to a sector such as the marketing of agricultural products. This is supported by 'early warning system' that is intended to prevent disruption of productive sectors. These protective measures are intended to encourage local economic transformation in line with the agenda of reviving the ailing economy. The agreement's offensive measures are intended to aggressively market Zimbabwean products in the European market. These include improved market access through flexible and improved rules of origin in which Zimbabwe is allowed to cumulate within the ESA configuration and with other EPA signatory countries in addition to source inputs for cumulation from countries that have FTA with Europe; and provision to redress supply-side constraints, support integration into the regional and global market, and develop value chains in support of diversifying the economy.

Re-engagement milestones and macroeconomic policies

Ideally, the re-engagement in support of iEPA implementation should be embedded in national development strategies and overall economic growth and development programmes and policies. Therefore, the re-engagement process should support parts or components of four-strategic clusters and sub-clusters[179] of the adopted Zim-Asset economic blue print of 2013 in order to accelerate growth and prosperity. This policy, *inter alia,* provides an enabling environment for sustainable economic empowerment and social transformation for the citizens of the country. The policy further acknowledges and articulates the importance of other national macro-economic policies such as IDP, NTPs and the national Micro, Small and Medium Enterprise (MSME) policy framework (2014-2018) in driving the country's economy including the trade agenda. In so doing, Zim-Asset elevates trade as the engine for sustainable economic growth and development, stimulating productive sectors of the economy towards higher productivity, efficiency, and international competitiveness. However, the above

---

[179] Food Security and Nutrition; Social Services and Poverty Eradication; Infrastructure and Utilities; Value addition and Beneficiation; Fiscal Reform Measures; and Public Administration, Governance and Performance Management.

policies (NTP, IDP, Zim-Asset and MSME) are all silent about iEPA goals and associated implementation benefits, opportunities and challenges within the context of the country's economic growth and development agenda.

The main features of these policies are summarised in Table 6.2 below. Firstly, the policies seek to potentially transform the economy from a low-income country producing primary raw materials to an industrial economy through strengthening the private sector's role in agriculture, mining, manufacturing, and services. Secondly, they seek to establish strong backward and forward linkages between the main national economic sectors as well as with cross-cutting infrastructural sectors. Thirdly, they seek to stimulate productivity in agriculture at all levels (communal, small scale, and large scale) thereby ensuring food security while providing raw materials for the agro-manufacturing industries that are essential for stimulating export-led growth. Fourthly, they seek in the medium to long-term to facilitate the transformation of the mining sector from exporting raw materials to exporting "value added" mining products. Lastly, they seek to improve the linkages between the manufacturing sector and other sectors such as agriculture and mining. In this respect, the policies support the manufacturing sector which supplies the machinery, inputs, and other needs of the above economic sectors.

Table 6.2 Zimbabwe's macroeconomic policy objectives, 2012 – 2018

Industrial Development Policy (2012-2016)
To restore the manufacturing sector's contribution to GDP from the current 15% to 30% and its contribution to exports from 26% to 50% by 2015;
To transform Zimbabwe from a producer of primary goods into a producer of processed value added goods for both the domestic and export market through the promotion of viable industrial and commercial sectors;
To create additional employment in the manufacturing sector on an incremental basis and reduce unemployment levels by 2016;
To increase capacity utilization from the current levels of around 57% to 80% by the end of the planning period;

To re-equip and replace obsolete machinery and new technologies for import substitution and enhanced value addition; To increase the manufactured exports to the SADC and COMESA regions and the rest of the world; and To promote utilisation of available local raw materials in the production of goods.
National Trade Policy (2012-2016)
To increase exports and promote the diversification of the country's export basket by altering the product composition of exports and/or range of export destinations as well as by harnessing comparative advantage in key priority sectors with the ultimate target of increasing export earnings by at least 10% annually from US$ 4.3 billion in 2011 to US$7 billion in 2016; To increase exports to sustain growth, diversifying the export portfolio and increasing its technology content; To promote enhanced value-addition of primary commodities in all sectors of the economy thereby restoring the manufacturing sector's contribution to export earnings from the current 16% in 2012 to 50% by 2016; To consolidate and expand existing export markets and explore new markets; with the main focus being to expand into regional markets in the context of deeper regional integration; To enhance trade facilitation in order to expedite trade flows by reducing and/or eliminating barriers to trade; To give guidance on trade policy instruments, as well as improving access by consumers to a wider range of goods and services; To support the trading environment with a view to maximize attractiveness of Zimbabwean products in the region and globally; To nurture private sector competitiveness and support the productive sectors of the economy thereby creating wealth and employment opportunities as well as enhancing social welfare; and To identify causes of failure to realise the targets of both the NTP and IDP in the first three years of their respective implementation with the view to update the two policies as well as design future implementation strategies and action plans.
Zimbabwe Agenda for Sustainable Socio Economic Transformation (2013-2018)
To promote equitable development and prosperity for all Zimbabweans whilst leveraging own resources;

239

To ensure sustainable growth and development of the economy by, among other things, engendering unity of purpose among the different stakeholders;

To provide an enabling environment for sustainable economic empowerment and social transformation to the people of Zimbabwe;

To boost economic growth and development thereby creating employment and increasing economic opportunities.

To address systemic institutional weaknesses by allowing the full exploitation of benefits arising from horizontal and vertical linkages, hence fostering the spirit of collaboration and partnerships among Government Agencies; and

To prioritise attainment of optimal generation of power, the production and use of bio-fuels as enablers for economic productivity and growth; ensuring that all primary commodities across sectors create more value through processing and beneficiation.

National Micro, Small and Medium Enterprise Policy Framework (2014-2018)

To enhance the creation and maintenance of an enabling legal and regulatory environment for MSMEs development and growth;

To facilitate coordination of different policies and programmes at national level;

To provide an appropriate institutional mechanism to facilitate MSMEs development and growth efforts;

To commit MSMEs growth over a longer term rather than dependence on any quick fix solutions;

To coordinate resource mobilization strategies and set priorities to ensure appropriate allocation of limited public resources;

To rationalize and coordinate support programmes; Delegate tasks, responsibilities and accountability to all the stakeholders; and

To promote formalization and graduation of informal to formal, and from micro to small, small to medium, and medium to large enterprises

Sources: IDP (2012), NTP (2012), Zim-Asset (2013) and MSME (2014).

The EU sustained its institutional collaboration with FAO Zimbabwe, which for more than a decade received financial support as the leading technical partner for coordination and policy support services. FAO Zimbabwe coordinated the implementation of humanitarian activities and agricultural sector services, policies and strategies including conservation agriculture, irrigation and livestock. The programmes that FAO Zimbabwe has implemented are estimated at €55.8 million (EU-Republic of Zimbabwe ToR, 2015). Ongoing support in agricultural related activities, especially for smallholder farmers are summarised in Table 6.3 below. Over the last 4 years, the EU has been financially supporting pilot projects in community based wildlife management (community based natural resources management) in the better use of indigenous plants for medicinal, nutrition and cosmetic purposes. In early 2014, the EU launched a new natural resources management programme with specific support for fishery, wildlife and forestry. This intervention also focuses on community based initiatives, support to local technical government institutions, coordination of national policy and strategy at both local and national level, market linkages and demand driven research (EU-Republic of Zimbabwe ToR, 2015).

Table 6.3 Ongoing EU Interventions in Zimbabwe implemented or approved[180] by FAO between 2013 and 2015

Contract title	Contract period	Planned amount	Action location
Support to the roll out and implementation of the Food and Nutrition Policy through the strengthening of the Food and Nutrition Council	2013 - 2016	€500,000	Zimbabwe – National
Increased household food, income and nutrition security through commercialisation of an integrated and sustainable smallholder livestock sector in Zimbabwe	2013 - 2017	€7,000,000	National with special emphasis on Nkayi and Lupane Districts in Matabeleland North Province
Smallholder Irrigation Support Programme	2013 – 2017	€6,000,000	Zimbabwe, Provinces of Manicaland and

---

[180] One project is expected to be signed by mid-June 2016

			Matabeleland South
Forests forces – Forests Sustainability Managed for Communities, Environmental and Shocks Resilience	2013 – 2017	€3,500,000	Masvingo; Manicaland; Mashonaland West; Mashonaland East; Matabeleland North and Matabeleland South
Support to improve multisector food and nutrition security coordination and integration of nutrition in the Agriculture sector in Zimbabwe	2015 – not indicated	€3,000,000	Key government departments in ministry of Agriculture[181], Mechanisation and Irrigation Development and the Food and Nutrition Council
Create an enabling environment for increased agricultural growth in the smallholder sector	Signature expected in mid-June 2016	€5,600,000	Zimbabwe – National

Source: EU-Republic of Zimbabwe ToR (2015)

The EU has to date successfully consulted both government and CSOs[182], culminating in the approval of NIP, reflecting progress in the bilateral re-engagement between the EU and the Mugabe government in support of national social and economic development programmes and projects. NIP also reflects the end of politically

---

[181] Operational, financial and technical resources to support effective implementation of key actions.

[182] The EU considers CSOs to include all non-state, not-for-profit structures, non-partisan, and non-violent organisations through which people organise to pursue shared objectives and ideals, whether political, cultural, social and economic. Operating from local to region al and international levels, they comprise urban and rural, formal and informal organisations including NGOs, faith-based organisations, foundations, research institutions, trade unions and employers' organisations, cooperatives, professional and business associations, and the not-for-profit media" (COM, September 2012, page 3).

induced contestations that characterised ZANU (PF) government and civil society relationships for more than a decade. It is not surprising therefore that the EU has observed that the country's civil society has since the post-July 2013 electoral outcome, undergone a retrospect, reflection and strategy process towards a more focused and effective engagement with the government with a view to influence decision-making processes (European Commission Report, 2014]. The ZANU (PF) government has been displaying some gestures towards engaging with CSOs and the international community. As such, the government consulted both CSOs and the international community during the process of preparation and implementation of the Zim-Asset macro-economic policy blue-print.

Based on experiences of engagement and regular consultations with the different stakeholders at all levels, the EU has decided to scale up their support in the area of natural resources management and climate change smart initiatives, to support sustainable and resilient sources of income in rural areas. The EU has not only implemented a number of interventions, but also continues to support the consultative process aimed at identifying and elaborating future programme interventions in support of the country's socio-economic development. Already agreed EU-Zimbabwe NIP under the 11th EDF, support 'natural resources management' as part of agriculture-based economic development. The rationale and overall purpose of EU's support for agriculture-based economic development is not only the recognition of its key role as a major engine of economic and social development in the country, but also the creation of a diversified, competitive and efficient sector which assures food security at both the household and national levels. This support also contributes to enhanced economic growth and stability, employment and income generation; improves the supply of raw materials for industry; and improves export earnings. The above interventions also complement efforts towards the domestication of iEPA, *inter alia,* via redressing existing constraints to the country's bilateral, regional and global trade agenda, improving the prevailing macro-economic policy environment, enhancing the performance of rural sectors such as agricultural smallholder farming, and increasing peoples' and/or households' disposable incomes. The interventions also complement efforts aimed at attracting domestic and foreign investors who appear hesitant, despite the presence of abundant natural resources. Pilling and England (2016) argue that foreign investors are waiting for the end of the Mugabe era.

Ongoing EU and other donors' programmes are summarised in the table below. All of them are designed to support social and economic development. These programmes also have strong synergies with the 'Identification Fiche and Action Document' that was drawn up in September 2015 to support the implementation of iEPA in Zimbabwe with a total resource envelope estimated at €7.5 million. Compared to other iEPA signatories (Madagascar, Mauritius and Seychelles) in the ESA configuration which had access to similar support, Zimbabwe has not made much progress. Further, the slow pace of finalising the identification of the proposed programme activities, throws into doubt Harare's political willingness and commitment to fully implement the new trade regime, which, *inter alia*, demands immediate tariff liberalisation of some imported EU products as per the agreement. It is therefore anticipated that the 22-26 February 2016 bilateral meetings held in Harare and another round of meetings scheduled towards the end of June 2016 between the parties' negotiators will unlock any potential logjam in the domestication of iEPA.

Table 6.4 EU interventions in support of Zimbabwe trade and development programmes' issues and objectives

Trade and Private Development Project (€3 Million)
Enhance the role of the private sector and intermediary organisations in the economic recovery and diversification of the country and to strengthen the capacity of key actors concerned with the implementation of the iEPA. This is achieved by:
• facilitating SMEs access to market information and opportunities including those arising from iEPA implementation;
• capacitating intermediary organisations, business associations and umbrella organisations working in trade, private sector development and SME's issues; and

• strengthening the public-private sector dialogue and the participation of the private sector in the policy making as well as carrying out critical business environment reforms.
Zimbabwe Regional Integration Implementation Project (€4.3 Million)
Enhance the capacity of coordinating ministry and other relevant institutions responsible for domesticating regional integration programmes. This is achieved by: • improving the capacity to implement commitments under the COMESA regional integration agenda and create an enabling environment for trade; and • improving the enabling environment for leather and cotton value chain performance.
World Bank - Business Enabling Environment Project (US$7.19 Million)
Redress the regulatory and business environment constraints by: • improving the doing business environment; • reducing licencing and business set-up time-frames; • improving the investment climate and access to finance; and • building market-related skills.
Agriculture-based Economic Development (€88 Million)
Creation of a diversified, competitive and efficient sector which: • assures food security at both the household and national levels; • contributes to employment and income generation; • improves the supply of raw material for industry; • contributes to improved export earnings and therefore to enhanced economic growth and stability • enhances competitiveness of the agriculture sector through improved value chains (inputs, production, processing, marketing and trade) and an improved business and trade environment taking advantage of opportunities arising from iEPA implementation. • Increases the capacity of farmers and improved access to inputs and services for the development of a productive and competitive agriculture sector; and • increases competitiveness of agro-businesses (input, output, service delivery, processing, marketing) making use of opportunities from regional integration and implementation of iEPA.

Governance and Institution Building (€45 Million (Indicative amount)
Implementation of public finance management reforms required to maintain macro-economic stability; Support rule of law through judicial reforms and increased access to justice for all without discrimination.
FAO (€8 Million)
A four-year programme in partnership with Zimbabwe's Department of Livestock and Veterinary Services and two NGOs (Help Germany and Lead), which aims: • to control anthrax and foot-and-mouth disease; • to increase household food, income and nutrition security through commercialisation of an integrated and sustainable smallholder livestock sector in Zimbabwe.

Source: NewsDay Zimbabwe (2016); and EU-Republic of Zimbabwe Report (2015)

The intensification of the re-engagement between the former antagonists is reflected in the EC's commitment to fund the domestication of iEPA in addition to committing resources for the implementation of other existing and upcoming programmes in the country. The EU-Republic of Zimbabwe Report (2015) observes that Zimbabwe has access to NIP funded activities in the area of Governance and Institution Building (€45 million) and measures in favour of CSOs activities (€6 million) as well as to the 11th EDF regional envelope of COMESA Regional Integration Implementation Project (RIIP) (2014-2016) worth €4.2 million. Zimbabwe has since 2013 been benefitting from the SADC Regional Economic Integration Support (REIS) programme's financial and technical assistance in the area of regional trade integration, finance and investment, and standards and quality infrastructural development. Further, Zimbabwe is eligible for up to €1.4 million from the SADC Trade Related Facility aimed at assisting the country meet commitments under the SADC Protocol on Trade, mainly in the areas of customs cooperation, TBT, SPS measures, rules of origin, trade facilitation, industrial development, trade promotion and development, and trade in services (SADC Secretariat, 2015).

There is widespread recognition among all relevant stakeholders and policy makers of the importance of sound trade and economic policies, good governance structures and effective public institutions to create the necessary conditions for more rapid, poverty-reducing economic growth. It is also anticipated that the European Investment Bank (EIB) may consider extending lines of credit to the Zimbabwe domestic banking sector for onward lending purposes to local companies and SMEs, thereby enhancing their respective entrepreneurial productive and export capacities, and market competitiveness. While the decision to bilaterally re-engage has attracted other funders including DFID, DANIDA, USAID, UNDP, AfDB, GIZ and the World Bank (Chatham House Report, 2014), success in the transformation of the economy, including consistent implementation of regional, bilateral and global trade agreements depends upon the political sincerity, commitment and willingness of the governing ZANU (PF) party.

How can Zimbabwe reap the greatest benefit from iEPA?

The iEPA is considered to be a major stepping stone to a wider, deeper and more comprehensive deal that supports sustainable economic revival and social development. This has huge potential to foster both vertical and horizontal integration with Europe, sub-regional economies and the global economy. This also fosters freer trade flows and creates stronger ties between Zimbabwe and European countries. However, this depends on how and when Zimbabwe is ready to domesticate the provisions and clauses of the agreement. Ramdoo (2014) argues that a trade agreement, however well negotiated and flexible in itself, is just the starter towards achieving expected developmental objectives. It requires a powerful commitment and willingness to unlock the full potential of the new trade regime. Firstly, this can happen if Zimbabwean authorities are committed to implement iEPA provisions and clauses. Thus, for the implementation of iEPA, Zimbabwe should establish and modernise relevant pieces of legislation and technical regulations as well as reform the management of relevant technical institutions in order to operationalise the prescriptions and achieve the stated policy objectives. Key to the implementation of iEPA is the reforms in the areas of tariff policy, competition policy, consumer protection policy, trade protection measures and other trade related issues. These institutional reforms are intended to adapt the national and regional administrative authorities to the requirements of trade liberalisation and strengthen the capacity of the productive sectors in Zimbabwe (EU-Republic of Zimbabwe Report, 2015). By undertaking the necessary reforms to reinforce a much-needed business friendly environment, which will subsequently attract local, regional and foreign investors, Zimbabwe must create opportunities to structurally transform the economy.

A good measure of capital injection through the current re-engagement will create the conditions for replacing obsolete machines and equipment necessary to revamp low industrial capacity, utilisation capacities and facilitate a value-added competitive export-led economy. The NTP predicts that such an economic trajectory facilitate the development and growth of value chains, especially in the agriculture, manufacturing and services sectors. Secondly, this can happen if Zimbabwe is supported to reap the most from the new trade regime through domesticating its provisions and clauses. In this regard, the EU has specifically availed €7.5 million to assist Zimbabwe in building the institutional capacities of all relevant stakeholders that are central to the implementation of iEPA by enhancing productive and export capacities, redressing all impediments to smooth trade flows between the parties, improving technical coordination mechanisms in the process and institutionalising public-private dialogue sessions and sensitisation platforms. Through this financial resource envelope and other current and future programmes, Zimbabwe will stand a better chance of benefiting from the post-July 2013 re-engagement with Europe. This enables the economy to improve current and future production and marketing related supply-side constraints; and build its production and export capabilities as well as technical competences in such areas as government procurement, regulatory environment, trade in services, competition and investment. Zimbabwe also has to build the technical capacities necessary to properly sequence iEPA domestication within the sub-regional trade integration milestones.

Further, there is need to ensure that the domestication of the new trade regime is embedded in the agenda of redressing the prevailing social and economic ills, particularly increasing poverty, inequalities and unemployment. This can be done if government works together with all key stakeholders, ensuring in the process that the iEPA regime becomes a truly developmental tool, especially in light of the fact that the agreement takes into account the differences in the level of development in terms of economic and social conditions between the parties.

Besides the €7.5 million iEPA support, the country has also received sub-regional (COMESA and SADC) trade and integration-related envelopes and sectoral interventions, especially in the agricultural sector as well as other areas, as reflected in table 6.2. All these funding opportunities should lead to a scaling-up of the process of industrialisation and modernisation of the private sector, which is necessary for structural economic transformation, especially of sensitive sectors such as agro-processing.

It is imperative to ensure that most renewed bilateral economic cooperation commitments orient current and future resource envelopes towards redressing institutional priorities, capacities and needs of stakeholders that are central in the implementation of trade agreements including the iEPA regime. Their requirements in terms of functions and needs are summarised in the table below. The intention is to build their respective requisite capacities to support the implementation of iEPA in order to enable the economy to reap the full benefit of the new trade regime in terms of socio-economic development through a sustainable and inclusive increase in trade and investment. The stakeholders (government institutions, private sector bodies and civil society groups) have the capacity to assist the country in the implementation of the iEPA regime. They are also key facilitators of trade, playing leading roles in trade policy formulation and implementation, trade facilitation, product testing and development, and market development.

Table 6.5: Leading Zimbabwean institutions in the implementation of iEPA regime

Area of focus	Needs in support of iEPA implementation
Government and quasi-government institutions	
Industry and Commerce ministry	
Government policy maker, trade agreement negotiator and manager of trade policy, trade negotiations and trade agreements.	Institutional capacity building (technical assistance, training, information and technology equipment, studies and technical dialogue sessions) to sensitise, domesticate, implement and monitor the alignment of iEPA regime with both current and future national trade and industrialisation policies within the context of the conduct of trade and regional integration reforms.
Competition and Tariff Commission	
The custodian of competition policy and a watchdog on tariffs and safeguards measures, which have a direct impact on competitiveness and rules of the game in Zimbabwe.	Institutional capacity building to effectively implement tariff reforms, competition policy and trade defence measures including export taxes, agricultural safeguards and transitional safeguards.
National Economic Consultative Forum	
A mechanism of cooperative governance through dialogue and consensus building between Government, the private sector, labour, academia and civil society.	Strengthening the public-private policy dialogue on critical iEPA provisions and clauses in line with the agenda of private sector development reforms including competition law, tariff policy and non-trade-barriers as well as regional economic integration.
Zimbabwe Revenue Authority	
Responsible for, *inter alia*, providing integrated border services and enforcing various import and export controls on behalf of government ministries as well as foreign exchange controls on behalf of the Reserve Bank of Zimbabwe.	Improving trade facilitation through mapping exercises of import and export processes, expanding the Authorised Economic Facilitator, and implementing a fully automated single window platform.

Standards Association of Zimbabwe and other SQAM institutions	
Facilitates market access through providing laboratory testing services for export oriented products to accredited and internationally accepted levels. SQAM institutions which operate at all the borders include Agriculture ministry (plants and plant products); the Department of Veterinary Service (animals); the Environmental Management Agency (hazardous substances); the Medicines Control Authority of Zimbabwe (medicines and allied substances); and the Vehicle Inspection Department (fitness of vehicle and load shipped).	Institutional capacities of current National Quality Institutions (*Standards, Quality Assurance and Metrology* - SQAM, laboratories) that are responsible for setting up, developing and implementing National Quality Infrastructure strategy such as expediting the treatment of quality issues at ports of entry and improving product quality to meet export standards (especially in agriculture and mining).
ZimTrade	
Organisation provides the information platform, export development and guidance to exporters as part of market access process	Facilitating SMEs access to iEPA related market information and opportunities including matching needs, value chains and creating business linkages.
Business support organisations	
Intermediary Organisations	
These represent the broad interests of their members at the national, regional and international levels and are important players in articulating the priorities and needs of the private sector as well as dialoguing with government to improve the business environment; o Confederation of Zimbabwe Industries, which represents a large component of the manufacturing sector of the economy. CZI is responsible for industrial production including beneficiation of raw materials from within and outside the country; o Zimbabwe National Chamber of Commerce, which represents mainly the commercial sector, majority of whom are registered as SMEs with a significant	o Improving advocacy skills and capacities of intermediary organisations with a view to Improve business competitiveness and export capacities at the level of companies; and o Improving quality and provision of business development services at the level of intermediary organisations, with a particular emphasis on finance,

presence of businesswomen's organisations; and o Empretec Zimbabwe, which is central in delivering entrepreneurship development programmes for SMEs and businesswomen, thus catering for the needs of these often marginalised, but significant, groups.	innovation and new technologies, entrepreneurship and macro- to micro-businesses.
Business Sector Associations	
They represent either important economic subsectors or important value chain activities. Envisaged support to be provided via call for proposals; o Zimbabwe Clothing Manufacturers Association, which represents the interests of the cotton and textile value chain. IDP priorities the sector while COMESA has identified its potential for development under EU funded cluster initiative. o Leather and Allied Industries Federation of Zimbabwe, which represents the interests of sector entrepreneurs. IDP prioritises the sector while COMESA is developing sector value chains under EU funded cluster intuitive. o Engineering Iron and Steel Association of Zimbabwe, which represents the interests of iron and steel entrepreneurs, and is an IDP prioritised sector; and o Livestock and Meat Advisory Council, which represents the interests of sector entrepreneurs. This is also a specialised subsector with export growth potential and require high product standards to be competitive.	o Improving advocacy skills and capacities of business sector associations; and o Improving the quality and provision of business development services at the level of intermediary organizations, with a particular emphasis on finance, innovation and new technologies, business entrepreneurship and micro- and macro-businesses.
Businesswomen's Associations	

They are an important, but marginalised, economic group; o Women Alliance of Business Association, an apex body that coordinates the interests of business women in the country. o Professional Women Executives and Business Women's Forum, which represents the interest of professional and executive women with respect to trade and development agenda. o Women in Business Zimbabwe, which represents a number of registered SMEs and some informal cross border traders; and o Zimbabwe Women in Trade and Development, which represents the interests of marginalised women at grassroots level in both urban and rural areas.	o Improving advocacy skills and capacities of business women associations; and o Improving quality and provision of business development services at the level of intermediary organisations, with a particular emphasis on finance, innovation and new technologies, women entrepreneurship, informal and micro-businesses.

Small and Medium Size Enterprises

Those entrepreneurs that have potential to develop value chains in the economy.	Improving SMEs productive and export capacities, and market competitiveness; and Facilitating SMEs access to iEPA related market information and opportunities including matching needs, value chains and creating business linkages;

Thematic organization

Zimbabwe Cross Border Traders Association, which represents marginalised but significant economic group. Its main role is policy advocacy on behalf of informal sector in general, and cross border informal traders in particular.	Improving institutional advocacy skills and activism capacities in pursuant of the interests of informal entrepreneurship and cross border traders.

Research, innovation and training organisations

Institutions of higher learning and other training and research institutions working on trade, and private sector and SMEs developments.	Improving institutional research skills and capacities by orienting research studies, outputs and outcomes with sectoral and national productive and export capacities including the development of value chains; market competitiveness at national, sub-regional, bilateral (with the EU) and global levels; national trade, industrial and SMEs policies including sectoral forward and backward production and

	marketing linkages; and innovation and new technologies.
Civil society groups	
Those formations seeking to influence trade and development policies and private sector activity with a view to foster and maximise sustainable social development and poverty alleviation agendas.	Improving advocacy skills and activism capacities in support of implementing iEPA in line with the pro-development agenda via trade and industrial policies, regulations and laws. The emphasis being a sector inclusive, labour-intensive and social development orientation trade and development agenda

Source: Author's construction from EU-Republic of Zimbabwe Report (2015) and Ramdoo (2014)

In order to maximise the benefits from implementing the iEPA trade deal, all relevant stakeholders should be assisted to build their respective capacities as reflected in the table above. Firstly, this entails building the coordination capacities of Ministry of Industry and Commerce in the iEPA implementation as well as technical capacities of other trade-related Ministries and quasi-government institutions (customs/revenue authority and competition and tariff commission). Secondly, this entails directly funding private sector associations such as the Chamber of Commerce or industries with a view to build the necessary technical capacities to support the productive and export capacities of companies. Thirdly, this entails funding SMEs with a view to establish or develop value chains with large manufacturing firms, whose products are destined for both the local and the EU markets. Fourthly, this entails encouraging EIB to set up a financial window in partnership with local financial institutions (banks) for the purposes of lending money at concessional rates to private companies that are currently experiencing difficult in accessing investment funding. Indeed, EIB partnership with local banks has potential to encourage domestic borrowing thereby improve production capacity utilisation, leading to improved production of goods and market competitiveness of local products both domestically, in Europe and beyond. Fifthly, this entails mobilising active participation of private sector constituencies through private-public sector dialogue sessions (such as breakfast meetings, seminars and workshops) involving government officials, MPs and representatives of the business community, civil society groups and donor community to interrogate the appropriateness of policies, laws and regulations in the context of implementing iEPA. Lastly, this entails extending financial support to civil society groups and trade promotion organisations for lobbying both the EU institutions and Zimbabwean corridors of power in support of iEPA implementation. This also entails convening national sensitisation dialogue sessions targeting various constituencies and broader sections of society with a view to explore potential benefits and search solutions to current challenges thereof of iEPA implementation.

Conclusion

The EU bloc and its member states, opposition political parties and civil society, have since 2014 realised the importance of re-engaging the ZANU (PF) government and the business sector. In this respect, they have adopted a policy of appeasement in which smart sanctions remain in force for President Robert Mugabe, wife Grace Mugabe, and five members of Zimbabwe's security apparatus in order to maintain relations with traditional allies in support of democracy, governance, human rights and electoral reforms while intensifying re-engagement with government to accommodate the interests of some constituencies in Europe, Zimbabwe and beyond (O'Kane, 2016). This position reflects a shift from a democracy, governance, human rights and electoral-centered approach to one that is focused on the profitability of its economic and political cooperation with Zimbabwe. This also equates re-engagement with fixing the country's economic framework via investment flows and friendly policies, laws and regulations at the expense of democratic, governance, electoral, legal and human rights reforms. More specifically, re-engagement should generate a comprehensive trade policy framework that is in line with the country's overall strategies and its regional and international trade agenda, and complemented with capacity building of trade-related institutions and structures in order to support the implementation of the new trade regime.

Zimbabwe is expected to take policy measures on fiscal reform in anticipation of compensatory possible effects of enhanced tariff liberalisation. Notwithstanding a fall in diamond production from 660,000 carats in the first five months of 2014 to 420,000 carats during the same period in 2015, Ndlovu (2016) argues that the ruling ZANU (PF) party in February 2016 unilaterally cancelled respective mining licences of six[183] firms' operating in the Marange diamonds sector and consolidated them under a single-state-owned entity – the Zimbabwe Consolidated Diamond Company – in order to control the flow of revenues into the fiscus. However, reformers in government who are projecting the economy as increasingly safe for FDIs, are yet to convince ruling party hardliners to desist from implementing the 51% indigenisation and empowerment law promulgated during the GNU regime (Ndlovu, 2016). The above efforts should be complemented by the current re-engagement, which seeks to improve the business environment (stable macroeconomic framework, predictable trade and industrial polices, and regulatory instruments) in order to strengthen local private sector competitiveness and improve the standards of export and/or market competiveness. Success in this regard has the potential to facilitate the implementation of iEPA which is currently slow due to various problems including revenue protection. The full implementation of iEPA will benefit Zimbabwean businesses, exporters, importers and investors both large and small. For instance, the private sector can use iEPA to increase exports of goods not only to the EU market, but also to sub-regional markets and beyond. Further, the re-engagement that is oriented towards the implementation of iEPA would enable some companies to start exporting new goods to the EU market, sub- regional markets and beyond. Thus, the renewed re-engagement has a potential stimulus effect on the country's productive and export capacities, and market competitiveness, leading to increased trade flows between the parties. Further, re-engagement would help Zimbabwe to redress some 'behind the border' barriers to trade that currently are slowing the flow of goods and services not only between the parties, but also between Zimbabwe and other sub-regional economies and beyond.

---

[183] Anjin Investments, Diamond Mining Co., Jinan Mining, Kusena Diamonds, Marange Resources and Mbada Diamonds

Chapter Seven

Conclusion

Theory versus practice in bilateral trade relations

Conventional trade theory argues that the differences in productivity and costs of production between countries are the underlying reasons why it is advantageous for countries to engage in trade. However, this has to be considered against the *realpolitik* of trade, especially negotiated agreements between sovereign states that set tariff levels, sequence liberalisation and establish concessions such as the protection of sensitive sectors or products. This is especially true when it comes to the provision of development aid assistance to support the integration of negotiating parties' economies as well as their subsequent integration into the global economy. These complications have, since independence in 1980, characterised the EU-Zimbabwe trade and development bilateral relationship, culminating in the most recent round in which Zimbabwe was unable to access development aid assistance from the EU, including individual member states. The proponents of FTA argue that, under competitive free market conditions, trade maximises economic welfare by moving both parties to a situation where no country can be made better off without the other becoming worse off. Trade relations between the EU and Zimbabwe have reached the point that the EU will maximise its economic welfare in the short to medium term while Zimbabwe struggles to improve the industrial capacity utilisation and competitiveness of its productive and export sectors. In other words, these trade relations don't work in Zimbabwe's favour.

FTA is a process in which countries agree to eliminate tariffs and quotas on most goods traded between them. According to the FAO Report (2003) trade is an important development tool, though not an end in itself, meaning that an increase in the volume or value of trade is not necessarily an indicator of industrial productivity and development. Similarly, Ramdoo (2014) argues that a trade agreement, however well negotiated and flexible, is just the beginning, meaning that strong political commitment and willingness is necessary if the country is to unlock the full potential of the new trade regime. Following trade liberalisation in the early 1990s, Zimbabwe recorded an improvement in trade flows but simultaneously a decline in industrial production value chains, caused in part by ageing machinery, equipment and tools. Even with the modernisation of the underlying capacity, the structural trade deficit remained. It is feared that the most recent round of EPA-driven trade liberalisation and Zimbabwe's commitment to subject 80% of trade value to the EPA in 2022 when the agreement enters into force, will fail to modernise the country's industrial production, even though trade flows may improve because of outflows of mineral commodities and unprocessed agricultural products. Zimbabwe will continue to have weak industrial output and innovation, which will open the floodgates for manufactured European products to enter the local market. These will include agricultural outputs, leading to Zimbabwe's unprocessed agricultural products becoming less competitive, given the power of transitional agribusinesses in the EU and other global agricultural markets.

By dangling a developmental assistance envelope, the EU made sure that the EPA would work in its favour before the process even started. The ACP countries were enticed into accepting adverse terms, despite empirical evidence indicating an absorption rate of less than 48% of the promised assistance since 1975. This enabled the EU to effectively employ its policy of divide and conquer from above, while from below the potential for solidarity between the civil societies of the EU and ACP (especially Zimbabwe) failed to materialise. The EU member states have been able to defend a common position with a single voice throughout the negotiation process and also maintain political pressure on Zimbabwe's rulers through sustained smart sanctions and travel bans on the ZANU (PF) leadership, while refusing all contact with the Zimbabwean government except in the context of the ESA. By allowing ZANU (PF)'s former Trade and Industry minister, Samuel Mumbengegwi, to attend EU-ESA or ACP-EU trade talks, including EPA meetings in Brussels, the EU succeeded in ensuring that its dispute with

Zimbabwe regarding human and property rights would not derail the EPA process. The bloc continued to bankroll 'democratic' CSOs while denying funding to CSOs which were critical of the EPA process. Its 'invisible hand' in the market (forces of supply and demand) while at the same time exercising a very visible hand in bilateral trade politics will result in the EU dominating Zimbabwe's economy. Zimbabwe's political elite has been fairly effective at political grandstanding, but much less so in operating within the confines of market forces of supply and demand, which are now set to further degrade the economy. Normally, such forces would have reacted by lowering the price of exports and raising import prices through currency devaluation, but without control of the currency – Zimbabwe has used a hard currency basket led by the US dollar since early 2009 – this option is not available.

Civil society influenced a change in the EU's attitude towards the 31 December 2007 deadline as well as subsequent missed deadlines. CSOs succeeded to some degree in forcing African negotiators in general and ESA negotiators in particular to confront and mitigate the dangers associated with rushing through the process. However, in Zimbabwe, the CSOs failed to effect any change in attitude, partly because of complications associated with the intrusion of party politics into economic policy and the EPA negotiating process. Civil society was generally understood as being allied with the MDC formations, and so the EU's refusal to provide financial support for their EPA activities (despite the fact that they maintained a critical stance) failed to convince the authorities that they were not agents of European political and commercial interests. A combination of CSO advocacy inadequacies and state shortcomings delivered the Zimbabwean domestic market to the EU while severely constraining the country's future trade in EU markets.

Since 2014 the EU and its member states have realised the importance of re-engaging the ZANU (PF) government and the business sector, largely due to changes in the post-July 2013 political landscape, in which its alliance with the country's main opposition parties (MDC formations) and civil society groups was curtailed. Thus, the EU bloc has maintained the restrictions imposed on President Robert Mugabe, wife Grace Mugabe, five security chiefs and the Zimbabwe Defense Industries while demonstrating its commitment to bilateral re-engagement by scaling-up developmental assistance (financial and technical resources) in support of the ZANU (PF) government's social and economic development agenda. For instance, Brussels recently supported the domestication of the iEPA regime with €7.5 million. This is expected to build the capacities of trade-related government and quasi-government institutions, and business sector associations and their respective memberships. This further suggests that the re-engagement agenda is that of a profitable bilateral economic and political cooperation relationship, in which the prevailing trade policy framework is based on the country's overall strategies in the context of a regional and international trade agenda.

Lessons for future studies

The study forming the basis for this book provides valuable methodological lessons for future enquiries into public policy (both economic and social) in an environment dominated by tense and suspicious state-society relationships. Structural problems are often disguised in shallow public commentary on the government's weaknesses or leadership style, especially between belligerent rival parties. In order to undertake a study of this nature it is necessary to gain trust and make government officials feel that they are not being criticised in face-to-face interviews.

Informants occasionally referred to the "IMF way" of extracting information, in which critical questions are posed haphazardly and without recording the responses, while absorbing as much as possible of the overall essential points in the conversations. However, this method calls for a certain status on the part of the researcher as well as the patience and time to build trust, and the resources to make frequent visits. Sources of information must be protected, and the objective of the mission concealed. The Zimbabwean academic community is as polarised as the rest of society. Thus, any association with critics of the state is construed as being supportive of the regime-change agenda. In a country suffering what Elijah Munyuki[184] terms 'high levels of political surveillance,' the possibility of having a field visit abruptly terminated, or inviting state control of the researcher's movements or access to data sources, and confiscation of information gathered, is always present. Conversely, associating with pro-regime academics invites the mistrust of other intellectuals and CSOs, who will withhold cooperation. It is important to request permission[185] from the relevant authorities before undertaking research as well as finding ways to share research findings with the relevant stakeholders, government and the general public.

There is no substitute for direct participation in national or regional policy dialogue sessions (conferences, round-table discussions, seminars, workshops and the like) all of which assist the researcher to refine research questions, objectives and concepts. Regional policy dialogue sessions facilitate engagement with government officials. Junior officials, too, share their views on unfolding socio-economic and political developments, especially with regard to policy. All this calls for resources – including affiliation to a reputable institution.

The prospects for a positive outcome from the EU-Zimbabwe EPA negotiations are remote, at least in the short to medium term. In order to arrive at a positive conclusion the Ministry of Industry and Commerce, as well as all the other stakeholders[186], must come to understand the importance of collective and constructive consultation in trade negotiations, regardless of economic and political differences. CSOs must reassess the focus, relevance and capacity of their advocacy activities with respect to economic policy in general and trade negotiations in particular. Failure to heed the important lessons of this round of EPA negotiations will result in the state and civil society merely repeating their mistakes in future regional, bilateral and multilateral trade talks.

---

[184] Interview discussion with Elijah Munyuki, Gaborone, 24 August 2012.

[185] In Zimbabwe it is mandatory to obtain written permission before undertaking any research anywhere in the country, including fieldwork in rural areas.

[186] Trade-related Ministries, ZIMRA, Tariff Commission, MPs, CSOs, business community and the labour movement.

This book gives an insight into why Zimbabwe was one of the first countries to agree to the iEPA and to hasten to ratify it, even when the country's industrial capacity utilisation was less than 20%, and the GNU's political dysfunction and economic policy contradictions had alienated both foreign and domestic investors and donors. The need to depoliticise and contextualise the economic policy and trade and development debate in Zimbabwe is obvious. For instance, the EU sanctions and travel prohibition targeted at the ZANU (PF) leadership and associated companies may not have had much impact upon the state of the economy over the period, but given the high level of politicisation, it is nevertheless necessary to demystify the economic sanctions debate. This is also true of the debate about indigenous economic empowerment and transformation, especially prior to 31 July 2013, which were directed towards a partisan election outcome. Following the July 2013 electoral victory, Robert Mugabe revived some of his most vitriolic anti-western rhetoric in line with the indigenous economic empowerment and transformation campaign message. Indeed, a week after being sworn into office, Mugabe threatened 'tit-for-tat' retaliation against companies from Britain and the USA if sanctions persist. "Over the next five years the country is going to witness a unique wealth-transfer model that will see ordinary people taking control of the economy, targeting over 1,000 foreign companies including banks" (Zim247.com, 13 August 2013). Though the 'threat' did not materialise, its effects continue to haunt the economy as evidenced by the continued struggle to attract foreign and regional private sector investment as well as access GFI external financial and technical resources. That threat dashed the prospects of attracting potential investors and donors, and accessing international financial resources, especially from western economies. As a result, any predictions of reviving the economy in the short to medium term remain a pipe-dream. This explains to a large extent Harare's hesitation to domesticate the iEPA that came into force in 2012.

In the wake of the country's default on its foreign debt starting in 2008, Zimbabwe's inability to access global financial credit – including on occasion vitally needed trade finance – severely limited the country's ability to put in place appropriate remedial measures to revamp and sustain industrial production and raise export capabilities. Sanctions against Zimbabwe's access to finance meant that there would never be a conducive environment for state officials to consult deeply and widely with all the relevant stakeholders and constituencies. These problems are not unique to Zimbabwe, of course. According to Diamond Chikhasu, the principal trade officer of the Malawian Industry and Trade ministry, the 'EPA process through its best endeavour language is likely to mirror the negative implications and outcomes of the structural adjustment programme (SAP), including closure of several companies in most regional economies including Malawi'[187]. Zimbabwe's iEPA trade liberalisation will now intensify, but under conditions of extremely low industrial capacity utilisation, use of ageing machinery, hesitant domestic and foreign investors, and an unpredictable political landscape. These all threaten the goal of economic recovery. The country's 1990s SAP experience should have compelled negotiators and the relevant authorities to carefully align iEPA tariff liberalisation and commitments with current plans (if any) to revamp and build industrial production and export capabilities, as well as market competitiveness for local products.

The ongoing EPA process in the ESA configuration has, since December 2007, achieved the aim of creating individual, small, weak and vulnerable economies whose rulers were so divided that they eventually signed and ratified iEPAs in 2009. Even the Zimbabwean government, which since 2000 had had very little bilateral contact with the EU, finally signed and ratified the iEPA. This was a major climb-down from ZANU (PF)'s earlier revolutionary pronouncements, and reflects the success of the EU's 'guerrilla' negotiating strategies and tactics. It also signals a short to medium term victory for the EU and its allies (business lobbies, multinational corporations and global financial institutions) since market competitiveness favours EU entrepreneurs in both markets (the EU and Zimbabwe). Kamidza (2010) exposed the hypocrisy of the EU's strategy of 'divide and conquer' in EPA negotiations. The EU is currently the main sponsor of all sub-regional economic integration

---

[187] Interview discussion with Diamond Chikhasu, Lilongwe, 9 March 2013.

schemes, and yet promoted individual iEPA tariff liberalisation schedules and commitments that are at variance with those obtained regionally. The EU strategy to win markets in the sub-region necessitated disruptions of regional and national markets.

The Zimbabwe government's reluctance – alongside others in the ESA region – to regularly interface with civil society groups, particularly those critical of the process, was an unfortunate development that should not have been allowed to continue. One outcome of this failure has been a process of intense lobbying and resource mobilisation in support of the programmes of the SADC Council of NGOs, based in Gaborone, which signed a MoU with the SADC secretariat to engage regional heads of states and government at their annual summit. To date, the organisation has developed a comprehensive regional integration programme that links CSOs with the SADC secretariat's Trade, Industry, Finance and Investment Directorate, which is the engine of the regional trade and integration agenda.

Many other countries engaging in EPA negotiations have platforms that allow all the relevant stakeholders to provide input into the process, including those with critical opinions. This has not happened in the EU-Zimbabwe trade talks. This book shows how civil society has been unable to engage in the EPA process, thus directly undermining lobbying - not only between Zimbabwean negotiators, officials and other state organs that are central to the process and the implementation of this agreement, but also regional EPA units (COMESA and SADC) in terms of resisting or at least harmonising iEPA liberalisation and commitments. Regional CSOs should have lobbied other SADC countries' officials involved in EPA negotiations to reconcile iEPA provisions with regional integration and development plans.

Policy recommendations

Stakeholders should strategically engage in the process of the EPA as well as sub-regional integration, sharing information on the emerging challenges and opportunities. The book recommends a new round of intensive, inclusive debates on the EPA process in particular and economic policies in general. Such discourses should also include ways in which the country can sustainably develop and mobilise human, financial and technical resources in support of existing public, quasi-government, and independent research institutions, and establish these where necessary. This has huge potential to solve potential problems associated with state shortcomings, poor stakeholder relations and civil society's inadequacies with respect to trade advocacy and trade policy development and application. A more robust analysis of the process would also require increased human, financial and technical support for the generation of reliable statistics and information and the analysis of such thereof. All key stakeholders should support related policy and data storage institutions so that all constituencies as well as the general population are well informed about the process that has culminated in the new trade regime with Europe as well as related implications to the economy in general and to their lives in particular.

The book shows that the state did not engage all the relevant stakeholders in the EPA process. This is likely to remain a problem if the political divide continues unchecked. For instance, state-private sector relations have been characterised by mistrust and a lack of cooperation with regard to major economic policy or economic programme decisions. This is underscored by the appeal from Katuruza, the former chief negotiator, for the private sector to submit a list of sensitive products for onward sharing with the EU at future negotiations. Equally important is the need to ensure that the current re-engagement with the EU and other broader sections of the international community unite all relevant stakeholders in the economy, including trade and development, beyond their respective political affiliations.

The state-CSO relationship has been tense throughout. As a result, the state has mainly consulted those CSOs which are not critical of government's approach to economic empowerment issues. The book recommends institutionalising regular state-society platform dialogue sessions (conferences, workshops, seminars and roundtable discussions) with a view to encourage stakeholders appreciate diverse opinions on social, economic, and political developments. Indeed, frank and honest state-society platforms have a huge potential for addressing the many shortcomings and advocacy challenges that arise in economic and trade debates. Ideally, such state-society debates should galvanise all available resources (human, financial and technical) and commitments, to collectively and constructively engage on economic policies, and institutional systems and structures with a view to promote smooth implementation – or a revisiting – of iEPA outcomes. State-society relations should link the implementation or mitigation of the iEPA with development assistance in order for them to become tools for development. Already, the EU, during the signing ceremony with iEPA ESA-countries, promised to support the establishment of EPA Implementing Units in trade ministries. To this end, the EU has through the 11ᵗʰ EDF envelope made available €7.5 million towards supporting the domestication of iEPA regime. In addition, Zimbabwe is eligible to access resources in support of iEPA implementation from regional envelopes (COMESA RIIP, and SADC REIS and TRF). This encourages state-society alliances to apply collective efforts and wisdom for monitoring and evaluating the implementation of the iEPA agreement.

Scholars should interrogate the ideological underpinnings and concrete processes associated with bilateral trade negotiations and help map the stakeholder tensions arising from the EPA processes, with a view to rationally assessing how the process would benefit from greater collective preparedness, unity and consistency during the negotiations. Such a review has the potential to assist the country in future trade negotiations at various levels: regional, bilateral, and multilateral. The analysis should include specifying the institutional processes for negotiating constructively, thereby avoiding the recent negative experiences, and instead, promoting solid policy analyses and evidence-based advocacy in support of the process, including strengthening negotiation skills.

The book has emphasised the fact that, since independence in 1980, Zimbabwe's economy has become agricultural, and trade with the EU will adversely affect the country's ability to compete with EU agricultural products in both the local and European markets. Yet, de-agriculturalisation triggered by the Bretton Woods Institutions' neoliberal policies of the 1990s, has increased. At the same time, both the Bretton Woods Institutions and subsequent World Trade Organisation interventions and the ZANU (PF) government's interventions in terms of unconventional fast-track land redistribution and indigenous economic empowerment were premised on the potential economic and social transformative power of the agricultural sector. In other words, both interventions recognise the agricultural sector as being the backbone of the economy. This book recommends a combination of trade policy and specific trade promotion processes based on agricultural trade, particularly under the iEPA. Sector-specific policies and interventions, especially from Zimbabwean authorities in line with the draft Regional Agricultural Policy (SADC, 2013), are needed in order to inspire confidence in new farmers who might feel out-maneuvered by the outcome of the EPA process, through farmer associations and other stakeholders. This might one day produce a competitive surplus for local and other markets – including the EU – to meet food security and food sovereignty objectives, contribute to economic development, improve farmers' returns on investment and enable modern technologies to be adopted to sustain good agricultural practices.

If these recommendations are pursued, an improved EU-Zimbabwe bilateral institutional relationship within the 11th EDF funding framework has the potential to return the Zimbabwean economy to its past glory and confirm the practical developmental aspect of EPAs in Zimbabwe, especially if accompanied by liberal democratic values and acceptable governance practices. This book therefore recommends that the EU makes an effort to remove the remaining smart sanctions and travel bans imposed on President Robert Mugabe, wife Grace Mugabe, and five members of Zimbabwe's security apparatus as well as related companies in the defence sphere (Zimbabwe Defense Industries) in the spirit of re-engagement and the unfolding changes in the country's political landscape. Regional political efforts to decisively tackle governance and electoral disputes in order to avoid another disputed electoral outcome, such as that of 2008, or the questionable 2013 poll, would provide new space for rational, constructive and inclusive state-society engagement on economic policy and future trade negotiations and assist in mobilising foreign and domestic resources. It would unlock the potential of Zimbabwe's entrepreneurs, especially in agro-processing value chains and SMEs, in order to exploit the economic opportunities arising from the iEPA. A successful political and economic transition opens up development opportunities based on mutual interests, not only in trade and development, but also in technology transfers, technical expertise, capacity and skills development in all areas of the economy, by combining EU grant resources with private or national government capital. Cooperation with development partners satisfies the nation's desire to have a deeper and more wide-ranging partnership in sustainable pro-poor developmental strategies.

Given that the negotiating parties have already signed the iEPA and that both the EU and the ZANU (PF) leadership are working towards the normalisation of the bilateral relationship (easing sanctions and maintaining political co-existence with the opposition political parties including MDC formations), the book recommends the creation of a predictable financing mechanism through the ongoing re-engagement including scaling-up by means of which Zimbabwe can access the 11th EDF in order to facilitate industrial rehabilitation and modernisation, and improve physical supply-side related bottlenecks (rail and road networks, reliable electricity and communications, and water provision). The financial window would attract the technology and essential knowledge that is needed to meet product standards, including sanitary and phytosanitary measures and the technological barriers prevailing in high value markets such as the EU. The ongoing EU-Zimbabwe bilateral re-engagement must improve the economic and political relationship between the parties to levels that leverage Zimbabwe to unlock global financial resources (from the IMF and World Bank) in support of social and economic development. Coupled with stakeholder collaboration, an improved EU-Zimbabwe bilateral relationship has the potential to promote Zimbabwe's commercial interests in Europe as well as in regional and other markets in the wider world.

Stakeholder interaction in policy dialogue sessions can stimulate debate. Interaction in such fora has enormous potential for improving future economic policies in general, as well as trade policy, and trade negotiations and their subsequent implementation and evaluation. The interactions could also lead to the development of capacities and skills to support future trade negotiations and trade agreement reviews at all levels.

The Zimbabwean authorities should make efforts to access 'Aid for Trade' resources. This would be possible with improved bilateral relations with the EU through the ongoing re-engagement and other international organisations, including the World, Bank, IMF, OECD, UN organisations, the WTO and other donor agents. Access to funding would allow Zimbabwe's products to penetrate not only the European market, but also other regional and global markets as well as facilitating integration into the multilateral trading system. This would sustain sectoral and industrial development, create opportunities for economic growth and development, and generate welfare gains for citizens, leading to improved livelihoods.

The book recommends making extensive use of public-private sector and state-civil society dialogue platforms in order to ensure not only that the laws and regulations are in harmony with the implementation schedules of the new trade regime with Europe, but also to relieve the tensions that have dominated the policy making environment over the period under review. Thus, as interaction between the state and other stakeholders working on trade and development gathers momentum, it should be possible to attract funding in support of projects and programmes for modernising and restructuring industrial export diversification and upgrading competitiveness, particularly in agriculture, which is likely to face challenges following the implementation of the iEPA.

The book also recommends strengthening the national trade facilitation committee chaired by officials from the Ministry of Industry and Commerce and composed of representatives from other trade related government ministries including the Office of the President and Cabinet, trade-related quasi-government institutions, the private sector and CSOs working on trade and development, who should meet regularly to identify challenges and opportunity in the ongoing EPA negotiations as well as obstacles to full implementation of iEPA provisions. Already, limited fiscal space has stalled the domestication of iEPA, resulting in a high level visitation by Brussels officials for talks with authorities and other stakeholders with a view to unlock the logjam which is not only unfair to European producers, exporters and consumers, but also prevents Zimbabwe from reaping the most from the new trade regime.

The above recommendations support the ZANU (PF) leadership and assist it to normalise the political and economic bilateral relationship with the EU and in accessing the financial, technical and "Aid for Trade" resources that currently benefit other ACP countries, especially iEPA signatories.

The future and new lines of enquiry

In line with Prasad (2005), it is time that an in-depth study of Zimbabwe was conducted, to assess the contribution of existing supply-side constraints to current export sector development and growth. Such a study - employing linear programming models of export receipts and building scenarios of causal relationships between the level of export receipts and reductions of supply-side constraints - would help the country to identify and analyse the impact of supply-side constraints on its export receipts.

There should be an effective working collaboration between the CZI and the ZNCC in order to identify signs of sectoral or industrial distress resulting from the implementation of the iEPA. This can be institutionalised as periodic monitoring of the performance of sectors and industries whose products are in competition with those from Europe either locally or in the EU market. Such periodic studies should be comprehensive and cover production-marketing value chain processes with a view to making the necessary recommendations for improving productivity levels and market competitiveness. Both the CZI and the ZNCC should work closely with the Ministry of Industry and Commerce to periodically undertake trade competitive diagnostic sectoral and industrial studies in line with Reis's (2011) argument, to assist companies to understand their position, performance and capabilities in the EU and other global export markets as well as factors that underpin prevailing levels of competitiveness and constraints to trade. Such an analysis would also enable firms to explore existing and potential market

270

opportunities vis-à-vis the factors that underpin the adjustment process.

There should be a critical review of the role and function, as well as the challenges and successes, of the NDTPF or trade committee as an EPA-institutionalised consultative platform for the state and stakeholders to debate not only national issues, interests, positions and offers with respect to negotiations, but also implementation challenges and opportunities of iEPA and any future trade agreement. Equally, there should be an honest assessment of the role, function and inclusiveness of the trade committee, housed in the Ministry of Industry and Commerce in terms of driving the trade agenda of the country. A critical assessment is needed of the collaboration and synergies between CSOs working on trade and development and private sector bodies and the parliament's Trade and Development Committee, as well as a critical review of the state-stakeholder working relationship with regard to economic policy and trade negotiations, with a view to identifying challenges and opportunities that may require immediate attention. The exercise would also review the trade regime's socio-economic impact vis-à-vis trade provisions, thereby increasing the scope for alternatives that might lead to a truly development-oriented EPA agreement.

The book has identified the difficulties CSOs have experienced in engaging with the sub-regional secretariats' EPA units and their respective CTAs. The book argues that this has kept CSOs at the periphery of the process, thus contributing to weak advocacy on shortcomings of the state. In this regard, the book recommends conducting an assessment of the roles and functions of sub-regional EPA units in the EPA process, with a view to recommending future working relationships in the implementation of iEPA, along with an overall assessment of trade negotiations and regional economic integration processes.

After the eventual exit of the UK from the EU, the book strongly recommends an enquiry on potential UK-Zimbabwe trade negotiations and the impact analysis thereafter. It further recommends comparative analysis of EPA with the future UK-Zimbabwe new trade regime.

Can Zimbabwe make social and economic progress?

The Zimbabwe economic and trade scenario is bleak, especially in the context of continuing hostile EU-ZANU (PF) relations following the ZANU (PF) 31 July 2013 electoral victory, as most countries in the EU expressed doubts about the outcome. The GNU's failure to fully normalise relations with the EU and other western countries meant the continuation of smart sanctions[188] and Zimbabwe's inability to restructure its international financial relations. An estimated US$10.7 billion worth of Zimbabwean sovereign debt is outstanding, of which 70% is accumulated arrears. The GNU administration could not access any direct overseas development assistance, cheap credit, grants or concessional capital from GFIs (mainly the World Bank, the IMF and the AfDB). The anticipated debt cancellation did not occur.

Darracq (2010) says that the EU-ZANU (PF) sanctions debate has divided the European Council into two camps: hardliners led by the United Kingdom, Germany and the Netherlands on the one hand, and more moderate forces led by Portugal, France and Denmark on the other. Hove (2012) describes the division as being Euro-centric versus Afro-centric. Mawere (2009) argues that many African heads of state and government, as well as the general public, see the EU-Zimbabwe bilateral crisis as representing neo-colonialism, the north-south divide and imperialist power. The ZANU (PF) election victory was endorsed by AU and SADC observers and by most regional and African governments, and the failed MDC-T electoral challenge in the national courts[189] was endorsed by traditional backers, mainly Australia, the EU and the USA. Since the process of re-engagement started, only Denmark has visited Harare. The fear though is that this dispute has the potential to entrench pre-existing divisions.

---

[188] The EU partially removed sanctions imposed on the ZANU (PF) leadership a few months before the 2013 elections.

[189] The growing perception of Mugabe's party controlling both legal and political institutions in the country not only reduces the MDC-T legal challenge to an academic exercise unlikely to worry ZANU (PF) and allies (SADC and AU head of states and government), but also influences the party's decision to withdraw the case.

The continued EU-Zimbabwe debacle may pave the way for emerging economies to engage with the country, especially Asian commercial interests through the government's 'look east politics' and perhaps also create better conditions for South African corporate investors, as a reward for the quick endorsement of the electoral process by SADC facilitator, Jacob Zuma. South Africans have recently expressed interest in retail expansion through conglomerates such as ShopRite and Checkers, Pick 'n Pay and Wal-Mart (which has inherited the Makro warehouses in Harare and Bulawayo). Russian investors are also gaining access to Zimbabwe's platinum and gold through preferential arrangements associated with military relations. Therefore, besides affecting EU-Zimbabwe trade, residual sanctions create conditions for Asian, South African and Russian producers and exporters to become potential drivers of the 'new trade tsunami', resulting in rock-bottom prices that may well equally drive domestic producers, including new entrepreneurs (new farmers and small-scale industrialists) from the local market. Furthermore, with foreign debt arrears of about US$11 billion, any re-engagement with Bretton Woods Institutions would introduce new trade conditionalities. Coupled with the current power outages and water shortages, the decay of physical infrastructure and the outdated technology and machinery in operation in most firms, we can expect not only reduced prospects for economic growth and development, but also a more difficult environment for trade with Europe. It may still be the case that "an iEPA outcome is an onslaught on the Zimbabwean economy in the short to medium term," but the onslaught may now emanate from different sources, of which mistrust in the EU-Zimbabwe bilateral relations are but an important symptom. 'A typical underdeveloped economy, Zimbabwe, would not be allowed to concentrate on those sectors of the economy which in turn would generate growth and raise production to a new level altogether' (Bond and Kamidza, 2009: 2) in order to survive the three market-led tsunamis: made-in-Europe products, made-in-China and-India products (especially clothes and electronics following the 'look east' policy), and made-in-South Africa products consistent with Pretoria's sub-imperial commercial agenda. It remains to be seen how Mugabe's government will unlock FDI flows and multi-donor resources through the ongoing re-engagement with the EU bloc in order to stimulate the current weak agricultural and industrial production processes, and support economic transitional trade and development policies and debates – given that the multiple challenges described here are not likely to be addressed within the foreseeable future. Already there is currently growing contestation between hardliners and reformers ZANU (PF) cadres with regards to attracting foreign investors. While reformers in government are marketing the country as an investment destination, hardliners insist on implementing the indigenisation law, which is expected to hand over a 51% controlling stake in foreign owned firms to indigenous Zimbabweans (Ndlovu, 2016). The above dashed any significant hope of competing with EU products in both markets (Europe and local).

The change of heart of the EU bloc in favour of direct engagement with ZANU (PF) government, a move likely to be followed up by other western governments and donors, calls for properly contextual analysis with respect to the extent to which the country will attract FDIs and donor resources as well as institutionalise security guarantees on foreign investment and bilateral investment treaties. Thus, by 2014, the EU bloc and the ZANU (PF) government embarked on re-engagement journey that has since seen the former committing developmental assistance direct to government programmes based on its policies. The former has also removed all but seven of ZANU (PF)'s leadership and a military defense company from the previously imposed sanctions and restrictions list. Similarly, the Mugabe regime has made overtones including scaling down previous threats to European firms, public grandstanding and charges of a 'regime change' agenda. However, the launch in March 2016 of Zimbabwe People First political party under the leadership of a widely perceived former ZANU (PF) party reformist with inclinations towards the western governments, Joice Mujuru, is a litimus test of the ongoing re-engagement in terms of how the parties will pull together towards a shared vision based on shared analysis of the nature of the political state, the quality of governance, national institutions and fragility of the legal systems and unfolding social and economic challenges.

References

Primary documents

Eastern and Southern Africa and European Union (2006). Text of the 4th Draft EPA/8th RNF/24-8-2006, Brussels, http://www.acp-eu-trade.org/library/library_detail.php? library_detail_id., accessed 5 June 2013.

Eastern and Southern Africa and European Union report (2011). Economic Partnership Agreement Technical negotiations, 28-30 November, Port St Louis, Mauritius. http:// www.mcci.org, accessed 5 June 2013.

European Commission (2013). Trade negotiations step by step. Director General Trade, http://ec.europa.eu/trade/creating-opportunities/bilateral-relations/agreements/, accessed 28 June 2013.

European Commission Report (2014). EU country roadmap for engagement with civil society 2014 – 2017, Zimbabwe, http://eeas.europa.eu/delegations/zimbabwe/documents/pres s_corner/20140711_en.pdf

EU-Republic of Zimbabwe ToR (2015). Programme Evaluation of the past and ongoing EU Implementations in Zimbabwe implemented by FAO, EuropeAid/132633/C/SER/

EU-Republic of Zimbabwe Report (September 2015). Identification of a programme in support of the implementation of the iEPA in Zimbabwe. Ministry of Industry and Commerce, Project No. 2015/360179

Republic of Zimbabwe Ministry of Trade and International Trade (2007). Progress Report on Southern Africa Development Community – Economic Partnership Agreement negotiations, MTI/NCTPN/12th/2007/9. 12 September 2007, Harare, http://www.miit.gov.zw, accessed 25 June 2013.

Republic of Zimbabwe (2011). Understanding Indigenisation and Economic Empowerment. Ministry of Indigenisation and Economic Empowerment, National Indigenisation and

275

Economic Empowerment Board, http://www.nieeb.co.zw, accessed 13 March 2014

Republic of Zimbabwe (2012). Industrial Development Policy (2012-2016). Ministry of Industry and Commerce, Harare, Printed by Printflow Pvt Ltd, 29 March 2012, http://www.miit.gov.zw, accessed 10 July 2013.

Republic of Zimbabwe (2012). National Trade Policy (2012-2016). Ministry of Industry and Commerce, Harare, http://www.zimtrade.co.zw/IMG/pdf/, accessed 10 July 2013.

Republic of Zimbabwe (2012). Zimbabwe Agenda for Sustainable Socio-Economic Transformation: Towards an empowered society and a growing economy, 2013 – 2018, http://www.zw.one.un.org/resources/publication, accessed 5 May 2016

Republic of Zimbabwe (2012). Micro, Small and Medium Enterprise policy framework (2014-2018), Ministry of Small and Medium Enterprises and Cooperative Development, http://www.smecd.gov.zw/, accessed 5 May 2016.

Republic of Zimbabwe (October 2015). Strategies for clearing external debt arrears and the supportive economic reform agenda, Ministry of Finance and Economic Development, http://www.rbz.co.zw/assets/clearing-zimbabwe-external-debt-arrears-february2016.pdf, accessed 10 June 2016

Southern Africa Development Community Secretariat Report (July 2011). EU sponsored consultancy on the establishment of SADC Development Fund, prepared by Technical Assistance coordinated by ADE in association with Coffey International Development and TDI, Gaborone, Botswana, http://www.sadc.int, accessed on 15 June 2013.

Secondary sources: books and book chapters

Benoliel, M. and Hua, W. (2009). *Essential Managers Negotiating.* London: Dorling Kindersley Limited.

Bond, P. (1998). *Uneven Zimbabwe: A Study of Finance, Development, and Underdevelopment.* Trenton: Africa World Press.

Bond, P. (2006a). *Looting Africa: the Economics of Exploitation.* London, Zed Books and Pietermaritzburg: University of KwaZulu-Natal Press.

Bond, P. (2006b). *Talk Left and Walk Right: South Africa's Frustrated Global Reforms* (second edition). Pietermaritzburg: University of KwaZulu-Natal Press.

Bond, P. and Manyanya, M. (2002). *Zimbabwe's Plunge, Exhausted Nationalism, Neoliberalism and the Search for Social Justice.* Pietermaritzburg: University of Natal Press, and London: the Merlin Press.

Chang, H-J. (2007). *Bad Samaritans: Rich Nations, Poor Policies and the Threat to the Developing World.* Random House, London.

Chizema, R. and Masiiwa, M. (2011). Trade and trade policy. In Kanyenze, G., Kondo, T., Chitambara, P. and Martens, J. (eds), *Beyond the Enclave: Towards a pro-poor and inclusive development strategy for Zimbabwe.* Weaver Press in association with Alternatives to Neo-liberalism in Southern Africa, Labour and Economic Development Research Institute Zimbabwe and Zimbabwe Congress of Trade Unions, Harare, Zimbabwe. (pp. 444–472)

Collins, P. (2009). *Negotiate to win! Talking your way to what you want.* Sterling Publishing Company, New York/London.

Das, B. L. (2004). Coping with WTO Needs New Institutions in South Countries. In Tandon, Yash and Megan Allardice (eds). *Paved with Good Intentions: Background to the GATT, Uruguay Round and WTO.* Seatini, Harare, Zimbabwe.

Doroh (2011: 143). Manufacturing. In Kanyenze, G., Kondo, T., Chitambara, P. and Martens, J. (eds), *Beyond the Enclave: Towards a pro-poor and inclusive development strategy for Zimbabwe.,* Weaver Press in association with Alternatives to Neo-liberalism in Southern Africa, Labour and Economic Development Research Institute Zimbabwe and Zimbabwe Congress of Trade Unions, Harare. (pp. 129–159).

Hartmann, T. (2008). *Bad Samaritans: The Myth of Free Trade and the Secret History of Capitalism.,* New York: Bloomsbury Press.

Hodge, J. (2002). Liberalisation of Trade in Services in Developing Countries. In Hoekman, B., Mattoo, A. and English, P. (eds), *Development and the WTO.* World Bank, Washington, DC.

Irwin, D. A. (1996). *Against the Tide: An Intellectual History of Free Trade.* Princeton: Princeton University Press, 1996.

Kachingwe, N. (2004). Partners or Predators? How Europe's Expansionist Trade Agenda has Hijacked Development Cooperation. In *Gobalisation and Africa.* edited by Peter Custers, http:// www.petercusters.nl/file/44, accessed 15 June 2013.

Kahler, M. and Odell, J. (2004). Developing Countries and the Global Trading System. In Tandon Yash and Megan Allardice (eds), *Paved with Good Intentions: Background to the GATT, Uruguay Round and WTO.* Seatini, Harare, Zimbabwe.

Kalenga, P. (2011). Making the Tripartite Free Trade Area work. In the *Cape to Cairo – An Assessment of the Tripartite Free Trade Area.* RSAM Printers, Trade Law Centre for Southern Africa, Stellenbosch, Cape Town.

Kamidza, R. (2008). Can SADC-EU Trade Negotiations Unblock Development and Regional Integration? In Brito, L., Castel-Branco, C., Chichava S. and Francisco, A. (eds), *Southern Africa and Challenges for Mozambique,* Tipografia Peres, IESE. Maputo.

Kamidza, R. and Mazingi, L. (2011). Inequality in Zimbabwe. In Deprose Muchena and Herbert Jauch (eds), *Tearing Us Apart: Inequalities in Southern Africa.* Johannesburg: Open Society Initiative for Southern Africa.

Kanyenze *et al.* (ed), (2011). *Beyond the Enclave: Towards a pro-poor and inclusive development strategy for Zimbabwe.* Harare: Weaver Press in association with Alternatives to Neo-liberalism in Southern Africa, Labour and Economic Development Research Institute Zimbabwe and Zimbabwe Congress of Trade Unions.

Kramarenko, V. L. *et al.* (2010). *Zimbabwe: Challenges and Policy Options after Hyperinflation.* Washington, DC: International Monetary Fund.

Kramer, R.M., and Messick, D.M. (1995). *Negotiation as Social Process.* in R.M. Kramer and D.M. Messick (eds). London: Sage.

Matondi, P. (2011). Land, Agriculture and Rural Development. In Kanyenze, G., Kondo, T., Chitambara, P. and Martens, J. (eds), *Beyond the Enclave: Towards a pro-poor and inclusive development strategy for Zimbabwe.* Harare: Weaver Press in association with Alternatives to Neo-liberalism in Southern Africa, Labour and

Economic Development Research Institute Zimbabwe and Zimbabwe Congress of Trade Unions. (pp. 75–128).

McCandless, E. (2011). *Polarisation and Transformation in Zimbabwe: Social Movements, Strategies and Dilemmas.* Lanham: Lexington Books.

Meunier, S. (2000). *What Single Voice? European Institutions and EU-US Trade Negotiations.* Cambridge: Cambridge University Press.

Myerson, R. M. (1991). *Game Theory: Analysis of Conflict.* Cambridge: Harvard University Press.

Raghavan, C. (2004). From Free Trade to Managed Trade. In Tandon Yash and Megan Allardice (eds), *Paved with Good Intentions: Background to the GATT, Uruguay Round and WTO.* Harare: Seatini.

Rege, V. (2004). Developing Countries and Negotiations in the WTO. In Tandon Yash and Megan Allardice (eds), *Paved with Good Intentions: Background to the GATT, Uruguay Round and WTO.* Harare: Seatini.

Rothstein, R. L. (1979). *Global Bargaining: UNCAD and the Quest for a New International Economic Order.* Princeton NJ: Princeton University Press.

Sandrey, R. and Vink, N. (2011). Agricultural production in the tripartite region. In the *Cape to Cairo – An Assessment of the Tripartite Free Trade Area.* RSAM Printers, Trade Law Centre for Southern Africa, Stellenbosch, Cape Town, South Africa.

Sebenius, J.K. (1996). Sequencing to build coalitions: With whom should I talk first? In Zeckhauser, R. Keeney, R. and Sebenius, J.K. (eds), *Wise Choices: Decisions, Games and Negotiations.* (pp. 324-348).

Todaro, M. (1990). *Trade Development and the Theory of Comparative Advantage.* London, Longman Press.

Ugarteche, O., (2000). *The false dilemma: Globalisation opportunity or threat?* Ottawa: Inter Pares, Zed Books.

UNECA (2005). Economic and welfare impacts of the EU-Africa economic partnership agreements. ATPC Work in Progress, No.10. Addis Ababa, Ethiopia: The African Trade Policy Centre of the United Nations Economic Commission for Africa.

World Bank (2006). *World Bank - Civil Society Engagement: Review of Fiscal Years 2005 and 2006.* New York: The World Bank.

Zartman, I.W. (1991). The structure of negotiation. In Kremenyuk V.A. (ed), *International Negotiation: Analysis, Approaches, Issues.* (pp. 65-77). San Francisco: Jossey-Bass.

ZCTU (2006). *Beyond ESAP: Framework for a Long-Term Development Strategy for Zimbabwe.* Harare: Zimbabwe Congress of Trade Unions.

Academic journals, thesis, reports and working papers

African Development Bank (2011). Zimbabwe: Country Brief 2011 – 2013.

Balchin, N. and Kamidza R. (2008). Angola Economic Partnership Agreement Hand Book. Mthente Research and Consulting Services, http://www.mthente.co.za, accessed 15 June 2013.

Bilal, S. and Rampa, F. (2006). Alternative to EPAs: Possible scenarios for the future ACP trade relations with the EU. Policy Management Report No. 11. European Centre for Development Policy Management, February 2006, http://www.acp-eu-trade.org/tni, accessed 15 June 2013.

Bilal, S. and Szepesi, S. (September 2003). EPA Impact Studies: SADC and the Regional Coherence. InBrief 2B, European Centre for Development Policy Management, http://www.ecdpm.org, accessed 15 June 2013.

Bond, P. (2007). Competing explanations of Zimbabwe's long economic crisis. *Safundi, Journal of South African and American Studies*, Vol. 8, No. 2, June 2007. (pp. 149-181).

Bond, P. (2009). Lessons of Zimbabwe: An exchange between Patrick Bond and Mahmood Mamdani. *International Journal of Socialist Renewal*, http://www.links.org.au/node/815, accessed on 15 June 2013.

Bond, P. and Kamidza, R. (2009). How Europe underdevelops Africa and how some fight back. *Pambazuka News*, Issue 381, http://www.pambazuka.org, accessed 15 June 2013.

Brander, J.A and Spencer, B.J. (1992). Export subsidies and international market share rivalry. *Journal of International Economics*, Vol. 9, No. 2.

Burnett, P. and Manji, F. (July 2005). Economic Partnership Agreements: Territorial conquest by economic means? *Pambazuka News,* Issue 216, http://www.pambazuka.org, accessed 15 June 2013.

Chigora, P. (2006). On Crossroads: Reflections on Zimbabwe's Relations with Britain at the New Millennium, *Alternatives: Turkish Journal of International Relations,* Vol. 5, No.3, Fall 2006.

Christian Aid (2003). What works? Trade, Policy and Development, London, http://www.christainaid.org.uk, accessed 15 June 2013.

Christian Aid (2005). For Richer or Poorer: Transforming Economic Partnership Agreements between Europe and Africa, London, http://www.christianaid.org.uk, accessed 20 June 2012.

Christian Aid briefing (2004). Why EPAs Need a Rethink. London, http://www.epawatch.net, accessed 20 June 2013.

Confederation of the Zimbabwean Industries (2008). Manufacturing Sector Survey. 31 October 2008, Harare: Confederation of Zimbabwe Industries, http.://www.czi.co.zw, accessed 20 July 2013.

Confederation of the Zimbabwean Industries (2009). Manufacturing Sector Survey. 26 May 2009, Harare: Confederation of Zimbabwe Industries, http.://www.czi.co.zw, accessed 20 July 2013.

Coorey, Sharmini, Clausen, J. R. *et al.* (2007). Lessons from High Inflation Episodes for Stabilising the Economy in Zimbabwe. *International Monetary Fund Working Paper,* Washington DC, https://www.imf.org/external/pubs/ft/wp/2007/wp0799.pdf. accessed 20 June 2013.

Cotonou Monitoring Group of European Development NGOs and networks (May 2002). Discussion Note: Addressing Supply Side Constraints, Brussels, http.://www.eu-ldc.org/downloads/EPASSUPP.DOC, accessed 0 March 2013.

Crump, L. (2005). Concurrently Linked Negotiations and Negotiation Theory: An Examination of Bilateral Trade Negotiations in Australia, Singapore and the United States. *Griffith University,* School of International Business and Asian Studies, Brisbane Australia.

Crump, L. (June 2006). Global Trade Policy Development in a Two-Track System, Griffith University, School of International Business and Asian Studies, *Journal of International Law,* Vol. 9, No. 2., (pp. 487 -510), Brisbane Australia.

Dorman, S. R. (2001). Inclusion and Exclusion: NGOs and Politics in Zimbabwe. Department of Politics and International Relations in the Division of Social Studies, *the University of Oxford*, D. Phil Thesis.

Draper, P. (2007). EU-Africa trade relations: The Political Economy of Economic Partnership Agreements, Jan Tumlir Policy Essay No. 2, *European Centre for International Political Economy,* http://www.ecipe.org, accessed 20 January 2013.

Dunn, B. (2009). Neither free trade nor protection but international socialism: contesting the conservative antinomies of trade theory. Marxist interventions, http:/www.anu.edu.au/polsci/mi/1/mi1dunn.pdf. (pp. 23-45), accessed 20 August 2012.

European Commission (May 2012). EU's first EPA with Africa region goes live. Brussels, http://www.trade.ec.europa.eu/doclib/press/index.cfm?id=80 0, accessed 10 August 2013.

European Commission Staff Working Paper (September 2011), 10th EDF Performance Review. SEC (2011) 1055 Final, Brussels, http://www.eumonitor.nl/9353000/j9vvik7m1c3gyxp/vj6ipnw 6my0, accessed 5 May 2013.

European Research Office (December 2006). Understanding the Possible Gains to African Countries from EPAs. Brussels, http://ero@be/content/documents/trade_negotiations-01/pdf/1.1.epa-general/costs-epa-related   -adjustments.pdf, accessed 8 May 2013.

European Union (1999). European Parliament resolution on the communication from the Commission to the Council and the European Parliament on the EU approach to the WTO Millennium Round. *Official Journal of the European Communities.* Brussels, http://eur-lex.europa.eu, accessed 5 February 2013.

Food and Agricultural Organisation (2003b). WTO Agreement on Agriculture: The Implementation experience – Developing

Country Case Studies, Economic and Social Development Department, Rome, http://www.fao.org/docrep/005/y4632e/htm, accessed 5 June 2013.

Food and Agricultural Organisation (2003c). WTO Agreement on Agriculture: The Implementation experience – Developing Country Case Studies (Zimbabwe), Study Prepared for the FAO by Moses Tekere (with assistance of James Hurungo and Masiiwa Rusare), TRADES Centre, Harare, http://www.fao.org/docrep/005/y4632e/y4632e0y.htm, assessed 15 June 2017.

Food and Agricultural Organisation (2003a). Trade Reform and Food Security: Conceptualising the Linkages. Commodity Policy and Projections Service, Economic and Social Development Department, Commodities and Trade Division, Rome, http://www.fao.org/docrep/005/y4671e00.htm, accessed 5 June 2013.

Garfield, S. and Knudsen, U.V. (1997). An Electric Negotiation Theory of Trade Policy Behaviour. *University of Copenhagen,* Discussion Paper No. 97.

Gideon, R. (1998). Review: Neoclassical Realism and Theories of Foreign Policy, *Cambridge University Press,* Vol. 51, No. 1, (pp. 144-172), Stable URL: http://www.jstor.org/stable/25054068, accessed 15 May 2012.

Goodison, P. (2007). The Future of Africa's Trade Relationship with Europe: New EU Trade Policy. *Review of African Political Economy,* Vo. 34, No. 111.

Goodison, P. and Stoneman, C. (2005). Trade, Development and Cooperation: Is the EU Helping Africa? *Review of African Political Economy,* Vol. 31, No. 102.

Grynberg, R. and Clarke, A. (2006). The European Development Fund and Economic Partnership Agreements, Commonwealth Secretariat Economic Affairs Division, http://www.secretariat.thecommonwealth.org, accessed 5 June 2013.

Hammouda, H. B. and Osakwe, P.N. (2008). Global Trade Models and Economic Policy Analysis: Relevance, Risks and

Repercussions for Africa. *Overseas Development Institute: Development Policy Review,* Vol. 26, No. 2, (pp 151-170).

Harrison, G. W. and Rutström, E. E. (May 1991). Trade Wars, Trade Negotiations and Applied Game Theory. *The Economic Journal,* Vol. 101, No. 406, (pp. 420-435), Published by Blackwell Publishing for the Royal Economic Society.

Hove, M. (2012). The debate and impact of Sanctions: The Zimbabwean Experience. *International Journal of Business and Social Science,* Vol. 3, No. 5, March 2012, (pp. 72-84).

ICCO Study, (September 2008). Dialogue of the deaf, An assessment of Europe's development approach to trade negotiations. Postbus 8190, 3503 RD Utrecht, http://www.icco.nl, accessed 15 March 2013.

International Monetary Fund Report (May 2011). Zimbabwe Article IV Consultation Country Report, No. 11/135. IMF, Washington DC, Publication Services, http://www.imf.org, accessed 5 May 2013.

Kahuika, *et al* (2003). Trade Assessment: Namibia and Angola. *Namibian Economic Policy Research Unit* Occasional Paper, XIV, 82 Series.

Kalima-Phiri, B. (2007). Financial Flows to Civil Society in Southern Africa: Key Lessons and Policy Implications, Pretoria, http://www.osisa.org/file/openspace, accessed 27 May 2013.

Kamidza, R. (2002). Budget 2002: A mismatch of policy objectives and allocations. *Southern African Political Economy Monthly,* Vol. 14, No. 8.Kamidza, R. (2004a). EPAs Negotiations: Sub-regional Development Challenges in the EU – ESA Relations. *Seatini Bulletin,* http://www.seatini.org, accessed 5 May 2011.

Kamidza, R. (2004b). EPAs: Unequal Partners, Unequal Outcome against ESA countries. http://www.aidc.org, accessed 5 June 2011.

Kamidza, R. (2004c). ESA-EPA negotiations still lack substance and direction. *Seatini Bulletin,* Vol. 7, No. 15, 2004.

Kamidza, R. (July 2005). Predictions for EPAs Negotiations: EU=1, ACP=0. *Pambazuka News,* Issue 216, http://www.pambazuka.org, accessed 5 May 2012.

Kamidza, R. (February 2006). EPAs: How the poor are excluded from trade negotiations. *Pambazuka News,* Issue 243, http://www.pambazuka.org, accessed 5 May 2012.

Kamidza, R. (2007a). Southern African Trade Talks with EU. *Institute of Global Dialogue, Tradewinds,* Vol. 1, No. 1, http://www.igd.org.za, accessed 5 September 2009.

Kamidza, R. (January 2007b). EPAs road show rolls on. *Pambuzuka News,* Issue 284, http://www.pambazuka.org, accessed 5 May 2012.

Kamidza, R. (July 2007c). SADC-EPA Information Seminar Failed Civil Society, *Seatini,* Unpublished.

Kamidza, R. (2008). Southern Africa – EU Fisheries Agreements: The case of Angola and Mozambique. *Open Society Institute for Southern Africa Resource Watch publication,* Unpublished.

Kamidza, R. (May 2009a). Donors won't cough up without change: Zimbabwe future in jeopardy amidst Unity government impasse. *Pambazuka News,* Issue 432, http://www.pambazuka.org, accessed on 5 January 2010.

Kamidza, R. (2009b). Zimbabwe's Post-conflict economic transition: State shortcomings and civil society advocacy, Unpublished.

Kamidza, R. (March 2009c). Government and civil society in Zimbabwe's economic recovery. *Pambazuka News,* Issue 425, http://www.pambazuka.org, accessed 5 January 2010.

Kamidza, R. (2010). The SADC Free Trade Area's Impact on the Socio-economic and Environmental well-being on the People of Southern Africa. *Economic Justice Network, Unpublished,* http://www.ejn.org, accessed 5 May 2013.

Kaminski, B. and Ng, F. (2011). Zimbabwe's Foreign Trade Performance during the Decade of Economic Turmoil: Will Exports Recover? http://www.worldbank.org/INTRANETTRADE/Resources, accessed 5 May 2013.

Keet, D. (2007). Economic Partnership Agreements: Europe's latest Economic Policy offensive against Africa, http://www.info@aidc.org.za, accessed 5 October 2012.

Kohnert, D. (2008). EU-African Economic Relations: Continuing Dominance Traded for Aid? *German Institute of Global Areas Studies*

Working Paper, Transformation in the Process of Globalisation, No. 82, July 2008.

Lamy, P. (January 2010). Quoted in *Cheickna, S. D.,* Banana Producers Turn to Regional Markets, *Inter Press Service,* http://www.ipsnews.net, accessed 5 May 2013.

Linder, S.B. (1961). An Essay on Trade and Transformation, Stockholm: Almqvist and Wicksell.

Mamdani, M. (2008). Lessons of Zimbabwe. London Review of Books, December 2008.

Menkel-Meadow, C. (2001). Negotiating with lawyers, men and things: The contextual approach still matters. *Negotiation Journal,* Vol. 17, No. 3: (pp. 257-293).

Moyo, S. and Yeros, P. (2007). The Radicalised State: Zimbabwe Interrupted Revolution. *Review of African Political Economy,* ROAPE Publications Ltd.

Moyo, S. *et al.* (2010). The Land Occupation Movement in Zimbabwe: Contradictions of Neo-liberalism. *Journal of International Studies,* Millennium.

Nalunga, J. (October 2004). ESA EPA third meeting of the Regional Negotiating Forum, Antananarivo, Madagascar, *Seatini Bulletin.* http://www.seatini.org/publications/factsheets/agreements.htm, accessed 5 May 2012.

New Agriculturist (June 2011). Country profile – Zimbabwe, WREN media production, http://www.new-ag.info/en/country/profile.php?a=2073, accessed 5 May 2013.

Organisation for Economic Cooperation and Development (October 1999). Open Markets Matter: The Benefits of Trade and Investment Liberalisation. *OECD Observer,* http://www.oecd.org/dataoecd/18/51/1948792.pdf, accessed 5 October 2013.

Osakwe, P.N. (2007). Foreign Aid, Resources and Export Diversification in Africa: A New Test of Existing Theories. *MPRA Paper,* University Library of Munich.

Oxfam (2002). Rigged Rules and Double Standards: Trade, globalisation and the fight against poverty, Brussels. http://www.oxfam.org, accessed 5 May 2013.

Prasad, C., B. (2005). Explaining the Supply-side Constraints to Export-led Growth in Selected Pacific Island Countries. *ARTNet website*, http://www.unescap.org/tid/artnet, accessed 5 May 2013.

Putnam, R., D. (1988). Diplomacy and Domestic Politics: The Logic of Two-Level Games. *International Organisation*, Vol. 42, No. 3, 42(3): (pp. 427-90).

Ralph, O. (2008). A New Trade Theory of GATT/WTO Negotiations. *Centre for Economic Performance, London School of Economics and Political Science*, No. 877. London.

Rattso, J. and R. Torvik, (1998). Zimbabwe trade liberalization: Ex post evaluation. *Cambridge Journal of Economics*, (pp. 325-46).

Reimer, J. K. *et al* (2006). Evidence on Imperfect Competition and Strategic Trade Theory. *University of Wisconsin-Madison*, Department of Agriculture and Applied Economics, Staff Paper Series, No. 498.

Rodrik, D. (1990). How should structural adjustment programmes be designed? *World Development*, Vol. 18, No. 7.

Roux, W. (February 2008). EPAs demystified, Insight, www.insight.com.na/login.html.

Seatini Bulletin, Vol. 10, No. 7, July 2007.

Shell, R. G. (March 1995). Trade Legalism and International Relations Theory: An Analysis of the WTO. *Duke Law Journal*, Vol. 44, No 5.

Shivji, I. (2004). Reflections on NGOs in Tanzania: What We Are, What We Are Not and What We Ought To Be? *Development in Practice*, Vol. 14, No. 5.

South Centre (March 2010). EPAs: The wrong development model for Africa and options for the future, http://www.southcentre.int/analytical-note-march-2010/, accessed 5 May 2016.

Southern Africa Trade Hub (June 2011). Technical Report on the Impact of Derogations from Implementation of the SADC FTA Obligations on intra-SADC trade, http://www.satradehub.org, accessed 5 May 2013.

Southern African Development Community secretariat report (2000). Industry and Trade Annual Report. July 1999 – June 2000, http:// www.sadc.int, accessed 27 July 2013.

Southern African Development Community secretariat study (2012). SADC Framework for the establishment of a Trade Related Facility, Southern African Development Community House, Gaborone, Botswana, http://www.sadc.int, accessed 27 July 2013.

Southern and Eastern African Trade, Information and Negotiations Institute Bulletin, (2004). Cotonou Agreement, Vol. 7. No. 6.

Stephen S. G. and Chang-Tai, H. (2002). Classical Ricardian Theory of Comparative Advantage Revisited. *Review of International Economics,* Volume 8, Issue 2, published online, 17 DEC 2002.

Stolper, W.F. and Samuelson, P.A. (1941). Protection and Real Wages. *Review of Economic Studies*, Vol. 9: 58-73.

Structural Adjustment Programme Review Initiative Network (2004). Structural Adjustment: The Structural Adjustment Programme Review Initiative Network Report: The Policy Roots of Economic Crisis, Poverty and Inequality. London: Zed.

Subbarao, D. (November 2012). What are Supply-side constraints? http://www.livemint.com/Money/TMgrNtZDTSag6iLrNdlHg L/Dejargoned--Supply-side-constraint.html, accessed 5 May 2012.

Tandon, Y. (2004). The ESA-EU EPA Negotiations and the Role of COMESA. *Seatini Bulletin,* Harare, Vol. 7, No. 9.

Tandon, Y. (1999). The World Trade Organisation and Africa's Marginalisation, *Australian Journal of International Affairs*, Vol. 53, Issue 1.

Tekere, M. (2001). Trade Liberalisation under Structural Economic Adjustment – Impact on Social Welfare in Zimbabwe, Harare: *University of Zimbabwe,* paper for the Poverty Reduction Forum, SAPRNI Initiative.

Tekere, M. (February 2013). State of play of Eastern and Southern Africa and European Union Economic Partnership Agreement negotiations. COMESA, Unpublished.

TRADES Centre Study (2002). Compatibility of Trade Policies in the Context of Current Regional Economic Integration Processes:

The Case of SADC region, Available on line at www.acp-eu-trade.org, accessed on 5 May 2016.

United Nations Economic and Social Council (2004). Addressing Supply-side Constraints and Capacity-Building. Subcommittee on International Trade and Investment, 27-29 October 2004. Bangkok.

Valodia, I. and Velia, M. (2006). Macro-Micro Linkages in Trade: Trade, Efficiency and Competitiveness of Manufacturing Firms in Durban, South Africa. *Journal of African Economies*, Vol. 15, No. 4, (pp. 688-721).

Watkins, M., and Passow, S. (1996). Analysing linked systems of negotiations. *Negotiation Journal,* Vol. 12, No. 4: (pp. 325-339).

Wise Men's Report (2005). The Sutherland report and the WTO's Institutional Law. Do parallels with other institutional organisations help?, International Organisation Law Review 2: 191 – 199, http://heinonline.org/HOL/LandingPage?handle=hein.journal s/, accessed 5 May 2016.

Newspaper opinion pieces, presentations, papers and speeches

Abugre, C. (March, 2010). Law violates trade ideals: UN official, 13 March 2010, http://www.thezimbabwetimes.com/?p=27921, accessed 5 May 2013.

Basevi, G. (2008). Regionalism vs Multilateralism: Trade Negotiations. Notes for the course on "Theory and policy of international trade". *University of Bologna:* University Press.

Bhebhe, T. (July 2012). Zimbabwe: Bulawayo factories shut up shop. The Africa Report, http://www.theafricareport.com/index.php/sectors/zimbabwe -bulawayo, accessed 20 June 2013.

Bell, A. (29 MAY 2014). Zimbabwe: EU Pledges Millions to Zanu-PF As Part of Re-Engagement, SW Radio Africa (London), http://allafrica.com/stories/201405300637.html, accessed 20 June 2016.

Chatham House Report (April 2014). Zimbabwe's International Re-engagement, The Long Haul to Recovery, Africa Programme, https://www.chathamhouse.org/africa, accessed 20 June 2016.

CIDSE-Caritas Internationalis, (2000). Make a Difference for Poverty Reduction. A paper presented at the Sixth WTO Ministerial Conference in Hong Kong, a *CIDSE-Caritas Internationalis,* Position Paper, http://*www.wto.org/english/forums_e/ngo_e/posp51_cidse_e.pdf,* accessed 5 May 2013.

Confederation of the Zimbabwean Industries Report (2012). The Annual CZI Manufacturing sector survey, Unpublished.

Commonwealth Secretariat (2010). Hub and Spokes Project Phase I Performance 2004 – 2010, http://www.secretariat.thecommonwealth.org, accessed 5 May 2013.

Commonwealth Secretariat Hub and Spokes Project Phase II (April 2012). Building trade capacities in Africa, the Caribbean and Pacific regions, Discussion and Consultation paper, http://www.secretariat.thecommonwealth.org, accessed 5 May 2013.

Darracq, V. (2010). The EU in Zimbabwe: What to do now? ISS opinion, European Union Institute for Security Studies, http://www.iss.europa.eu/uploads/media, accessed 21 February 2011.

Deve, T. (October 2006). Wither ACP trade relations with the EU in the context of EPAs negotiations: Challenges and opportunities for poverty eradication in sub-Sahara Africa, Regional Roundtable Discussion Paper, South Africa. Unpublished.

Deve, T. (September 2009). EPA Negotiations and Non-State-Actors in SADC and ESA configurations. Speech given to regional CSOs and social movements during the southern Africa social forum, Mbabane, Swaziland. Unpublished.

European Commission Press Release (May 2012). EU's first EPA with an African region goes live. European Commission, Brussels, http://www.trade.ec.europa.eu, accessed 5 February 2013.

Kadzere, M. (September 2012). Zimbabwe Trade Deficit Widens. Senior Business Reporter, *The Herald,* Harare, Zimbabwe, http://www.herald.co.zw, accessed 5 May 2013.

Kadzere, M. (March 2010). Zimbabwe: Exports to EU up. *The Herald,* Harare, Zimbabwe, http://www.herald.co.zw, accessed 5 May 2013.

Kapoor, K. (ed) (1995). Africa's Experience with Structural Adjustment: Proceedings of the Harare Seminar, 23-24 May 1994, Washington DC: World Bank, *World Bank Discussion Paper. (pp.* 288).

Madambi, P. (March 2013). Zimbabwe must take advantage of EU beef market. *Sunday Mail,* Harare, Zimbabwe, http://www.sundaymail.co.zw, accessed 5 May 2013.

Mananavire, B. (May 2015). EU sets re-engagement agenda with Zimbabwe, 8 May 2015, https://www.dailynews.co.zw/articles/2015/05/08/eu-sets-re-engagement-agenda-with-zim, accessed on 5 May 2016.

Magaisa, A. (June 2016). Britain Leaving the EU: How will #Brexit Affect Relations with Zimbabwe?, http://alexmagaisa.com/2016/06/24/will-brexit-affect-zimbabwe/, accessed on 5 September 2016.

Makanza, T. (2007). The nexus between EPAs and WTO negotiations, SADC Parliamentary Forum Annual Meeting Presentations, Johannesburg, South Africa, unpublished.

Matsaka, A. (April, 2014). Where to Zimbabwe, Daily News, https://www.dailynews.co.zw/articles/2014/04/10/where-to-zim, accessed on 5 May 2016.

Mawere, M, D. (2009). The EU-Africa relationship post-colonialism, http://newsdesk@newzimbabwe.com, accessed 5 June 2013.

Meyn, M. (June 2005). The progress of Economic Regionalisation in Southern Africa. Challenges for SADC and COMESA, Conference paper for *Namibian Economic Policy Research Unit,* Windhoek.

Mukori, W. (31 October 2014). EU confirm re-engagement with Zanu PF, snuff out our hope for free and fair elections, http://bulawayo24.com/index-id-opinion-sc-columnist-byo-56619.html#sthash.nsZbK8bc.dpuf, accessed on 5 May 2016.

Mushowe B., (2012). Addressing Supply Side Constraints Presentation on ZIMTRADE Annual Exporters Conference, http://www.zimtrade.co.zw/pdf/presentations/mushowe.pdf, accessed 5 June 2013.

Mutsaka, F. (2010). Zanu PF stance threat to EU re-engagement, 15 July 2010, http://allafrica.com/stories/201007161135.html, accessed 5 June 2016.

Nalunga, J. (May 2004). Implication of EPAs on Regional Integration in COMESA and SADC. Discussion paper presented at the ESA civil society policy dialogue workshop, Nairobi, Kenya. Unpublished.

Ndlovu, R. (2016). Trust breaks down, Franancial Mail, 10 March – 16 March 2016, (page 33), Vol 234, No. 9, http://www.financialmail.co.za, , accessed on 5 May 2016.

NANGO/EU Report (2014). CSO Roadmap Consultative Meeting Report, Governance and Human Rights Cluster, 29 April 2014, accessed on 5 May 2016.

NewsDay Zimbabwe, (19 February 2016). EU donates €8m to fight foot and mouth, 19 February 2016, https://www.newsday.co.zw/2016/02/19/eu-donates-e8m-fight-foot-mouth/, accessed on 5 May 2016.

Ngwenya, R. (1 August 2014). Zimbabwe EU Ambassador Blunders as Civil Society Trembles, Konrad-Adenauer-Stiftung, http://www.kas.de/zimbabwe/en/publications/38577/, accessed on 5 May 2016.

Nyakazeya, P. (August 2009). Manufacturing sector needs major rebuilding. Zimbabwe Independent, Harare, Zimbabwe, http://www.theindependent.co.zw/, accessed 5 May 2010

O'Kane, M. (17 February 2016). EU lifts most of its Zimbabwe sanctions, COUNCIL REGULATION (EU) 2016/214 of 15 February 2016, amending Regulation (EC) No 314/2004 concerning certain restrictive measures in respect of Zimbabwe, accessed 5 January 2016

Pilling, D. and England, A. (February, 2016). Plotting and planning for a Zimbabwe without Mugabe, The Zimbabwe Mail, Monday, 29 February 2016, http://thezimbabwemail.com/headline-

19850-plotting-and-planning-for-a-zimbabwe-without-mugabe.html, accessed 5 January 2016

Raftopoulos, B. (June 2005). The Zimbabwean Crisis and the Challenges of the Left. Institute of Development Studies, *University of Zimbabwe,* Public lecture delivered at the University of Kwa-Zulu Natal.

Ramdoo, I. (2014). ECOWAS and SADC Economic Partnership Agreements: A Comparative Analysis, ECDPM Discussion Paper No. 165, September 2014, http://ecdpm.org/wp-content/uploads/ecowas-sadc-economic-partnership-agreement-dp-165-september-2014.pdf, accessed on 5 December 2015.

Reis, G., J. (March 2011). Identifying supply-side constraints to exports. OECD Workshop presentation on 'Aid for Trade Implementation', http://www.oecd.org/dac/aft/47441603.pdf, accessed 5 May 2012.

Robinson, R. (1998). The Poverty of International Trade Theory. Lecture Notes, 1998, http://www.rrojasdatabank.info/capital5.htm, accessed on 5 May 2013.

Shonhiwa, A (2015). Opening speech at the Validation Workshop for the Designing of a programme to implement the iEPA with the EU, 22 July 2015, at Crown Plaza Monomotapa Hotel, Harare, Unpublished.

Sibanda, G. (November 2012). Trade with South Africa declines. *The Herald,* Harare, Zimbabwe and South Africa Foreign Policy Initiative of the Open Society Foundation for South Africa, http://www.safpi.org, accessed 5 May 2012.

Stop unfair trade campaign (2007). Stop unfair trade deals between Europe and ACP countries, http://www.epa2007.org/stories_quotes.html, accessed 5 May 2012.

SW Radio Africa (London) (20 MAY 2014). Zimbabwe: European Engagement With Zanu-PF Slammed As "Travesty of Justice", http://allafrica.com/stories/201405210347.html, accessed 5 August 2014

Zapiro (2006). An adopted Catoon.

ZEN Conference Report (10 December 2014). Report on Conference held in Brussels on 10 December 2014, A new era in EU – Zimbabwe relations? Exploring terms of engagement, http://zimbabweeurope.org/wp-content/uplods/2015/03/ZEN-Conference-Report.pdf, accessed on 5 May 2016.

Zim247.com (August 2013). Zanu-PF Government faces Tough Economy Fight, http://www.zim247.com, accessed on 5 September 2013.

ZimTrade, (2012). ZimTrade Database, www.zimtrade.co.zw, accessed 5 May 2013

ZimTrade, (2015). ZimTrade Database, www.zimtrade.co.zw, accessed 5 May 2016

Wikipedia (2008). Zimbabwe general election, 2008, https://en.wikipedia.org/wiki/Zimbabwean_general_election,_2008, accessed 5 May 2012

Personal interviews

Angelica Katuruza, Zimbabwe government former chief negotiator, now with the Zimbabwean Embassy in Pretoria, South Africa, Johannesburg South Africa, 28 May 2012.

Christina Zakeyo Chatima, Malawi Trade Director, Lilongwe, Malawi, 24 November 2016

Diamond Chikhasu, Malawian Industry and Trade ministry's principal trade officer, Lilongwe, Malawi, 9 March 2013.

Elijah Munyuki, trade law consultant, Gaborone Botswana, 24 August 2012.

Gabriel Chipare, deputy clerk of the Zimbabwean parliament, Lilongwe, Malawi, 24 November 2012.

Godfrey Kanyenze, director of LEDRIZ, the research wing of the ZCTU, Harare, Zimbabwe, 28 June 2011.

Medicine Masiiwa, lecturer at the University of Zimbabwe, Gaborone Botswana, 25 August 2012.

Rangarirai Machemedze, SEATINI deputy director, Harare, Zimbabwe, 25 June 2011.

Richard Mandebvu, ZIMCODD social and economic programme officer, Harare, Zimbabwe, 24 June 2011.

Tedious Chifamba, Zimbabwean Regional Integration and International Cooperation permanent secretary and current government chief negotiator, Harare, Zimbabwe, 14 September 2012.

Tendayi Makanza, senior researcher: ZCTU Alternative to neo-liberalism in southern Africa project, Durban, South Africa, 10 August 2011.

Willie Shumba, former Zimbabwean revenue commissioner and regular government delegate to EPA-related meetings, now SADC secretariat's customs senior programme officer, Gaborone, Botswana, 14 March 2012.

Junior government officers and other informants were not directly quoted as per their request.

Appendix

A.   Questionnaire to government officials and/or negotiators

1.

List key civil society organisations (CSOs) and private sector chambers that
have been or are still involved in the EPA negotiations

Name of civil society organization	Name of private sector chamber
1.	2.
3.	4.
5.	6.

2.   Explain why government?

Participated in the EPA process	
Participated under the ESA configuration	

3.   With respect to EPA process, what are your views on?

The old Zanu (PF) government's[190] strategy at Seattle, Doha and Cancun WTO negotiations;	
Explain	
The GNU's approach;	
Explain	

4.   With respect to EPA process, what are your views on?

COMESA Secretariat	
Explain	
SADC EPA Unit	
Explain	

---

[190] In particular, the role that the former minister of Trade and Industry,
Nathan Shamuyarira, played in putting Zimbabwe at the cutting edge of critical
diplomacy during the WTO processes since Seattle Ministerial Conference.

South Africa's Trade and Industry's Minister, Rob Davies	
Explain	

5. Describe key constraints that undermined government effective leadership in the EPA process.

6. With respect to the EPA preparedness in the EPA process, describe how the EU – Zimbabwe bilateral relations affected?

Government's preparations	
Government-civil society relationship	
Government stakeholder mobilisation	

7. How do you describe government - civil society consultative relationship on the process with respect to?

Challenges	
Opportunities	

8. With respect to the EPA preparedness, what are your views on the effectiveness of?

National Development Trade Policy Forum[191]	
Stakeholders' consultations	

9. With respect to the EPA preparedness, how would you describe civil society's inputs on?

Skills and capacity development	
Negotiating strategies and tactics	
Identifying issues	
Identifying interests	

[191] The National Development Trade Policy Forum is a stakeholder forum comprises of government officials and representatives of the private sector and civil society organizations working on trade and development issues in the country.

Developing positions	
Developing offers	

10. With respect to stakeholders' consultations on the EPA process, describe government's:

Strengths	
Weaknesses	

11. Describe how government shared issues, interest, positions and offers with civil society?

12. With respect to negotiating guiding principles on the EPA process, how would you describe government's negotiating approaches, strategies and tactics?

At ESA configuration level	
At the EU level	

13. Which sectors of the economy are vulnerable to the EPA outcome and why?

Sector	Reasons

14. With respect to supporting the EPA process, which donor(s) funded the following?

	Funding donor(s)
Government officials/negotiators participation in EPA meetings	
Impact assessment study	
Stakeholders consultations	
Other, specify	

15. Any other information, specify.

B. Questionnaire to the representative of civil society organisations

1.

ist key civil society organisations (CSOs) and private sector chambers that have been working with you in the EPA negotiations process.

Name of civil society organisation	Name of private sector chamber
1.	2.
3.	4.
5.	6.
7.	8.

2. Describe the working relationship in the EPA process with other CSOs, government and donors.

Other CSOs	
Government	
Donors	

3. With respect to the EPA process, describe government's:

Strengths	
Weaknesses	

4. With respect to EPA process, what are your views on?

The old Zanu (PF) government's[192] strategy at Seattle, Doha and Cancun WTO negotiations;	
Explain	
The impact of the International Trade Minister, Welshman Ncube's new political portfolio;	

---

[192] In particular, the role that the former minister of Trade and Industry, Nathan Shamuyarira played in putting Zimbabwe at the cutting edge of critical diplomacy during the WTO processes since Seattle Ministerial Conference.

Explain	

5. With respect to EPA process, what are your views on?

COMESA Secretariat	
Explain	
SADC EPA Unit	
Explain	
South Africa's Trade and Industry's Minister, Rob Davies	
Explain	

6. How do you describe negotiators'- civil society consultative relationship on the process with respect to?

	Zanu (PF) Government	Government of National Unit
Challenges		
Opportunities		

7. With respect to the EPA process, how would you describe negotiators' appreciation on?

Implications	
Challenges	
Opportunities	

8. With respect to participation on trade and industrial policy debate, how would you describe the EPA process and why?

Category	Reason(s)	
	Zanu (PF) Government	Government of National Unity
Transparency		
Inclusive		
Democratic		
Sensitive to socio-economic conditions		

9. With respect to the EPA preparedness, what are your views on?

National Development Trade Policy Forum[193]	
Stakeholders' consultations	

10. Describe key constraints that undermined civil society's effective participation in the EPA process.

11. With respect to the EPA preparedness, how would you describe civil society's inputs on?

Skills and capacity development	
Negotiating tactics	
Negotiating strategies	
Identifying issues	
Identifying interests	
Developing positions	
Developing offers	

12. In your view, what has been the role of donors in the EPA process?

13. With respect to the EPA process, which donor(s) funded your organisation's activities in terms of?

Participation in the EPA process at the:		
	National Development Trade Policy Forum	
	Regional Negotiating Forum[194];	

---

[193] The National Development Trade Policy Forum is a stakeholder forum comprises of government officials and representatives of the private sector and civil society organizations working on trade and development issues in the country.

[194] The Regional Negotiating Forum is a platform in which member states belonging to the same configuration meet to prepare their negotiation positions and offers with the European Union.

	African Union meetings;	
	Brussels meetings	
Dialogue sessions:		
	Conferences;	
	Workshops;	
	Seminars; and	
	Roundtables	
Advocacy at:		
	National level;	
	ESA level;	
	EU level	
Consultations with:		
	Government negotiators;	
	Other civic bodies;	
	Other constituencies;	
Other activities, *specify*		

14. How would you describe civil society's advocacy strategy in the EPA process at the:

National level	
Regional level	
AU level	
EU level	

15. Given the politically-charged environment, how would you describe CSOs' advocacy with respect to?

Implications	
Challenges	
Opportunities	

16. With respect to the EPA preparedness, describe how the EU – Zimbabwe bilateral relations affected your organisation's' participation in the EPA process?

17. Given the tense EU-Zimbabwe bilateral relations, how would you describe CSOs' advocacy strategies with respect to?

Implications	
Challenges	
Opportunities	

18. Any other information, specify.

www.ingramcontent.com/pod-product-compliance
Lightning Source LLC
Chambersburg PA
CBHW050628280326
41932CB00015B/2571